READING AND
RESPONSE

CLIMBER.

Open University Press

English, Language, and Education series

General Editor: Anthony Adams

Lecturer in Education, University of Cambridge

This series is concerned with all aspects of language in education
from the primary school to the tertiary sector. Its authors are
experienced educators who examine both principles and practice of
English subject teaching and language across the curriculum in the
context of current educational and societal developments.

TITLES IN THE SERIES

Narrative and Argument
Richard Andrews (ed.)

Time for Drama
Roma Burgess and Pamela Gaudry

Computers and Literacy
Daniel Chandler and Stephen Marcus (eds)

Readers, Texts, Teachers
Bill Corcoran and Emrys Evans (eds)

Thinking Through English
Paddy Creber

Developing Response to Poetry
Patrick Dias and Michael Hayhoe

Developing English
Peter Dougill (ed.)

The Primary Language Book
Peter Dougill and Richard Knott

**Children Talk About Books: Seeing
Themselves as Readers**
Donald Fry

Literary Theory and English Teaching
Peter Griffith

**Lesbian and Gay Issues in the
English Classroom**
Simon Harris

Reading and Response
Mike Hayhoe and Stephen Parker (eds)

Assessing English
Brian Johnston

Lipservice: The Story of Talk in Schools
Pat Jones

**The English Department in a
Changing World**
Richard Knott

Oracy Matters
Margaret MacLure, Terry Phillips and
Andrew Wilkinson (eds)

Beginning Writing
John Nicholls et al.

Teaching Literature for Examinations
Robert Protherough

Developing Response to Fiction
Robert Protherough

Microcomputers and the Language Arts
Brent Robinson

English Teaching from A–Z
Wayne Sawyer, Anthony Adams and
Ken Watson

Collaboration and Writing
Morag Styles (ed.)

Reconstructing 'A' Level English
Patrick Scott

Reading Within and Beyond the Classroom
Dan Taverner

Reading for Real
Barrie Wade (ed.)

English Teaching in Perspective
Ken Watson

Spoken English Illuminated
Andrew Wilkinson et al.

The Quality of Writing
Andrew Wilkinson

The Writing of Writing
Andrew Wilkinson (ed.)

READING AND RESPONSE

EDITED BY
Mike Hayhoe and Stephen Parker

Open University Press
Milton Keynes · Philadelphia

To Margaret Meek,
with affectionate admiration

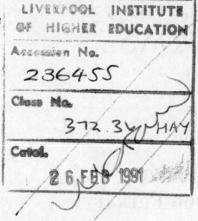

Open University Press
Celtic Court
22 Ballmoor
Buckingham MK18 1XW

and

1900 Frost Road, Suite 101
Bristol, PA 19007, USA

First Published 1990

British Library Cataloguing in Publication Data

Hayhoe, Mike
  Reading and response. – (English, language, and education
  series).
  1. Education. Curriculum subjects: Reading
  I. Title   II. Parker, Stephen   III. Series
  428.407

  ISBN 0-335-09439-2

Library of Congress Cataloging-in-Publication number is available

Typeset by Rowland Phototypesetting Limited
Bury St Edmunds, Suffolk
Printed in Great Britain

Contents

List of contributors   vii
Preface   viii
General editor's introduction   ix

1   **Why response?**   1
Margaret Meek

2   **Research on reader response and the National Literature Initiative**   13
James R. Squire

3   **Children's recognition of stories**   25
Robert Protherough

4   **The experience of literature and the study of literature: the teacher-educator's experience**   34
Ben Nelms and Don Zancanella

5   **Reading as framing, writing as reframing**   49
Ian Reid

6   **Feminism, Romanticism and the New Literacy in response journals**   62
Deanne Bogdan

7   **Safety and danger: close encounters with literature of a second kind**   73
Peter Medway and Andrew Stibbs

8   **Molesting the text: Promoting resistant readings**   84
Marnie O'Neill

9   **What do students learn from literature teaching?**   94
Tanja Janssen and Gert Rijlaarsdam

10 **Children's books: always back of the queue?** 107
    Stephanie Nettell

11 **US censorship: an increasing fact of life** 115
    John S. Simmons

12 **Home stories** 124
    Nicholas Tucker

13 **Reading, re-reading, resistance: versions of reader response** 132
    Bill Corcoran

Bibliography 147
Index 159

List of contributors

Deanne Bogdan, Ontario Institute for Studies in Education, Toronto, Canada.
Bill Corcoran, Department of Communication and Resource Studies, Brisbane College of Advanced Education, Brisbane, Australia.
Tanja Janssen, Department of Linguistics, University of Amsterdam, Amsterdam, The Netherlands.
Peter Medway, School of Education, University of Leeds, Leeds, England.
Margaret Meek, Institute of Education, University of London, London, England.
Ben Nelms, University of Missouri, Columbia, Missouri, USA.
Stephanie Nettell, Children's Book Editor, *The Guardian* newspaper, London, England.
Marnie O'Neill, Department of Education, University of Western Australia, Perth, Western Australia, Australia.
Robert Protherough, School of Education, University of Hull, Hull, England.
Ian Reid, Centre for Studies in Literary Education, Deakin University, Victoria, Australia.
Gert Rijlaarsdam, Department of Linguistics, University of Amsterdam, Amsterdam, The Netherlands.
John S. Simmons, Department of English Education and Reading, Florida State University, Tallahassee, USA.
James R. Squire, Executive Consultant and Lecturer.
Andrew Stibbs, School of Education, University of Leeds, Leeds, England.
Nicholas Tucker, Department of Developmental Psychology, University of Sussex, Brighton, England.
Don Zancanella, University of New Mexico, Alberquerque, New Mexico, USA.

Preface

In recent years, what is understood by the word 'reading' has become increasingly complex. We now know far more about what is involved when someone reads. A reader is not at the mercy of a text, passively absorbing its surface and hidden values and messages, but is busily *making* significance through an active engagement with what is being read.

The increasing use of the term 'response', with its origins in a Latin word to do with agreeing to be part of an alliance, is a recognition of this interaction. Most of the chapters in this book support and investigate this vision of reader and text actively engaged in a collaboration. Some question that reading should be such a collusive process. For them, a text is something to be questioned, an opportunity for debate and 'resistance' instead.

The international contributors brought together here mirror the main issues in this exciting debate about the nature of reading and response. Occasionally divided in debate, they are united in their commitment to empowering young people through successful reading in a problematic world. Their work is not a matter of abstruse academic enquiry and theory: across the world, the stances that teachers adopt towards reading affect students of all ages, each and every day, in the classroom and beyond.

Mike Hayhoe
Stephen Parker

General editor's introduction

The biennial conference on issues to do with English teaching at the School of Education in the University of East Anglia has become a firm date in the diaries of academics in the English-speaking (and -teaching) world. We are glad in this series that we have been able to make available a permanent record of some of the papers delivered at each of these conferences.

It is good to see that, despite the impending retirement of Professor Andrew Wilkinson, whose tireless work first established these conferences, they will continue to take place. The present volume represents some of the pieces that were delivered to the Conference held in Easter 1989. The two editors will already be known to many readers for the work that they have done on literature teaching and it is appropriate that they should have edited a volume concerned with literature and response.

Reader response theory has been one of the most persuasive developments in English teaching in the 1980s and has already been celebrated in an earlier volume in this series (Corcoran and Evans, eds, *Readers, Texts, Teachers*, Open University Press, 1987). Bill Corcoran (Australia) makes a welcome reappearance in the final chapter of this book; a further volume by Emrys Evans (UK) – *Reading Against Racism* – is in active preparation for the series. But a glance at the titles of this distinguished international collection of chapters shows that things have moved on from the 1980s to new concerns. Aspects of stylistics are present in the work of Ian Reid (Australia); feminist concerns in that of Deanne Bogdan (Canada). In this sense, the present collection stands, as the date of its publication symbolizes, on the edge of an old and a new tradition in thinking about the role of literature in the classroom.

As the editors themselves recognize, no book can do full justice to the excitement of the conference itself. Many papers were given that had to be omitted for reasons of space. Some of these will find publication in later volumes that are planned or being written. But the real excitement (perhaps the real response) was in the conference itself and the discussions that took place. In my experience, as a dedicated conference goer, it was a unique event and much of its flavour, especially its international perspective, has been captured in this skilfully edited volume.

The 1990s will see the retirement of Margaret Meek Spencer (UK). It is right that the collection should open with her inaugural address to the conference and be dedicated to her. Her long and valued work has always placed both the child and the book together in context. This collection of papers celebrates her work in more ways than one. I doubt whether there is a contributor represented here who does not share my own indebtedness to her wisdom and inspiration.

Anthony Adams

1 Why response?

MARGARET MEEK

> You are perfectly free to leave that book on the table. But if you
> open it, you assume responsibility for it.
>
> Jean Paul Sartre

I often find that I am unwilling to think about response because I know I can neither define nor defy it. Apart from answers to requests and questions, I know response as agreement ('This is it, isn't it?') or disagreement ('Anything but that!'), as a form of greeting, and as the balanced *responsorium* of the psalms: 'Keep me as the apple of an eye, and hide me under the shadow of thy wings.' Tracked down through the thesaurus, its hair-veined network reveals thirty-two contingent meanings, including 'friendliness'.

The origins of my unease about discussing 'response' in relation to literature lie in the dominance that behaviourist psychology has always had over the teaching of reading: the notion that the text is the stimulus, and the reader's reaction to it 'the response', in the form of word or letter recognition, or some form of commentary, as 'comprehension' or interpretation. Also, my students often use the word with amorphous generality, like custard, to account for personal feelings which could not be either examined or gainsaid.

And yet, many critics and teachers whom I admire have found in reader-response theories of literature satisfactory replacements for the limitations of Leavis and New Criticism. Louise Rosenblatt's interactionist viewpoint has been a pillar of light to those who have valued, examined and urged the importance of what growing readers have had to say about texts and their understanding of them. Think of the years we spent examining children's reading by means of comprehension exercises without asking ourselves what the so-called 'wrong' answers indicated. However, despite challenging revisions of the definition of response, I cannot help nodding when Peter Hunt says that much reader-response theory 'paints a cretinous reader who has to lumber along each line of the text, constantly surprised by the next lexical, or grammatical development' (Hunt, 1988). My complaint is less imaginative, and shorter. The word has to do too much work. At best, it shows up aspects of reading, writing and criticism that need more balanced and refined awarenesses. At worst, it can induce a greater self-concern on the part of the reader, an egocentric, individualistic preoccupation (as in Holland's concern with *personality*) which distracts us from the nature of a text and what we do when we read it.

Therefore, I ask myself, when I engage with pupils or students in reading novels, poems, articles, and in the explorations of what the Cox Report (1989) calls 'all kinds of writing', what am I actually doing besides teaching them to read? What part does my response to their responses play in their understanding of what they are doing *when* they read?

In teaching anything we generate responses all the time, at every stage of the activity, by our habitual pedagogic practice of asking questions. Even our most rhetorical queries are voiced as if they are bound to be answered. We are never content with silence, amazement, stupefaction, despair, a grimace or a gesture, all of which constitute the range of responses of which our students are capable. Undoubtedly, there are refinements of these responses to which the social psychologists would draw our attention ('mental gestures', for example) if we were of a mind to let them. When we ask others about their reactions to a film, a poem, an event, some public activity, or to the state of the nation, our questions are about what *counts* as response. We also want to declare our own view of the matter. Our behaviour is always socially inter-responsive. Our thoughts and feelings are about something for which we feel a *responsibility* as the result of our intra-responsive consideration of them. My experience of responding suggests that I can no longer see a reader as a unitary self, not least because all human communication is interactive, embedded in sets of social practices. Response, therefore, is bounded by the conventions of its definition. We do not respond to letters as we do to arguments, to a metaphor as to badly fitting shoes, to the weather as to *Paradise Lost*. Most writers of narrative predict in their readers a range of responses. They invite surrender, a giving over of ourselves to the thoughts and actions of others. But writers cannot fully control the nature of the reader's engagement with their words. There is no inevitable, necessary response to any text, not even to *King Lear*. Literary criticism, as a way of passing the time or earning one's living, is the constant consideration of difference and of why we react as we do to what we see, hear and read, and why we mind about it. The only helpful response to response is to problematize it.

Our topic has a public history to which others will constantly refer. The publication of I. A. Richards' *Practical Criticism* in 1929 seems a reasonable starting point for me, as many of his questions have remained unanswered over the half-century that separates us from their asking. Richards complained that his students had very little confidence in their own judgements of literature. He blamed this failure on their authoritative schoolteachers who, he claimed, taught that all questions about poetry could be answered by reference to events in the lives of the poets, or to their subsequent reputations. Richards himself was not lacking in authoritative discourse. Here he is criticizing his students writing about literature; ask yourself if you still find this tone, in the context of GCSE, for example:

The extraordinary variety of views put forward, and the reckless, desperate character of so many of them, indicated the difficulty that was felt and how unprepared for such a testing encounter the majority of readers were.

— end

In Richards' view, good readers find reading literature hard work. Response has to be prepared for, earned, as something more than whatever we may mean by reading. Do you ever characterize your students' responses as reckless and desperate? In his later book, _How to Read a Page_ (1943), Richards lists the one-hundred most important words of 'systematic ambiguity' which are 'concerned in all that we do as thinking beings'. _Response_ is not one of them. _Responsibility_, however, sits between _respect_ and _right_. The memorable phrase from this text is: 'We all enjoy the illusion that we read better than we do.'

In the continuing English critical tradition, response to literature is the close reading of texts. Not a bad habit, I'd say, although the Humpty Dumpty question 'Who is to be master?' persists. I have begun with Richards to remind us how _Practical Criticism_ dominated the literary experience of students in English universities, and elsewhere, for three decades after its publication. We have to rattle in our heads all that has happened in literary theory in the last two decades if we are to shake ourselves out of Richards' mandarin certainties. For example, most of the books that Robert Protherough refers to in _Developing Response to Fiction_ (1983) – books about the feminist deconstruction of the male dominance of literary criticism, the growth of language studies, cultural studies, and the extension of theories of literature in relation to political and social analysis, the diversity of popular culture, and the whole new 'literacy' of television – have extended our interpretations of the interactive nature of our dealings with people, ideas, texts and the world. Response has to be part of that bigger pattern to connect. We cannot extract poems, plays, novels and other texts from their social context. By 'response' we can no longer mean a general or particular verbal sagacity in respect of certain chosen writings.

All this is just to indicate where we are. But our deliberations must include response as something socially learned as part of _schooled_ reading. Teachers of literature in higher education still, like Richards, take for granted the reading histories of their students because these competences are checked by the gate-keeping procedures of examinations. Whatever their tutors think of them, university students are experienced readers. Schoolteachers read texts with children who are still learning the different kinds of discourses that are in use in the world. They are usually dealing with the earlier stages of the relation of literacy to literature; that is, where children are still discovering (or failing to discover) what reading is good for, so our deliberations must include the nature of the more naive expressions of no less strongly felt reactions, expressions about which we have to be more cautious in our judgements. Consider, for example, the eight-year-old who said of _The Silver Sword_, 'I'll never be able to follow that; it was so brilliant and it's still in my head.' What, more precisely, is the 'that' in her response? Our particular concern with response will surely include the distinction we tend to make between what children actually say about what they read and what we, as experienced readers with responsibilities for their learning, are prepared to acknowledge and understand by it. But we do not stop there. Our pedagogic response to such a reader as this one includes our decisions about what will 'follow that'.

Here, then, are some simple signposts that point to the complexities of our topic. If we agree that the notion of 'response', as part of reading, has a history which it is important for teachers to understand, we must also agree that we are part of that history. Deeply, we interpret our responses and those of others, just as we learned how to make them over the years of our apprenticeship and how we have learned to remake them since then. To show how response, for me, is always a form of resistance to the ideas, let me quote Jane Miller in *Women Writing about Men* (1986). 'Reading and writing are social practices, learned within a culture which produces individual and sexed identities. Individuals become who they are within the discourses of their culture. As part of that culture, literature both makes and remakes its readers, especially but not only, in school.' At my high school in Scotland where I went with, but never spoke to, my brother, I learned the particular kind of androgyny that was a part of my professional life until modified by circumstances and, I guess, other responses. From the age of thirteen to twenty-three, I was taught entirely by men, who were the heads of all the departments of the subjects I studied for examinations, except, significantly, French. As an undergraduate, I had only male tutors. I learned early that there were accepted 'right' responses to deceptively open-ended questions. 'What do you think about . . . ?' was not an invitation to speculate about one's reactions, especially one's gut reactions, to, say, Burns' *Tam o'Shanter*. Instead of finding it in doubtful taste, as I did, I was expected to say it had verve and wit. (It has; it's the best possible pub tale, but I couldn't know that then.) On the other hand, my adolescent passion for Burns' love songs (which has not changed much) had to be modified in essays into acceptable statements about 'poetic diction', and so I learned to sing them in order to express what I thought they really *meant*. I memorized the hundred good words to defend Milton from Eliot, a strange deviance at that time – Edinburgh defying Cambridge, I guess. My own understanding of Milton – the blazing defiance of *Areopagitica* in all its clarity and the baroque splendours of *Paradise Lost* – restructured my consciousness, as Ong would say. But no-one noticed. Everyone knew that Milton was great. If I had even admitted at school that I enjoyed reading poetry I would have been mocked and shunned; dissimulation was part of all response. This hypocrisy, one of the darker strands of responses everywhere, was not in support of ambition; it was simply how you got through the school day, and the next one, keeping clear of scorn by standing in a devious relationship to authority.

Keeping secrets and silence about girls' school stories, Christina Rossetti, Virginia Woolf and the accidental discovery of Boccaccio, I spoke openly of Biggles, Aldous Huxley and pretended to read Zane Grey. I cleared my undergraduate essays of anything that was not supported by textual evidence. My reason for rehearsing all this is not simply to display selected parts of my reading history, but to show that I took a long time to see that these things *had* happened.

I had been taught to believe that to say 'I feel' or to say what I really thought in response to what I had read was to bring forth something indecent that no-one wanted to know about. So many responses were secrets, indulged in social silence. When I was turning the pages of more recent books of literary theory where 'reader-response' has a new respectability, I heard again the voices of these reasonable men, my teachers, confident in their understanding of what to me was always puzzling, ambiguous, double. Culler, whose work I like, announces 'A model of one's own literacy competence would be extremely valuable.' I agree. But this is half of the sentence, which concludes 'and doubtless have much general validity'. The exact nature of this 'general validity' needs analysis so that Culler's experiences and those of the bilingual children in London fifth forms, say, could stand alongside each other. The transformations of our 'understanding' brought about by engagements are dynamic and often fundamental. Reading is a particular example; others are looking at pictures and listening to music. I doubt if our best acknowledgements and comprehensions of the import of what we read are ever instantaneous, or complete.

If we are to problematize 'response' in respect of texts the better to understand what we mean, and what counts as evidence, then we cannot take for granted that we know what children do when they read, simply because they answer our questions. How, for example, do they learn what a story is? 'By being read to, and by gaining "experience" of different kinds of story, in the same way as they come to know dogs', is the usual answer. We assume that they recognize poems by their appearance on the page, and choose to distinguish them by rhythm and rhyme. How much and which kinds of their understandings are 'schooled' we are not sure. The evidence we have from writers who explain their reading history suggests that their important reading experiences were singular discoveries. Yet we also know that many young people, those we interview for admission to university courses, for example, owe their interest in literature to a good teacher and good classroom discussions. Still, we have been curiously incurious about the reflexive and recursive nature of readers' understanding; as usual, we lack the time to inquire. So we keep on asking questions or devising activities to confirm and extend interactions with texts, treating the outcome as 'responses' which, on the whole, we expect. Our persistent problem is to be open to responses that make us reconsider what is going on. To read *again* with the young, remembering that their generation is not ours, may be more of a challenge than we want.

Between the ages of nine and eleven, my son became addicted to the adventures of *Asterix the Gaul* which was, at that time, a novelty. I could not discover what attracted him and kept him reading what I believed were esoteric jokes and puns about cultural stereotypes and French politics. It never occurred to me to understand at the time what he explained quite clearly fifteen years later. He liked the books because each volume was *what it was*: a set of comic pictures about comic characters who did comic things. He was, if you like, against interpretation, but not against response. This is the kind of lesson I thought I needed to learn; namely, that my questions about the jokes and the intertextual references were, at that stage, irrelevant.

So now I listen more carefully and do not let myself believe that I always know what children are doing when they read. If I had a regular school class I would engage in some of the 'meeting, sharing and displaying' that Benton and Fox so intriguingly propose. But, more than doing things *with* stories and poems, I feel I want to know what young readers *do* in the course of their coming to know what reading is and how they *interpret* texts in the light of their understanding of their world and of other texts. When a five-year-old says at the end of *The Tiger who Came to Tea* (and ate everything up) 'They should have had more to eat', what has she in mind? The seven-year-old in the *Primary Language Record* who says 'I can be two people in a book' makes me want to ask 'How?', because her understanding seems to be common among children of that age. Some teachers are particularly good at evoking reflections in young readers. I am given to quoting the report of a colleague who visited the children she had seen learning to read in a nursery class when they went to the reception class in the 'big' school, in order to see what happened to them in reading lessons. One child explained very patiently that, although she had been able to read *The Very Hungry Caterpillar* in the nursery, it was no longer possible for her to do so in her new class. Asked why, she explained that the teacher had not put the words for the 'eatings on Tuesday and Thursday on a card yet'. That is, her early reading experience, which included many significant understandings of the relations of text to pictures and the nature of 'sequencing', had no validity in the new situation, where only word recognition counted as reading.

Although literary theorists, in their queries about what is literature, now give readers a more significant role, they are still incurious about how young readers become the kinds of readers that literary texts imply. We still need to hear more about how readers are made, and teachers are nearest to the neglected evidence. So far we have only picked at the problem of why some people seem (only seem, I think) to give up reading entirely, and why others are reluctant to diversify their tastes and skills. We are not absolutely sure how 'good' a reader anyone needs to be nowadays. I know that what keeps readers going lies in what James Britton once called 'a legacy of past satisfactions'. That is, we go on reading because we not only like what we read but we are also pleased by reading itself. We may do other things as the result of reading a novel or a poem – twenty or fifty, even – but reading, to be satisfying, has to be part of the experience of the thing read. Our response is also to the reading of it and some readers' responses are a refusal of the text. How do we learn that?

The differences between readers' readings are what the theorists find endlessly attractive. Terry Eagleton re-reads and rewrites the Book of Jonah which he calls 'a surrealist farce' to illustrate his understanding of Paul de Man's *Allegories of Reading* (Eagleton, 1988). Here is part of his response, to reading both Jonah and de Man:

> Rhetorical discourse, in the sense of language intended to have definite public effects, is marred and insidiously undone by 'rhetoric' in the sense of verbal figuration. Something like this, I would suggest, is the abyss or aporia, the vertigin-

ous collapse of meaning in which Jonah is finally embroiled. Even if he could console himself by surmising that this journey to Nineveh really *was* necessary, that his crying doom was performatively effective rather than farcically redundant, there is no way in which he can ever know whether he was doing anything or not. There is no means of precisely determining the hair-thin line between describing and yet getting something done, being a spectator and being a participant.

Critics teach us about reading and how they do it. At the same time, they privilege certain kinds of reading, the kinds that reflect 'the spirit of the age', a phrase that provokes wry smiles but is, nevertheless, being heard more frequently these days. My point now is that pupils could, if we let them, show us how they learn the rules of the reading game; how they begin to take risks in trying out new generic forms, to tolerate uncertainty, to discover that texts have power, and to read against the grain of the writing in the spirit of the age, as we teach it. My unanalysed belief is that they learn many of these things by mimicry and parody, just as they do in drama. But 'sending up' literature is usually left to their own devices, or, at least, to the jokey bits at the end of term not included in assessments. Harold Rosen tells a cautionary tale of how, looking for evidence of his son Michael's progress in writing, he found only an empty neat essay book. But in the muddled privacy of the rough notebook were scores of satirical versions, take-offs, of what had been required homework, all of them showing the writer's grasp of the necessary 'verbal configuration'. Imitation seems an almost inevitable response in children's early engagements with literary devices, or, in fact, of any musical or artistic endeavour. Think of the schools of music and painting where, without our modern concern about copying or 'just' copying, the apprentices began by composing variations on a theme. We are right to see literacy as something more than scribal reproduction, but until they have become used to 'all kinds of writing' children are bound to do a fair amount of imitative practice, even if we do not set it for homework. The kinds of re-reading we encourage our pupils to do for examinations, for example, can produce more than neat essays. That said, however, we still have to ask whether we are always best pleased when, as the song says, they do it our way. Would we not be better informed about both literature and learning if we gave them more responsibility for texts, the undoing and remaking of them?

Close reading is always re-reading, interpretation, after our initial surrender to the writer's invitation to an engagement with the text. What we now need is a series of inquiries into what the young do when they do this, inquiries which do not depend solely on our asking questions or promoting classroom activities. How, for example, do young readers relate what they have already read to what they are now reading? What kind of attention do they give to what they do not quite understand, or to texts they believe they understand but then discover they have been mistaken about? When Barbara Everett (1986) writes about Keats' *Ode to a Nightingale*, a text which, until recently, has appeared every year in 'A' level examinations since these began, she takes two and a half pages to discuss 'hemlock'. As interpretive sources she includes a wide range of references, her other readings. In doing so, she challenges the idea that, in reading the poem, we know at once how Keats heard the nightingale and that his is the way we are to hear it. How much idiosyncracy are we prepared to tolerate in our sixth formers' essays, or in that of a younger student who just had to pursue her own way through the poem? When are the responses of the young unacceptable? Is our refusal of them the turning-off point for some readers?

What I think we need is some kind of *Inquiry into Meaning*, of the kind that Anne Bussis and her colleagues (1985) undertook with such success when they investigated the early reading of young children. If writing really does change consciousness, as Ong suggests, then I believe that we should know more about the nature of the changes. If the proposals of the Cox Committee (1989), that children should understand and respond to 'all kinds of writing', are to carry any weight, then we need to know what counts as evidence of this kind of attainment.

If we agree that children's interactions with texts, i.e. reading, still need sensitive exploration at all ages and stages, we must agree to look at the relation of reading to all other forms of language use: speaking, listening and writing. We may also have to include what we often ignore: children's refusal to be involved in what they are expected to read, their belief that what we like is not likeable, as well as the reading they do that we think does not count. School 'reading and responding' is by no means the whole of children's literacy, but their wider literacy gives school reading much of its contextual reference. As Carlo Ginzburg, Shirley Brice Heath and Michael Cole make plain, we not only have our own reading history, but we are also part of the history of literacy. Before they come to school, and throughout their time there, our pupils absorb the lessons of the literacy events of their lives at home, in the street, and from television and video. So we are bound to be aware of differences in responding and, in most classrooms nowadays, of the pluricultural nature of most responses.

In my current work in the London borough of Brent, I watch children making their own *versions* of stories and books. A universal favourite with the very young is Raymond Briggs' wordless picture book *The Snowman*. In a classroom full of new pictures of snowmen made by the children, the Bengali one is quite different from the Turkish one. Many of these children have never seen snow, yet the pictures are recognizably wintry. Seeing the children at work I recognize the imaginative force that pictures, images and television have on them.

Those who study children's reactions to television say that they are capable of sophisticated judgements about the interactions of words and pictures (Davis, 1989). When I hear them discussing *The Snowman* I know they are teaching each other different ways of looking. The book itself lets them recognize the everyday things of their lives at home and also to see them differently. The Snowman likes the refrigerator, looks silly in ordinary clothes, and lets the child in the book, and thus, the reader, fly. So, from the earliest book experience, readers are offered a change of perspective. What do they make of it? What is the dialogue of the imagination like at this stage?

Surely, we know response in most domains as the making of alternative worlds. We have long known that this is what reading is good for, especially the reading of fiction. *The Cool Web* came together as an invitation to consider this in relation to

Winnicott's idea of a 'Third Area', the space between the internal and external worlds where the dialogic imagination works to investigate the possible alternative construing of experiences. Writing about children watching television (Spencer, 1987) helped me to locate what I still describe uneasily as response in that domain where I consider how I relate the social text of the world I live in to the musical, pictorial and verbal texts I choose to engage with. In discussing what happens in both domains, I recognize that my interactions are different from others', even when the world and the texts are things we share. We are all constantly examining by means of argument or storytelling what Bruner calls *possibilities*: the words that expand experience, change consciousness, deepen affectivity and the worlds that artists, musicians and writers have made. Here is Bruner's (1986) version:

> We construct many realities, and do so from different intentions. But we do not construct them out of Rorschach blots, but out of the myriad forms in which we structure experience – whether the experience of the senses, the deeply symbolically encoded experiences we gain through interacting in our social world, or the vicarious experience we achieve in the act of reading – the function of literature as art is to open us to dilemmas, to the hypothetical, to the range of possible worlds that texts can refer to.

It is the 'myriad' nature of responses that I want to hang on to, not least because it outwits test-makers and turns dilemmas into opportunities for both poetry and logical analysis.

This leaves, of course, one great gap, the response that teachers shy away from – boredom. We have many words for this state of mind; it has a long history, but somehow it escapes analysis. The serious aspect of boredom is not a lack of response, but when we are bored we do not want to do anything else. There is no denying the power of boredom, the inanition, the blocking of the escape routes of daydreaming, and interior narrative. Boredom is the response we need to know more about.

I tried to investigate boredom as part of a plan I had two years ago to read the same text with children at each year stage in school from six to sixteen. To do this, I chose Ted Hughes' (1968) *The Iron Man* to see what kind of evidence I could find to set against what Hughes wrote about his story in 'Myth and education' (1970). I have to report that I did not have a single chance to analyse boredom. Simply by asking children to read the story and to talk about it with others, I recorded some of the best classroom discussions I have ever heard. *The Iron Man* clearly inhibits boredom.

The 'myriad forms' of the children's responses included re-tellings, plays, models, poems, pictures, extensions of the fable and parallel narratives, oral and written. For the very young, the destruction and return of the Iron Man became metaphors, mirror images of family dramas and stories of loss. The eight-year-olds reshaped the events to highlight emotions of fear and excitement. Secondary school pupils grappled with the allegory, as we might expect. But at each stage, the same details in the text were the source of comment. For all readers and listeners the tale seemed to be essentially visual, iconic. The different *versions* of the narrative were evoked by the sharp-edged detail in the story. When it came to saying which part they liked best, children of all ages picked out precise words of the text. The six-year-old who said 'My best bit is "delicacies"' chose the same passage as the sixteen-year-old who said 'I like the high particularity of the prose.'

Leaving boredom behind, I decided to look in children's books for writing which gave young readers lessons in what I believe is *textual power*. I borrow this notion, of course, from Robert Scholes, and add it to Bruner's idea of 'recruiting' the imagination of readers. As I sorted out the books for *How Texts Teach What Readers Learn* (1988), I found that Janet and Allan Ahlberg, both of whom are teachers, had embedded in their continuing *oeuvre* a plan for helping young readers to learn the rules of storytelling and to discover how they can be changed. In *The Baby's Catalogue* (1982) they introduce the relation of life to text: five families here do the same things, but they are all different. In *Each Peach Pear Plum* (1978) they rewrite the old rhyme, introducing the best known characters in nursery tales: The Three Bears, Cinderella, Mother Hubbard, The Wicked Witch, Robin Hood, Bo-Peep, Jack and Jill. Then, they enchant more than a million readers with *The Jolly Postman* (1986), the most successful children's book of the decade. Here we have children's discovery that all texts imply other texts. Response, then, can never be singular; it is always multiple, layered, combining understanding and affect, involving mental images and gestures for which the surface features of words always seem inadequate. For me, and for the children I know, responses are other *versions*, rediscoveries, sets of possibilities, hazards, risks, a change of consciousness, a social interaction. Here is how eight-year-olds respond to the 'myriad forms' of *The Jolly Postman* with their versions. (They came to me by the generosity of the publisher and the teacher who collected them.)

Miss Muffett
Tuffet Cottage

Dear Miss Muffett,

I am deeply sorry for the inconvenience caused by prancing up behind you and frightening you away. I merely meant to make a friendly gesture to you. I hope in future we could be friends. P.S. I will try to leave you in peace to eat your curds and whey.

Yours faithfully,
B. Webb

---

24 November 1986

Squire & Co (Solicitors)
Shirley
Solihull
West Midlands B90 2RD

744 9289

Dear Mr Tortoise,

I'm writing to you on behalf of my client Mr Hare. He wants to take you to court for unlawful behaviour. He seems to think you took the trophy unfairly.
Please attend this court at 12.00 am on Friday next.
Here is the address:
Magistrates' Court, 3 Regent Street, London.
Please attend punctually.
Thanking you in anticipation.

Yours sincerely,
Paul Mosson

---

5 Yaxall Buildings
Derwent
England
24.11.76

Old Woman
1 Boot Lane
Wently
England

Dear Madam,

I am writing to you on behalf of the Social Services Department of Housing. I have the pleasurable duty of informing you of our plans to re-house you into larger accommodation. We are all hoping that you are not too hungry as we are informed by your husband that he has forgotten the code on his 'Family Express' card and therefore can send no maintenance. We are moving you to a larger mansion house and we hope you will be very happy there.

Yours sincerely,

Ben Palmer
Housing Director

Mr R Cow
Sweetfields Lane
The Woods
B90 QRP
West Midlands

Dear Mr Cow,

I am writing to say please don't jump over me, because it does hurt when your hoof hits me. I have already got a big cut on my side. If you don't stop it I will not have any strength to shine.

from Mr Moon

P.S. If you don't stop it I will tell the C.T.M.A. (Cruelty to Moons Association)

I offer these as evidence of responses of which young readers are capable with regard to forms of rhetoric. The contents are imaginary, the forms are directly social, exactly as in *The Jolly Postman*. The children had no explicit lessons, but some important sharing. There is nothing reckless or desperate about this, just a humorous understanding of the reader's responsibility to the author, and, more remarkable at this stage, of the author's to the reader. It is the beginning of certain ways of doing things with words in the world and in the imagination, ways that Eagleton must have tried out in his youth. The children are able to 'follow' their reading of *The Jolly Postman*, probably because their teacher encouraged it, knowing that this brilliant book had become a milestone in their reading history. She does not need to ask questions; instead she invites imitation. The children know what they are handling, so they take risks. The parodies reflect their text-to-text awareness, their close reading and observations of the Ahlbergs. They offer us a way of continuing our inquiries into their meaning making.

I will conclude with an apophthegm to say that the non-boring reading that children do is, essentially, about reading. Nowadays, literary text in books for the young, from the non-words of *The Snowman* to whatever is chosen for GCSE, embodies other texts, the stories, poems, discoveries that *keep them going*. Response to reading is always more reading, re-telling, versions, renewals as well as the text-to-life, life-to-text engagement of readers. But we still need to explore boredom, refusal, hazard and loss. We should know why some children give up reading, and why others never really begin to read in ways that make response possible.

2 Research on reader response and the National Literature Initiative

JAMES R. SQUIRE

Today's schools, particularly American elementary schools, are seeing a reawakening of interest in literature – on the one hand, concern with what should be taught and, on the other, a reassertion of the power of imaginative and literary studies after a decade of stress on accountability for specific skills and overt attention to the writing process. The California Literature Initiative (California State Department of Education, 1987; Barr, in press) is not only influencing the content and structure of basal reading programmes and the emphasis on 'whole language' strategies, but as it sweeps eastward seems to be redirecting attention to the significance of literature in the total educational programme. Coupled with the steady but perceptibly growing influence of Louise Rosenblatt's second study, *The Reader, the Text, the Poem* (1978), one senses a genuine chance, perhaps for the first time, for developing response-oriented programmes in our schools on a widespread basis. But the more one reads about James Madison Elementary School (Bennett, 1988) and its like, or of similar exemplary school projects, and the more one listens to supervisors in California talk about '*the* response approach' (a term that is anathema to what response-oriented teaching genuinely is about), it seems clear that a reinterpretation of what we know about response to literature and what it means for teaching is a critical priority. Too many practitioners today seem to be using 'response to literature' as an umbrella term to refer to any aspect of literature and its teaching: the study of literature, the study of the teaching of literature (which may or may not be designed to elicit response), or studies about and around literature – the author, the genre, the history, the cultural period from which the work emerged, and so forth. And even more one senses a lack of concern for the quality of reading and quality of the response. Response to literature does not mean response to just any kind of reading, nor does it mean that 'anything goes' when a child reacts to a particular text. Important as the experiences a child brings to the reading of a book are, the text itself imposes rigorous limits on the nature and direction of his or her response. One cannot give a child a predetermined response. But it does not follow that any response, regardless of stimulus, can be accepted in teaching literature.

Some historical views on reader response

Research in response to literature dates back sixty years to I. A. Richards (1929) and his analysis of the misreadings in protocols written by selected Cambridge undergraduates about thirteen poems. Concerned about 'the meaning of meanings', Richards pinpointed ten problems in responding which were reflected in the readings of his subjects. The fact that his talented undergraduate subjects included such future literary critics as D. W. Harding and L. C. Knights only underscores the fact that even the most literarily inclined readers can go wrong when they are young. And what Richards did for poetry, Wayne Booth (1988) has done today for fiction, detailing the strategies of readers as they confront the strategies of writers. A brilliant new study.

Ten years after Richards, Louise Rosenblatt gave us *Literature as Exploration* (1938), her personal study of the transaction between works and readers, and an assertion of the power of personal experience in shaping the experience of literature. Drawing on Dewey and on Bentley's transaction formulation for the social sciences, she called for exploration of the complex nature of literary response through the case study method, a practice which has been followed by many subsequent researchers. Rosenblatt's work grows steadily more influential (see, e.g. Clifford, 1988). *Literature as Exploration* remains the fountainhead of the analytical study of reader response – in research, in curriculum development, in literary theory; and coupled with Rosenblatt's subsequent work, *The Reader, the Text, the Poem* (1978), we have a literary theory which has influenced virtually all subsequent researchers and research on the transaction of book and reader (Farrell and Squire, 1990).

The research has been substantial and continual, if never dominant. Partly conditioned by other compelling interests at the time, we have seen studies of reader response in relation to personality variables (Meckel, 1946; Russell and Shrodes, 1950; Britton, 1963; Squire, 1968; Petrosky, 1975, 1985; Holland, 1975); prejudice and social outlook (Loban, 1954; Taba, 1955); aesthetic consideration (Beach and Brunetti, 1976; Purves and Rippere, 1963; McClure, 1986; Beach and Wendler, 1987); cultural background (Fanslow, 1973; Hansson, 1973); orthographic knowledge (D. Barone, 1989); teaching method (Wilson, 1966; Janssen and Rijlaarsdam, 1989; beliefs and expectations (Cullinan *et al.*, 1983); gender (D. Barone, 1989); personal style (Hickman, 1981), and reading competence (Purves, 1975; Anderson and Pearson, 1987; Meek *et al.*, 1977, 1983; Hynds, 1986). Few may have been significant on their own, but together they form a distinct pattern. Further, psychologist Robert Coles (1989) has now explored the ways in which readers organize their own perceptions of reality through the intermix of their own stories with the narratives that they encounter. Many of these have been summarized from time to time by Meckel (1953), Russell (1970), Squire (1969), Purves (1975), Applebee (1982), Purves and Beach (1972), Galda (1982), Hickman (1983) and, most recently, Beach and Hynds (1990) and Walker (in press).

From the 1940s to the 1970s, European psychological, philosophical and literary scholars were also studying the reader's response to literature. Particularly brilliant was D. W. Harding's (1937, 1962, 1963) analytical formulation of the differences in the reaction of the reader as *participant* in the text to which he is responding, and the reader seeing himself as *spectator* or *onlooker* of the action. The two stances clearly 'impact' the individual reader's involvement in the action and affect the ways in which he or she views the narrative. Harding's work influenced Britton's (1969) reflections about the role of literature in language learning, later studies by Applebee (1978, 1985), Margaret Meek *et al.*'s (1977) construction of 'the cool web' of patterning in children's reading, and others. Also influential has been the recent writing of Corcoran and Evans (1987), who have studied the response theories of Wolfgang Iser, whose *Act of Reading* (1978) examines the ways in which the reader's own predispositions are balanced against the role of the text. The European critics' concern with reader response continues to be vigorous. Witness, for example, recent volumes by Griffith (1987) and Van Peer (1988).

Whether stimulated by publication of Rosenblatt's (1978) second study, by the recommendations on response to literature emerging from the Anglo-American Seminar at Dartmouth College (Squire, 1968), or by reading research studies on the impact of prior knowledge and schema theory on reading comprehension (Pearson, 1986), recent years have seen a rise in concern with reader response theory in teaching strategies (Holland, 1968, 1985; Probst, 1988; Nelms, 1988; Barr, in press), in literary theory (Bleich, 1986; Griffith, 1987; Chew *et al.*, 1986; Milner and Milner, 1989) and in research (Cooper, 1985). Many of the studies of schema theory, studies of the impact of prior knowledge and prior experience on the comprehension of children and young people, supply empirical data to illuminate insights into reader response long since advanced by Rosenblatt, Carlsen, Loban, and others. Carlsen and Sherrill's (1988) most recent analyses of the reading autobiographies of more than 1000 readers, a delightful book illuminates with personal anecdotes many of the major findings of the empiricists. These diaries and case studies provide valuable insights into the richness of children's responses. Appearing at the same time as Robert Coles' brilliant study of the response of his college students to literature, they remind us that response to literature is fundamentally an individual experience. Indeed, once in a while, writes Coles (1989, p. 88) 'a bold student dares really immerse himself or herself in a particular novel or short story, dares give a literary creation a new private lease on life'.

A review, then, of both these studies and the methods used in research yields certain clear findings which should influence the teaching in our schools more extensively than I sense is happening today. It raises inevitable questions about the designs emphasized in researching children's responses. Here, I would like to deal with both dimensions of the research of the past seventy-five years: what we know that should inform our teaching and what we should find out.

What we know about the teaching response of the reader that should inform classroom teaching which purports to be literature-centred

1 *The teaching of literature must focus on the transaction between the reader and the work* (Rosenblatt, 1938, 1978; Probst, 1988). The task of teaching literary history is a task for the literary historian; the task of teaching about the lives of authors, a task for the literary biographer; the task of teaching about the structure of the text or characteristics of the genre, one for the literary critic. The task of the teacher of literature, on the other hand, is to focus on the transaction between the book and the reader, on the literary experience itself, and on ways of extending and deepening it. As Scholes (1987, pp.24–5) clearly puts it:

> Our job is not to produce 'readings' for our students but to give them the task of producing their own. Our job is *not* to inundate students with our own superior textual production; it is to show them the codes on which all textual production depends, and to encourage their own textual practice.

Sound literary insight and aesthetic judgement will never be taught by imposing from above adult ideas of what a work should mean (Rosenblatt, 1938; Beach and Hynds, 1990). But neither will such insight develop automatically, without guidance and nourishment from the teacher (Probst, 1988; Squire, 1969). Would that the recent spate of British titles on methods of eliciting response in the classroom were better known by American teachers (Benton *et al.*, 1988; Dias and Hayhoe, 1988; Protherough, 1983).

2 *Response is affected by prior knowledge and prior experience.* The reader brings to any work of literature personality traits, memories of past events, present needs and preoccupations, a particular mood, and a particular preoccupation (Rosenblatt, 1938). If, as research in reading comprehension has demonstrated (Pearson, 1986; Tierney *et al.*, 1987), prior knowledge is one of the most influential variables in determining adequacy of the comprehension of informational texts, how much more potent its power when affective, emotional experiences are involved. And how significant the prior experience of readers in determining their reactions to particular works. As Meek *et al.* (1983) make clear, prior experience includes not just events and books but 'must also include learning how to make inferences, infer points of view, and make predictions as one reads'. Certainly, emotional involvement with a text is critical to understanding. 'Feelings are facts', writes Margaret Heaton (1955), a gifted teacher who once summarized the ways of engaging children with books, and only recently Hynds and Chase reported that college readers who were 'feeling types' are more likely to make evaluative judgements on literature than readers who are 'thinking types' (Beach and Hynds, 1990; Squire, 1963). Yet too intense findings can adversely affect the capacity to respond (Russell, 1969). Meckel (1946), for instance, reported boys insecure in relations with their fathers blocking personal reactions to Hugh Walpole's *Fortitude*; Loban (1954) found adolescents' responses to

short stories intended to evoke sympathy varied with the readers in relation to their innate social sensitivity; Mosenthal (1987a, b) provided arresting insights on affective responses to the theme of alienation. How important it is, then, to select literature for teaching for which children and young people are likely to have sufficient personal experience to understand. John Middleton Synge's *Riders to the Sea*, for example, may be the greatest short play ever written, but it is a work that requires maturity on the part of the reader. One has to live for a time with the inevitability of death, with the endless waiting for the end, to really grasp what Synge's Irish drama is all about. As Robert Coles observes in his study of the impact of books, some readers come late to them. Men and women who return to school in their middle or late twenties or early thirties seem especially responsive to *The Moviegoer* or *The Last Gentleman*. They may have decided what occupation to pursue, but have not made their way with a personal life that they find worthy of respect and commitment. Why introduce such mature works too early? Why *King Lear* or *Hamlet*, with their hallmarks of ageing, when *Romeo and Juliet* works so well for young minds? Why an adult's intellectual treat like *Alice* to which few children really respond? If *Water Babies* once grasped the imaginations of young children, it no longer does so. Few of today's children can respond to Robert Louis Stevenson's tortuous sentences in *Treasure Island* at an age when they can also empathize with Jim Hawkins in the apple barrel. As the Dartmouth Report on Response to Literature recommended, we need to re-examine the canon and find works that speak to boys and girls today (Squire, 1968). Ann Terry's (1974) study of poetry preferences and its follow-up study by Fisher and Natarella (1979), help to distinguish good poems to which many children respond; and Norvell's (1950, 1958) older study of reading interests in the standard school canon reveals outstanding texts which still have meaning to boys and girls today. To liberate the imagination, we need to provide young people with a broad range of literature – works past and present, reflecting cultures different from our own (Farrell, in press). But we also need to ascertain those selections which are most accessible to young people. Why don't we use the many reading preference studies in deciding on the selections of literature to be taught (Walker, in press)? Dollerup *et al.*'s (1981–8) current analysis in the Danish Folktale Project of varying responses within and about cultures to familiar and less familiar folk-tales, offers an encouraging approach which might be applied to the standard curriculum.

3 *Response is affected by prior knowledge and prior experience and it differs with time and place.* One twenty-year-old study found American students responding to books on racial relations like *Black Like Me* and *To Kill a Mockingbird*, but equivalent British boys and girls preferring stories dealing with the working-class struggle like *The Loneliness of the Long Distance Runner* and *Sons and Lovers* (Squire and Applebee, 1969). National experience, geographic limitations, prevailing attitudes – these affect the capacity to respond. If one of the tasks of the school is to build background experiences so as to free children from the insularity of their limited experiences, we need to bear in mind those literary experiences that will

be really ennobling. An interesting attempt to suggest teaching strategies based on this research is offered by Bridge (1987).

4 *Response to literature varies with the rhetorical mode* (narrative, non-narrative; efferent, afferent: Rosenblatt, 1978; Beach, 1985). Children and young people need help in responding to texts of many kinds. 'The meanings readers derive from texts vary according to the prior knowledge of speech-act, of social, and literary conventions . . .' (Beach and Brown, 1987). This mandates programmes structured to introduce young readers to many modes, genres and conventions (Squire, 1985; Dixon and Stratta, 1987), not programmes which provide only repetitive experiences in reading the same kind of fiction.

Independent reading programmes require particularly careful scrutiny. Left to their own devices, children will choose to read extensively in only one kind of literature and at one particular level (Handlan, 1946). Personal guidance from the teacher – 'nudging' to use the word of one British headmistress – may be needed to enrich and advance the reading choices of boys and girls.

Further, our programmes in teaching children to read and our programmes for teaching them to respond to reading must distinguish sharply between what Rosenblatt (1978) calls 'efferent' texts – reading to take away information – and 'afferent' texts – those which provide genuine experience. Reading specialists like Calfee (1987) and Venezky *et al.* (1987) have warned that children taught to read only with literary texts will become disabled comprehenders of informational texts. One cannot but speculate whether the great emphasis today on literature-centred reading programmes does not risk creating a generation of youngsters who can read literature, but are unable to comprehend and respond to science, history, geography and even biography. Certainly one could be more sanguine about the long-range impact of these programmes if equal stress were placed on teaching boys and girls to read informational texts during content area instruction (Venezky *et al.*, 1987).

5 *Large numbers of readers generally share a common response to a particular literary text; yet no two responses are alike.* Still, both the central tendencies and the predictable dispersions must be considered in teaching (Rosenblatt, 1978; Probst, 1988). It seems particularly important that young readers learn to recognize the limitations that the author's text imposes on any particular reading: 'Though students should express freely their reactions to a selection in both writing and class discussion, the text must remain a constant restraint against total relativism' (Farrell, in press).

When Rudine Sims Bishop (in press) talked about children reacting to the 'people in feathers and fur' in *Charlotte's Web*, and the ways in which children see themselves and others in fat and lonely Wilbur, greedy and selfish Templeton, brilliant, beautiful, and loyal Charlotte, she was talking about the commonalities in response to the book. It is E. B. White's text that requires young readers to see *Charlotte's Web* as a book about friendship and loyalty and the cycle of life, and not otherwise, despite all personal predispositions (Sims Bishop, in press). Still, there remains much room for personal response.

6 *Works of genuine literary quality can evoke richer, more meaningful experience than those that I. A. Richards calls 'pseudo-literature'* – the trite hackneyed works which convey no real experience but depend on stereotypes already implanted in the reader's mind. 'The button is pressed', says Richards in talking about such stereotypic literature, 'and then the author's work is done, for immediately the record starts playing in quasi- (or total) independence of the poem which is supposed to be its origin or instrument' (Richards, 1929, pp. 16–17). Such texts provide few, if any, real points of contact between what the writer expresses and what the reader feels, because the writer is trying not to convey an experience but to capitalize on a stereotyped association. Much writing for children and adults, including many television scripts, but also the romantic fiction of the pulps on the local newsstands, or the formula mystery stories, etc., are this kind of writing. There is nothing wrong with such reading – almost all of us do it from time to time – but we cannot expect such books to convey real experience. A real literary text, to quote Dixon (in press), 'a poem, a novel, a play . . . is an event in the life of a reader. It is an experience s/he lives through, part of the ongoing stream of life.' In the classroom, do we need to distinguish between 'reading material' and works of genuine literary merit at every level? Literary sensibility is not likely to emerge from a diet of pseudo-literature, nor are genuine literary responses. Too many of today's 'response-oriented' reading programmes are not subjecting themselves to the criteria of quality, and tend, therefore, to confuse any kind of reading and any kind of child response with genuine experience.

Robert Coles (1989, p. 190) sees that matching books and readers has much to do with engaging the moral imagination:

> Over time I began to learn from the students that constructing a good reading list involves not so much matching student interest with author's subject matter . . . as considering the degree of moral engagement a particular text seems able to make with any number of readers. 'This novel won't let go of me,' a college freshman said to me about *Invisible Man* – and the student was white and from a wealthy, powerful family.

One finds no semblance of 'pseudo-literature' in the titles to which Coles' students respond. When these great books really work with a reader, they can have all of the power of life experience itself.

Yet this does not mean that we need the programme of great books that E. D. Hirsch (1987) or Ravitch and Finn (1987) recommend today, that Mortimer Adler advocated yesterday (1982), or even the multicultural prescriptions now becoming available (Simonson and Walker, 1988). There are many great literary experiences for children at every developmental level. Forcing children to confront classics in which archaic language or ways of life confound understanding does not contribute to the process of growth. Such works can await student maturity (Farrell, in press).

7 *It takes two to read a book.* This statement has become a truism since first advanced by Purves. We must realize that much of the value of the reading experience comes from thinking about, or talking about, or writing about the work (Purves, 1972). This is true from the pre-school days onwards. What other reason for Dolores Durkin's (1966) discovery of the power of oral reading of literature as contributing to children's response to stories; Hickman's (1980) finding that books read aloud by the teacher elicit rich art responses with young children; or Sulzby and Teale's (1987; Sulzby, 1985) reporting that 'integral to storytime experiences of young readers is discussion with the shared text, and that participation of the adult reader is important'? D. Barone (1989) has demonstrated how effectively first-graders can write about their independent reading. We learn from experience. Remember the words of John Dewey: 'An activity – even the activity of reading – doesn't become an experience until we think about it.' It is the thinking during and after reading that translates the activity of reading to experience. 'Response is a process of discovering meaning through talking and writing' (Beach and Hynds, 1990). 'Think alouds', as Susan Lytle conceived them, help to stimulate response (Beach and Hynds, 1990). Active construction and the processing of ideas about literature through language are stressed by Britton (1969) and Martinez and Roser (in press). Yet in too few of today's school programmes, even our whole language programmes, do we sense the linkage of talking and writing about books to the central goal of responding. This sharing is one of the central reasons, I think, for providing some common literary experience at every level.

In the context of schooling, such oral responding to literature can well occur within a group. John Dixon (in press) says it well when he talks about a:

> new classroom tradition internationally – group reading of a poem, group discussion of how a text is to be rendered, group consideration following such rehearsals, and reading help to alert each individual student to potential cues in the text and the latent potential in the experience that can be drawn on as they construct a human event. . . . As each reader's primary transaction with the text is directly communicated by the spoken voice, by gesture, and by action, it is possible for a sympathetic group to produce a joint discussion.

8 *Important developmental differences can be seen in the ways children respond to literature.* Applebee (1978) found differences across age levels – six-, nine-, thirteen- and seventeen-year-olds – in children's objective responses to such verifiable characteristics as character, theme and point of view. Favat (1977) and Lehr (1988) also explored the development of children's perceptions.

We know that analysis of structure and generalization about literary response emerges slowly, but that most children are summarizing and providing synopses by the end of the fourth grade (Beach and Wendler, 1987; Beach and Hynds, 1990). Certainly, interpretation of what is read, as distinct from factual retelling, emerges later (Squire, 1963; Purves, 1975), as does any tendency to be able to look for symbols and themes, or to evaluate what is read.

Cullinan *et al.* (1983) and Hickman (1981) reported strong developmental trends in both the form and content of response, with Hickman's study particularly valuable in suggesting the modes of response – overt listening, sharing, a sense of discovery, losing oneself in discovery of a book, writing, making things appropriate at different levels. Beach and Wendler (1987) found college responders far more likely to focus on social and psychological factors than on personal feelings. Galda (1982) reminds us that individual styles vary in response at different developmental levels. We now seem to know enough to suggest a range of appropriate response activities for different developmental levels.

This is not unimportant, as Carlsen and Sherrill's (1988) study of adult recollections of literary experiences is replete with recollections of required response activities which blocked any semblance of response – formalized book reports, imposed interpretations, factual tests, and the like.

9 *The sounds of words are often as important as the sense.* One dimension of literature that is too little understood, too seldom researched, and too infrequently stressed in the schools of America is experiencing it aloud. 'The association of literature and the human voice has a powerful influence on a young person's interest in reading', report Carlsen and Sherrill (1988, p. 45) in analysing how adults remember their literary experiences. Can one really experience the glories of Browning or Shakespeare or, for that matter, of Thornton Wilder or Tennessee Williams without the stimulation of sound?

Poetry, being a complex intermingling of sound and image, virtually requires oral experience. But the group sharing described by Dixon (in press), the parent readings and teacher storytelling of early childhood (Sulzby and Teale, 1987), and interpretative oral reading by teacher and students, are curriculum experiences that will occur only if planned at every educational level.

10 *The ways in which we teach literature will affect our students' responses* (Applebee, 1982, 1989). It follows, then, that we must emphasize in schooling the kinds of responses we think most important to develop for a lifetime.

Purves, in his international study of literature teaching, found sharp differences in the kinds of responses from culture to culture – historical concerns in Italy, for instance; *explication de texte* among Belgian boys, but not Belgian girls; personal responses in the United Kingdom – all reflecting the kinds of educational programmes to which the children had been subjected (Purves, 1981; Purves *et al.*, 1973).

Dixon has demonstrated that the kinds of questions about literature asked in examinations – even college entrance examinations – influence the nature of questioning at lower school levels (Dixon and Brown, 1985). A study by the Center for the Learning and Teaching of Literature finds that 70% of the questions being asked by secondary teachers today in the United States elicit textual knowledge (Beach and Hynds, 1990). The individual questions are of the 'efferent', not the 'afferent' type, says Purves (in press). And has anyone recently examined the kinds of questions in our 'reading books'? Indeed, Applebee (1989), in a related study, finds few of today's high-school teachers even aware of reader response theory (or, for that matter, post-structuralism, or deconstructionism, or any other recent literary theories). Most literary teaching remains textually based, the legacy of the new criticism of the 1940s and 1950s. Most teaching of reading still focuses on explicit understanding. Where reader response is seen as important, it is introduced as a method for engaging young readers immediately after reading, prior to the comprehension lesson, and not as anything more. Is there any wonder, then, why so few Americans respond deeply to literature? This is scarcely what we mean by response-oriented teaching. Corcoran and Evans (1987), in a recent helpful review of the response processes of 'good sensitive experienced/perceptive' readers of literature, identify six characteristics:

- They can comprehend verbal ambiguities, regularize complex syntax and discriminate among verbal rhythms.
- They constantly predict how a story will unfold.
- They *expect* to help the author *make* the story.
- They can evaluate an author's point of view.
- They fuse emotional and intellectual responses.
- They know that they could be authors, and that they are often enjoying the power of providing texts to be read by someone other than their teachers.

In short, such individuals have learned how to 'read like writers', to quote the influential metaphor advanced by Pearson and Tierney (1984).

Planning instruction to elicit and respect reader response is difficult, because responses are unpredictable, diverse and often digressive. But unless we explore better ways of redirecting the literary education of young people, based on what we know about response, we are unlikely to create the nation of literature readers about which we talk and write so much. I see little indication that today's literature-centred reading programmes are coming to grips with these issues.

These ten principles, I submit, should form the basic strategies for redirecting the attention of teachers and students to literature-centred teaching. From all that we have learned about the response of the reader, these seem to be the most important.

Suggestions for research

If this review of research in response to literature has made clear much that we know and do not use in teaching, it also yields new critical problems that must be addressed by research. Here I will identify only four.

1 *We need greater insight into the ways in which response develops during the complete process of reading of a work of literature.* Too often research is based only on written responses to whole texts secured after the reading of the text is completed (Martinez and Roser, 1989). Those few researchers who have studied reactions sampled during the course of a total reading effort (Russell and Shrodes, 1950;

Squire, 1963; Hansson, 1973) report final, cumulative reactions can differ sharply from those occurring in midstream. Research in comprehension finds that children must learn to predict as they read, to reorganize continually and adapt their interpretation (Meek *et al.*, 1983; Pearson, 1986; Flood and Lapp, in press), yet we know little about how such continued reiteration of meaning (and feeling) may affect responses to literature. Dias' (1987) use of oral think-alouds in response to poetry might well be adapted to students' responses to other literary genres (see also Dias and Hayhoe, 1988). With longer works, especially, we need to discover the kinds of questions (if any) to be asked *en route* which might enhance response.

2 *Considered study must explore concretely the ways in which programmes for teaching reading comprehension and programmes for developing response to literature can best be integrated (or dare I say, isolated) in the classroom.* Are they mutually supportive, or mutually incompatible? Whatever the teacher's stance in reading, some attention must clearly be paid to textual meanings, to explicit interpretation of vocabulary and statement, to text organization, to specific skills or broader strategies in reading taught through the text, to what Rosenblatt (1978) sees as 'efferent' reading. More attention must also be paid to the nature and quality of the literary selection, as T. Barone's (1988) recent analysis suggested. Necessary as such skills and strategy development are to reading comprehension, is it not likely over the long haul to deaden interest in literature? The long catalogue of classroom horrors recalled in Carlsen's and Sherrill's (1988) reading autobiographies reads like a compendium of classroom methods from a teacher's textbook in reading. There is nothing wrong with these methods. They are needed to teach children to develop competence in reading. Yet, if we must apply them in literature-centred reading programmes, do we not run the risk of teaching children to read but at the same time destroy their desire to read? In a very real sense, the aims of reading instruction and the aims of a literary education are in conflict. We need to learn more about the long-range impact of providing all skill and strategy instruction through literature, and about alternatives which promote both competence in reading and power in responding.

3 *We need clearer guidelines on how literary appreciation or mature responses develop over a period of time* – the kinds of reading experiences, the kinds of instructional experience that will lead children to be mature responders. In Australia, Bunbury (1985) and Thomas (1987) have been developing constructs of stages of appreciation through which most children must pass. Not since Margaret Early in the 1960s has any American leader advanced similar ideas, although Cullinan *et al.*'s (1983) work on developmental differences in knowledge of conventions offers a beginning. Juel's (1988) longitudinal study of the impact of wide independent reading is also helpful. Stage theory may ultimately prove to be unworkable in describing how responses unfold over time, but probing the possibilities may provide guidelines for the curriculum which we do not presently possess. Dixon and Stratta (1987) and Barr (in press) express concern about the

current mixing of goals and methods; Rosenblatt (1978) suggests that efferent and afferent reading are fundamentally different. It is the exploration of these differences that remains our present task.

4 *Finally, we need to bring together, in ways more useful for teachers and teaching, what we now know from research in cognitive development and the teaching of comprehension about the impact of schema and prior knowledge on reading, with the insights from literary theories of various persuasions, and findings from research on response to literature.* A parley at the summit which engages some of our most insightful scholars and critics – from reading comprehension, from literary theory, from studies of reading response – to focus on this very problem *and no other*, could clarify much that remains opaque about the intermix of the processes of comprehension and literary response.

These, then, are four major problems which need to be addressed by researchers and teachers, and ten broad findings still to be applied to the classroom. Unless we find better ways of addressing these issues, the current Literature Initiative is not likely to become more than one brief moment, however shining, in the history of English Education.

3 Children's recognition of stories

ROBERT PROTHEROUGH

Background: The term story

Words can develop new senses and significance when they suddenly seem to concentrate the thinking of a generation; their fresh usage lasts until the newly acquired sense is stretched too widely or fossilizes into cliché. 'Story' is one such word. The traditional uses recorded in the *Oxford English Dictionary* are all straightforward references to a simple narrative: an anecdote, a tale, an incident, a succession of events, 'intended for entertainment', 'to amuse or interest', or 'a euphemism for a lie'. Stories were seen as somehow sub-literary: the term did not even merit a definition in Beckson and Ganz's (1961) *A Reader's Guide to Literary Terms* or a reference in Warren and Welleck's (1949) *Theory of Literature*.

In recent years, however, fresh uses of the term 'story' have provided English studies with a new focus and helped us to open up new ways of thinking about that interlocking of story-making and story-hearing which is inseparable from human consciousness. We have become used to the helpful notion of story as a key term to describe an element in almost all thinking, and to the concept of storying as a universal human activity. We take it for granted now that we apprehend what it is to be human through stories. In Barbara Hardy's (1975) often-quoted words, 'in order really to live, we make up stories about ourselves and others'. Through stories we are socialized into particular societies because 'stories structure the meanings by which a culture lives' (Cohan and Shires, 1988). Aidan Chambers (Noel, 1984) said that 'telling stories is the way people discover meaning', and storytelling is increasingly being seen as an essential element in all kinds of intellectual activity, scientific as well as artistic. It is not unusual now (as it would have been some years ago) for academic, literary or educational texts to have that word in the title: *Telling Stories* (Cohan and Shires, 1988), *Story Telling Rights* (Shuman, 1986), *Play, Language and Stories* (Galda and Pellegrini, 1986), or *Teaching as Story Telling* (Egan, 1988).

The ways in which children acquire a sense of stories and of their conventions have been increasingly documented. Studies have shown how interlocking are the stories that children hear and those they tell. Applebee's (1978) important work, *The Child's Concept of Story*, has been followed by detailed small-scale studies, e.g. Crago and Crago's (1983) study of one girl's development through stories, or Vivian Paley's (1981) description of the place of stories during a year in the life of her class. So much valuable work has been done that there is now some danger of over-simplifying the issues. Within the new, wider sense of story, texts are still defined in the traditional way, but story-making in a new one. Is there really a simple relationship between the ability to tell a story, the ability to recognize one, and an understanding of what a story is? It is easy to assume that story is a straightforward and uncontentious term, that we all know what we mean when we use it and that we employ it in the same way. In *A Grammar for Stories* (Prince, 1973), one of the major theorists goes on from arguing that 'everyone in every human society . . . knows how to tell stories, and this at a very early age' to say that 'furthermore, everyone distinguishes stories from non-stories', with the implication that we all make similar if not identical distinc ns Surprisingly little seems to have been done to test this belief, to consider whether people do in fact identify the same texts as stories, or to examine on what basis they make such decisions and implicitly (if not explicitly) define stories.

The commonsense assumption that we all know a story when we see one, has persisted in part because so much academic work on story has been text-centred rather than reader-centred. The different attempts to formulate story grammars, and from these to propose definitions of story, have tended to use reader responses only as a kind of proving mechanism to suggest that certain structures are better remembered or better comprehended than others. With one significant exception (Stein and Policastro, 1984), such studies have rarely asked children what they actually recognize as stories and what the point is of reading them.

The kinds of stories actually used in these experiments are often quite unlike those that children normally read or hear. What, for example, were eight-year-olds supposed to make of one complete narrative that read, 'The cat put on his glasses, and then he flew his toy plane, and then he went riding on a bolt of lightning', especially when the accompanying picture-cards showed the cat playing with a small toy plane in one picture, and riding in it in another (Brown, 1975)? Too many of the stories (like the 'interleaved' ones) sound deliberately concocted to test a hypothesis, or are in some other way implausible.

What do we recognize as a story?

Our assumptions can easily be tested. Here are four very brief texts. Which of them would you call a story?

1 Once an elderly lady in south London was unhappy because her pet cat had got stuck up a tree and would not come down. She called the fire brigade and they quickly arrived with a long ladder. A fireman went up and brought down her cat. The old lady was so grateful that she invited all the men to come into her house for a cup of tea. Afterwards they thanked her, drove off in their fire-engine, and ran over her cat, killing it.

2 The cook got a big bowl and two dozen eggs and some butter and five pounds of flour and a pound of yeast. He mixed the flour and the eggs and the butter in the

big bowl, then put in the yeast. Then he lit the gas and when the oven was hot he put the cake in. Soon there was a lovely smell of baking cake.

3 Once upon a time the beautiful Princess Miranda fell very ill. Her father the king offered half his kingdom to anyone who could cure her. Famous doctors came flocking to the palace with their remedies, but none could cure the princess. Then there arrived a clever young man, the son of a magician, who said that he could kill the dragon. Next morning he took his magic sword and after a long battle he cut off the dragon's hideous head. There was much rejoicing in the city. He married the beautiful princess the same day, and they lived happily ever after.

4 We saw a lot of different animals at the zoo. There was this monkey there and he stole somebody's hat and put it on. We saw a shark with big teeth. It was coming right at me. We went around. There was this lady. She was washing the tiger. And the tiger it went over there and started roaring.

When this question was put to about forty participants at the International Convention on Reading and Response at the University of East Anglia in 1989, there was no unanimity in their responses. The majority classed no. 1 (taken from a book of anecdotes based on true stories from newspapers) as a story, but there were marked disagreements about no. 2 (description of a process taken out of context from a children's book, no. 3 (juxtaposing the beginning of one fairy tale with the end of another) and no. 4 (transcript from a boy asked to tell a story). The adults were almost as divided as the 700 children to whom the same passages had earlier been offered. In their responses, 68% believed no. 1 and 71% thought no. 3 to be stories, but only 21% called either nos 2 or 4 a story.

The story enquiry

The simple enquiry referred to here was concerned with the responses of just over 700 children across the ability range, drawn from the top three years of eight primary schools (now to be called years 4, 5 and 6) and from the first three years of three mixed comprehensive schools (years 7, 8 and 9). Thus they covered the age range eight to fourteen, with approximately equal numbers on each side of the primary/secondary transition.

The children were presented with ten brief passages of text: four of them (those printed above) common to all, the others varying between primary and secondary, though selected to represent the same categories (including a short narrative poem, the introductory paragraph of a story and a summary of the plot of a children's novel). The texts were drawn from published sources, with slight editing in three cases, and three of them were transcripts of young children's recorded stories. They were chosen for their brevity and from the kinds of source that children of their age might encounter. Each passage was read aloud twice while children followed the printed text. After each text, they were asked to record one of three simple options: YES (it is a story), NO (it is not a story) or I DON'T KNOW.

We hoped for clues that might help to answer a number of questions:

• Is it true that children of this age all distinguish between stories and non-stories?

- How clear are they about such a distinction in their own minds?
- How similar are their judgements?
- Do these judgements differ significantly according to age, to sex or to school?
- By what reasoning do they classify texts?

In a later stage of the enquiry, we were also concerned with what children saw as a 'good' story, and by what reasoning they reached this conclusion. Here, however, I shall summarize the information which bears upon the questions raised above.

Stories and non-stories

Prince's (1973) contention was borne out in so far as all the children did make an attempt to distinguish between stories and non-stories. However, it was also clear that, in practice, hardly any of them were prepared to make such a distinction about all ten of the texts they encountered. The dividing line that marked off stories from non-stories in their minds was very unclear, and their judgements were often tentative and uncertain, as the following points indicate:

1 Nearly one-third of the children changed their minds about particular passages in the course of completing the activity. Some of them altered their original opinions about as many as five of the ten texts, and although most of the changes were from YES or NO to I DON'T KNOW, some were from YES to NO or the other way round.

2 About 15% of the total responses were I DON'T KNOW. In other words, a general willingness to discriminate between stories and non-stories is not accompanied by an ability to do this in particular cases. The proportions choosing the DON'T KNOW option decreased with age both in the primary schools and in the secondary schools, but it is interesting that on the transition to secondary school, the proportions rose again. At all ages except top primary, girls were slightly more inclined to reply I DON'T KNOW than boys.

3 It will be apparent that some of the passages *are* (and were intended to be) more problematic than others. The important fact is that *none* of the ten texts was perceived as unproblematic. Only one (the dislocated fairy tale) attracted a DON'T KNOW response from fewer than one in ten (8%). More than 15% were unsure whether or not seven of the ten passages were stories.

4 In the cases where children *were* sure, they disagreed with one another about whether or not any text was a story. In no case were as many as three-quarters of the sample united in any one opinion. The strongest majority feelings were 71% believing that the fairy tale *was* a story and 69% agreeing that a brief narrative poem was *not*. In several cases, though, there was almost a balance between those opting for YES and those for NO.

5 There was a marked difference between pupils' relative willingness to see passages as stories. Several of them only picked out one as definitely a story, the majority selected several, and one deconstructionist in the making wrote 'All ten are stories and all of them are good.'

6 Increasing age seems to be associated with changing perceptions of some texts,

but in most cases there was only a minimal difference between the six years involved. The description of cake-making, for example, was classified identically in the primary and secondary schools, and in five of the six years the proportions calling it a story only varied between 19 and 21%. Those passages which showed more variation were:

- The fairy tale (no. 3), which was recognized as a story by 87% of the top juniors, but by decreasing numbers in the secondary years.
- Narrative poems, which were classed as stories by increasing numbers in each of the three years in the primary and secondary schools (though again with a fall after the transition).
- The newspaper anecdote about the cat (no. 1), which was increasingly classified as a story by each secondary year.
- The transcript of a young boy's visit to the zoo (no. 4), which was less likely to be called a story in secondary schools.

7 Variations by gender were more marked in the primary than in the secondary schools. The proportions identifying three of the passages as stories varied significantly between boys and girls in the primary schools. Girls were more likely than boys to see the fairy tale as a story (84% to 72%), but boys were more likely than girls to name the cookery description and a girl's oral narrative as stories.

8 At secondary level, in eight out of ten cases the difference between boys' and girls' ratings was only 4% or less (indeed, in five cases it was only 1%) and in the remaining two the differences were only 5 and 7%. Girls were rather more likely than boys to name the narrative poem and a summary of a novel's plot as stories. In the secondary schools, there was markedly more difference between classes and between schools than there was between the sexes.

9 The lack of assurance and the lack of agreement combine to suggest that 'story' is not a simple, unproblematic category. There seems little evidence that children have identical or even very similar perceptions of what a story is. They are even less likely to classify as a story other children's spoken narratives than printed ones by adults.

Discussion

There seems to be evidence, then, that in practice children vary considerably in what they recognize as a story. It is therefore important for teachers to identify the underlying concepts of story that lead individuals to their decisions. This is more difficult. What people know explicitly is quite different from the implicit understanding that they apply in actual situations. Only with caution, therefore, can we look at what children felt able to write (or to say to their teachers) when asked to give some indication of their reasoning. Their remarks provide us with some clues about those qualities that subconsciously or consciously they believe mark off stories from other kinds of texts. Two sets of their responses can be considered together:

- Why they felt uncertain about some passages.

- Why they decided that some texts were not stories.

We can sympathize with those who simply offered a gut reaction ('Because it's NOT') or expressed puzzlement:

- I dont no wether it is or not.
- I am just not sure.
- I'm not sure because it does not sound like a story.
- It sounds like a story but I don't think it is.
- To me it does not make sense, but it might be a story.

Most, however, made some attempt to explain their judgements, and the same basic reasons were advanced to justify both uncertainty and rejection. At all ages these judgements fell naturally into six major categories, each embodying some underlying criterion for what a story *should* be. These six can be illustrated by a few of many similar responses.

1 *Fictionality*
- This is not a story because it really could happen.
- It really is the truth and not fiction.
- It's a what happened thing not a story.

In other words, stories are imaginary, fictional, made up or false; they are not true or drawn from real life. This belief seemed at its strongest in year 5 Primary schools (perhaps when children are most used to hearing formulations like 'You're telling stories again!').

2 *Conviction*
- Its not realistick.
- Because I don't think that could happen.
- There is no such things as dragons.

This argument is the mirror image of 1. Stories are believable, realistic, true to life; they are not implausible. Some younger children seemed able to believe 1 and 2 simultaneously, and used both at different times for saying that texts were *not* stories.

3 *Evaluation*
- He could have wrote it better.
- It is not good English.
- Not what I like its too corny.

Stories are well written, in 'good' English; they are interesting and effective. Some children denied texts the title of story because they were 'boring' or 'stuwpid' or 'not exiting'. Some even thought that the narrative about the cat – the one most generally recognized as story – was not one because it was 'not very nice' or 'a bit cruel'.

4 *Categorizing*
- It is a poem so it can't be a story.
- It's the instructions, not a story.
- No story that I no of rimes.

Children seem to imply in comments like these that story is a literary form that can be clearly distinguished from other modes or kinds of writing; it is an exclusive genre; a text cannot be a story if it is more like some non-story category – diary, description, recipe or poem. Many children explained their uncertainty by an inability to categorize a text precisely, saying, for example, 'It's like a story but it's like a recipe' or 'I don't know if poems can still be called stories or not.'

5 *Content*

- Because you don't get stories written about that sort of thing.
- It is not like a story with people.
- Because it isn't about anything important.

A story has appropriate subject matter; essentially a sequence of events leading to a satisfactory ending. A common formulation was that a text was dubious or a non-story because it was 'only' about 'food' or 'talking' or 'describing', or was unsuitable in some way ('not a very nice thing to tell a small child'). The other common approach was to suggest that some vital ingredient was missing: 'Nothing really happened', 'There were no pictures in my mind', 'nothing exiting', 'no avenchers'.

6 *Structure*

- The story line changes as it goes along.
- This is a skeleton of a story, for we are left with a very vague idea.
- It's not really finished off.

In other words, stories are coherent; they have a structure that makes sense. An inability by the reader to construct a satisfactory meaning was one of the most common reasons for expressing uncertainty about a text. Children were sometimes scrupulously unwilling to say that a passage was *not* a story, but they recorded that they themselves were unable to read it like one: 'It sounds like a story at the beging, but when I got to the end I was not sure', 'It is more like a forward where it tells you what happened.'

The existence of these six implied criteria, despite their juvenile formulation and some inconsistencies, does suggest that children have internalized the major conventions of story form, but that they are uncertain in applying them. Older pupils tended to advance more reasons than younger ones, but all six categories were used by a number of children at all six ages. References to *fictionality* were used more often at primary level and *conviction* at secondary level. *Evaluation* was consistent (between 8 and 15% employing it) across five of the years (used rather more by the youngest primary year). *Categorizing* was the most common, mentioned by over 70% in all except the oldest secondary group (year 9), where it dropped abruptly to 38%.

The other two categories suggest something like a developmental pattern, though whether this is the case could not be substantiated without a longitudinal study (see Table 3.1). The increasing attention apparently paid with age to the two structural criteria is one of a number of indicators that the concept of a story develops significantly during these middle years. The question, of course, is how far this is learned as a result of direct and indirect teaching.

Table 3.1

Age group	Percentage of children referring to:	
	Content	Structure
8–9	18	26
9–10	19	27
10–11	38	38
11–12	58	68
12–13	64	60
13–14	76	79

Some implications for teaching

1 The fact that children in school will all have some idea what the term 'story' means, will be able to tell stories, will respond to stories they read or hear, and will be able in their own ways to distinguish between stories and non-stories, does *not* mean that different children will have the same idea of what a story is or of what stories in general are like. Stories told by one child will often not be recognized as stories by others. As teachers, we may have to remind ourselves that when we talk of stories, the word will have meanings and associations for particular children that we have not imagined (though some of which we may unintentionally have helped to create). There can be clear advantages in having such a variety within a group, providing that we are conscious of the range, but it may be desirable at times to work on sharing these ideas so that the variety is made explicit rather than remaining hidden.

2 The evidence suggests the importance of teacher and group influence in helping to mould ideas of story form. As was pointed out earlier, at secondary level the variations between schools were much greater than those between the sexes. In two classes, three-quarters of the pupils said that the dislocated fairy tale was not a story, but only one person in each of two other classes held this opinion. In some classes, a majority believed that a narrative poem was a story, but in others nobody expressed that view. Results like this suggest strongly that literary judgement is learned, acquired both through direct teaching and through the acted-out reading practices used in schools.

3 Some features of this enquiry (like the apparent increase with age in the proportions of those justifying their judgements in terms of structure or interpretation) seem to support my earlier work that pointed to a broad developmental sequence in the ways that children respond to fiction (Protherough, 1983). There is a continuing need for more work in this field, particularly for longitudinal studies, if teachers are to be provided with a reliable diagnostic tool, and if it is not to be misused in standardized assessment processes.

4 One purpose of such diagnostic work, and of bringing into the open children's existing preconceptions of stories, is to assess which stories will be appropriate

for individuals or for a group. An extension of this is to gain assistance in framing – within a school or department – a coherent programme of stories for use that will be developmental rather than working simply on thematic similarities or mechanical reading levels.

5 Some associated work suggests that there is much to recommend occasional periods in which classes are invited to share their ideas of those features that seem to mark particular kinds of story. In one recent lesson on fairy tales, a group of eleven-year-olds established together a wide range of markers: *formulaic* ('once upon a time', 'lived happily ever after'), *linguistic* (archaic registers like 'sought her hand in marriage'), *situational* (marriage-choice, tests and quests, riddle solving), *locational* (palaces, hovels, forests, far-off lands), and *conventional* in terms of character (kings and queens, old beggars, wicked witches, beautiful princesses), animals (horses, dragons and other monsters, frogs, birds) and objects (jewels, mirrors, spinning wheels, caskets, swords). Similar approaches to romances, thrillers, ghost stories and picture books for small children can help to bring to consciousness the implicit understanding that children have.

6 There is still a need for greater sharing across the primary/secondary transition. Several of the results suggest that on entering secondary school many children undergo a reversal of processes that had been maturing in the primary years. Concepts of story would be one suitable field for study by joint primary/secondary working parties.

7 The reading of stories cannot be separated from telling them and writing them. The evidence suggests that younger children may over-value surface features like punctuation or good 'describing' or 'doing' words, because those are the features that have been most stressed about their own writing.

8 Literary competence is largely a matter of learning what stories to tell about stories. (Protherough, 1987). This notion of competence varies from age to age, culture to culture and group to group. We have to start from what children themselves have to tell us, from *their* responses, not from any artificial ideas of what they *should* be able to do at any stage.

4 The experience of literature and the study of literature: the teacher-educator's experience

BEN NELMS AND DON ZANCANELLA

Experience and study: The tension

Valerie is an undergraduate English major at the University of Missouri who thinks that she may want to become an English teacher. In a classroom exercise, she was asked to list words that she associated with the word 'literature'. Her list included such terms as 'exciting', 'adventures', 'Sunday afternoons' and 'knowledge', but the most significant ones for her, she decided, were 'enjoyable', 'enlightening' and 'recreation'. She then compared her list with those of several of her classmates, reflected upon the similarities and differences in their lists, and discussed her thinking with a partner. Reflecting upon the experience, Valerie writes a paragraph that is not unusual among undergraduate teachers-in-training:

> This exercise reinforced something I already knew – I often struggle with the idea of reading literature for study and reading for pleasure. I enjoy 'literature' – the classics, what is considered 'good' literature, yet I also very much enjoy books which are 'non-literary' – to be read for only enjoyment's sake. When the directions said to write words we associate with literature, I did not even think of the mechanics. That scares me. I've spent three years studying literature and its mechanics, yet my words are all descriptive words or personal evaluations of literature.

Another student in the group, Laurel, had chosen such terms as 'relaxing', 'bedtime', 'children', 'cuddling' and 'hot chocolate' – probably reflecting in part her experience as a young mother. Valerie commented particularly on Laurel's contribution:

> I found one other person in the class [who] had very similar ideas/feelings about literature as me. Those feelings are what got me 'hooked' on the study of literature.

The ambivalence Valerie expresses is, of course, fairly typical of a young person embarking on a profession in the teaching of literature. What is a bit disconcerting is the genuine discomfort she feels in confronting the majority of her group, who had listed such words as 'characterization', 'setting', 'realism', 'symbolism', 'style', 'genre', 'epic', 'poetic', 'denouement', and the like. 'It scares me', she says. 'I've spent three years studying literature and its mechanics.' More interesting is the reinforcement she finds in Laurel's echoing of her responses in even more concrete terms. (Laurel is a more mature student and was generally a more outspoken one in group activities.) The sense of resolution Valerie reaches, almost unconsciously, balances her tensions and puts them in perspective: 'Those feelings [cuddling, hot chocolate, bedtime . . .] are what got me "hooked" on the study of literature.' Hence, without denigrating the years she has spent in study and her admiration of the 'classics', she realizes that her preoccupation with literary concerns has its roots in a deep sense of personal pleasure.

The comments of two of the other students, whose lists were more typical of the class's concern with critical terminology, betray their perhaps even more intense sense of ambivalence. Suzanne is also a more mature student, a young mother, who has been a speech teacher and director of youth activities for her church, but who only recently has turned to the profession of English:

> It amazes me how we (as a group) think the same when describing the word 'literature'. Many of us (including myself) looked at all the technical aspects of literature without focusing on the lighter side of the word. That is why I [divided the list made by our group] into two categories, light and heavy.
>
> What I have learned in this lab today is that I personally need to relax and let the literature I choose to read speak to me more clearly. Have fun and enjoy. Reading literature should be fun. My enthusiasm for life and teaching should spill over in my reaction to literature.

Though Suzanne concluded by saying that she thought this was 'an excellent lab activity', her resolve to let her enthusiasm for life and teaching spill over into her reading of literature was more easily spoken than acted upon. The choice of 'light' and 'heavy' – both somewhat pejorative terms to her – betrays her discomfort with both her reading of literature for study and her reading for pleasure. When she talked about her speech teaching and her church activities, one saw a more relaxed, enthusiastic, altogether pleasant person than the one struggling with the prospect of teaching literature to young persons.

Her partner, Jane, a librarian and French major, was even more direct in her analysis and reflection on the activity:

> My partner and I are a little paranoid about our lack of familiarity with literary jargon, so we both came up with fairly intellectual terms (less responsive than many others, like exciting, boring, etc.).
>
> I did answer honestly, though, about the things that are important to me, although I left out some. Probably the most important thing to me is beauty of expression.
>
> . . . The interesting thing I noticed is that the technical aspects work together to determine our responses and they're both equally important, and you don't have to analyze technical aspects to respond, though sometimes you want to, or can't help it.

Paranoia is certainly a strong descriptor for what these young teachers-in-training are feeling, but Jane locates the source of her ambivalence not in her technical expertise itself but in its newness to her and her sense of unfamiliarity with the 'jargon' of the literary establishment. Curiously, Jane seems to have got it about right in her last sentence, but she is yet a long way from actualizing the significance of her conclusion: 'You don't have to analyze technical aspects to respond, though sometimes you want to, or can't help it.'

We will return to these young teachers-in-training later and describe this exercise more explicitly, placing it in context. But first let us digress briefly to describe one class responding to a poem – a class of mostly unsophisticated fifteen-year-old American students, who illustrate the rhythms of response and analysis, of the experience of literature and the study of literature, in one rough-and-tumble community of learners. You will probably notice that their response sequence demonstrates that (a) you do not have to analyse technical aspects of poetry to respond, though (b) sometimes you want to – because the analysis grows naturally out of the response – or (c) sometimes you cannot help it, for analysis is required to clarify the text to which one is responding.

From experience to reflection: The practice

This poem by Judith Hemschemeyer (1984) is the one to which the students responded:

We Interrupt This Broadcast

They're still my grown-ups
and it's still Sunday afternoon
beneath the table.

It's raining blackjack
but my oak protects me
from the Plock! 'Hit me!' Plock!

Motionless, I scurry
in and out of their talk,
hauling back huge wisdoms.

A miscarriage is messy
and I think it has
high, wobbly wheels.

Time and a half
needs a fatter clock.
'Hit me!' Plock! 'Too hard!' Laugh.

War is coming but not yet.
There's still half a jug
of sour honey-colored beer

and mother just lit a cigarette.
Hitler could kill me
but he'd have to fight

Roosevelt, Joe Louis
and Daddy to get into the house.
Anyway, I'm a mouse.

The teacher, Mrs B, began by asking the students if they had ever played under a table when they were children. They responded with stories from their childhood. 'What were some card games that adults played?' she asked. In each class, two or three students mentioned blackjack, connecting it with gambling in Las Vegas. Then she mentioned the expression, 'We interrupt this broadcast . . .', and in each class the students connected it with the interruption of television programmes with live warnings of dangerous weather or important newsbreaks. Then Mrs B read the poem aloud twice, providing copies for students to follow. With no further discussion, she asked students (as they were accustomed to do in her class) to write their immediate responses in about ten minutes of quiet writing time. This was timed so that the class period ended at this point. She collected the poems and the students' written responses.

At the beginning of the next session, she handed out copies of the poem again and said, 'Let's dramatize this poem. What will we need?' Each class quickly listed essential props, which Mrs B provided or they improvised: a table, cards, chips (like poker chips), beer, a cigarette, chairs and a radio. Each class decided on six characters: the child under the table (they debated how old it should be), two adult couples (like the Waltons, someone said, or like Lucy, Desi, and their neighbours in the old Lucille Ball show – it's interesting how much their views of this family scene are drawn from television re-runs rather than from life or contemporary sitcoms) and, of course, a radio announcer. The students selected to play the characters looked for lines that told them what they should talk about. Usually, they improvised the women's and the men's conversations going in and out of one another. They spoke of a miscarriage, of work (time-and-a-half), of boxing (Joe Louis), the threat of war (Hitler) and politics (Roosevelt).

After the improvisation, Mrs B distributed a handout consisting of brief excerpts she had typed from the students' initial responses. The students read these silently, checking those that helped them understand, visualize or appreciate the poem, and writing out any questions they still had. In groups of three, they shared their responses to the excerpts and helped one another answer any remaining questions. The excerpts were organized according to a scheme derived by Eeds and Wells (1989).

Some of the students' responses provided what they called a simple construction of meaning:

> During this poem I think a blackjack game is going on and that the 'Plock' is the sound of poker chips or money being thrown on the table and that 'Hit me!' means 'give me another card'. While this card game is going on, the little kid under the table, moving around from place to place listening to what is said and remembering.

Other responses indicated personal involvement in the action of the poem:

> This poem shows youth and vibrance that is only a distant memory to me. When you're little and you hear things, they seem so far away, so distant that they could never touch, never reach you on your pedestal. . . . Few things have ever reminded me that at one time I was a little kid sitting on a dirt pile imagining I was king or a race car driver.

Some students raised questions in their responses or expressed confusion.

> What does 'Time and a half needs a fatter clock' mean?
>
> What does 'raining Black Jack' mean?

Sometimes, in the course of the written response, they answered their own questions or clarified what was confusing.

> Is the kid sitting under the table just to listen or do the people above not notice that s/he is there? The child feels small like a mouse under the table – safe from the outside world because s/he can't see it or feels it can't get to them. Hauling in the wisdoms of the people above is fun and fun to get away from reality sometimes.
>
> I don't quite understand the 6th passage, but maybe the child sees war as the card game and 'they can't play that yet, they're not done with their beer'. That could be an interpretation of it.

Some of the responses offered a tentative analysis or critique.

> This poem is really different. Just by the way it's worded, you feel like you're standing over the table watching all of this take place. The poem seems elementary, yet it holds a lot of issues a little kid might not understand. Even I don't understand all of it. It makes it even harder when I only hear part of the sentence. The author of the poem wrote 'A miscarriage is messy', and I wanted to know if that meant someone playing cards had lost a baby? The way the author plays around with the sound of the cards is very clever also. They're sounds that a 6–7 year old can imagine.

Thus, without Mrs B's overt intervention, these students 'taught' one another the poem. They facilitated a 'lived-through' experience for one another, and they moved on to interpretive and critical concerns. In the course of their conversation, of course, they had dealt with the mechanics of point of view, character, setting, diction, style and theme, though these terms may not have been used explicitly. Only after they had had the opportunity to sample a good variety of their classmates' responses and have most of their questions answered, did Mrs B confront them with the big interpretive question: 'What is the significance of this poem? How does it reflect human nature?' They spoke of a moment frozen in time. Life would never be the same after this radio announcement. The irony and the ambiguity of the penultimate sentence in the poem were not lost on these students. On the one hand, Hitler and all the awful consequences of the Second World War had just invaded that child's house and life on that quiet Sunday afternoon in 1941, and neither Roosevelt, Joe Louis, nor Daddy had been able to prevent it. On the other hand, the sentence is oddly predictive of the outcome of those dire events. Hitler did have to fight Roosevelt and the likes of Joe Louis and the child's father, and he could have won and killed children everywhere as he did in concentration camps throughout Europe, but he didn't.

The students reverted to their own experience, to moments frozen in time which had interrupted their quiet routine and changed the shape of a nation's thinking; for example, the assassinations of the Kennedys and Martin Luther King in their parents' youth and the *Challenger* tragedy in their own. They spoke of the 'under the table' fantasy and the 'above the table' reality, the security children feel and the threats adults deal with (miscarriage, work demands, war). This generation of youngsters is intensely aware of the possibility of catastrophe that lurks just beneath the surface of our apparent security, ready at any moment to interrupt a quiet Sunday afternoon and the established routines of family and neighbourhood with cataclysmic events.

Consider some of the factors that served to distance these students from this poem, making both the experience and study of it difficult for them. First, it is a poem, and these are students not accustomed to reading poetry. Nothing in their home, community or daily experience 'acclimatizes' them to the forms and structures of modern poetry, and not much in their English curriculum in prior years has foreshortened the distance. Secondly, it concerns a period of time (i.e. 1941) that is just about as remote from their experience as the events of 1066, 1215 or 1789. Consequently, in the third place, it embodies cultural codes with which they may be unfamiliar or only vaguely familiar – Joe Louis, Roosevelt, the radio when it occupied a central place in the conveying of information. And it represents a social class and a social era quite different from the cool middle-class environment most of them know (talk of 'time-and-a-half' was as foreign to most of them as to the child in the poem). Fourthly, the point of view is that of a child younger than themselves, but a child whose thoughts are represented in language decidedly adult, in some instances more sophisticated than they would be likely to use themselves (e.g. 'hauling back huge wisdoms').

And yet they were not daunted by the distance or the difficulties the poem entailed. Of course, they had been in Mrs B's classroom for several months, and no doubt they had picked up on some unspoken assumptions that Mrs B makes. It is obvious when you read their initial responses that they had incorporated these assumptions in their thinking about reading:

1 They assume that literature (including this poem, which some of them admittedly describe as weird and confusing) will make sense, it will somehow connect with their lives, and they will be able to make sense of it.
2 They assume that they may not understand all of it at first but that does not prevent them making a beginning.
3 They assume that they can rely on one another to help make sense of the text; they have learned to trust the learning community.
4 They do not assume that the 'meaning' of the poem will magically imprint itself on their mind if they just continue calling the words, but instead they assume that one way to figure out what a text means is to produce other text around it; so they paraphrase and retell, they draw word pictures and articulate

connections with their own experience, they ask questions and sometimes speculate about the answers to their own questions, and they point to parts of the poem that work for them and to parts that are confusing or unpleasant or unbelievable.

5 Finally, they assume that it is a good idea to withhold final judgement. Though they may not understand the poem, they do not dismiss it as 'dumb', and they are not timid about expressing enthusiasm or at least acceptance, though they may as yet have very incomplete understanding of the ultimate significance of the poem.

From experience to reflection: The theory

This classroom sequence approximates a model of reading and responding derived from the pedagogy of Robert Scholes. This model has been described elsewhere (Nelms, 1988), but we summarize it briefly here, relating it to Scholes' prior formulation, to Mrs B's classroom sequence, and to our immediate concern, the problem of teachers-in-training, groping between the personal experience of literature and the professional study of literature.

The model begins, as Scholes' does, with the assumption that the object of literary study 'ought to be *textuality*: textual knowledge and textual skills' (Scholes, 1985, p. 20). The act of responding to a text, according to Scholes, is completed only with the production of text. In practice, the responsive text may be spoken rather than written, may in fact be a dialogue between two selves of the reader (call them the private and public self, ego and superego, if you will); however, in the classroom, this exchange often should and does involve the production of written text – journal entries, impromptu writings like the ones Mrs B used, eventually critical essays or narratives, and the like. As the silent and essentially mute experience of literature becomes outer, spoken response, as the spontaneous becomes reflective, readers have to talk and write. The objects of literary study are both the literary works themselves and the responses of readers. Hence, students of literature – from kindergarten through graduate school – articulate their responses, examine the responses of others, and participate in a community of readers. Scholes (1985, p. 21) says:

> We have an endless web here, of growth, and change, and interaction, learning and forgetting, dialogue and dialectic. Our task as teachers is to introduce students to this web, to make it real and visible for them, insofar as we can, and to encourage them to cast their own strands of thought and text into this network so that they will feel its power and understand both how to use it and how to protect themselves from its abuses.

The process consists of four recursive stages, moving from inner to outer, (1) private to public, expressive to expository, (2) autonomy of literary text to autonomy of the reader, (3) individual transactions to communal negotiation of meaning and value, and (4) experience to study. The first stage is simply the evocation of the text. In Scholes' terms, what is produced here is 'text within text':

the reader enacts or performs the script provided in the work. We lose ourselves in a book; submit to the control of the text; for all practical purposes, we lose consciousness of ourselves as reader and of our world outside the world postulated in the text. The language we use is the language provided by the writer. Iser (1974) calls this stage *passive synthesis*.

When we emerge from this evocative stage, we begin to engage in conversation with the text. Scholes does not make this a separate, explicit stage, but it is implicit in this discussion of reading and interpretation. One produces 'text with text', i.e. dialogue between the now self-conscious reader and the text. The reader begins to appropriate the text, retelling and paraphrasing, selecting and repressing details within his or her memory, making guesses, asking questions, providing personal associations and parallel instances, decoding cultural codes. However, these activities do not go as far as interpretation in abstracting, gener-alizing or 'thematicizing' the text. Though inferences are drawn at this stage, Scholes calls them 'interpretation in the service of reading', not interpret-ation proper. They simulate what all of us do when we leave the movie theatre, talking with our friends about what we have just seen, or when, in a casual conversation, we exchange comments about books we have recently read. The mood is still essentially private or intimate and personal, the mode expressive, and the audience oneself or one's close companions.

With interpretation and criticism, stages 3 and 4 in the process, the discourse becomes public and the mode transactional (exposition or argumentation). Interpretation involves consideration of the significance of the text, not just what it 'says' but what it 'means'. The reader provides inferences derived not just from the text but by application to the text of certain schema not dependent upon the text for their authority (for example, we might provide a Freudian, Marxist or feminist reading). Scholes calls this 'text upon text'; we think of it as 'text around text'. We have in mind the familiar metaphor of the stone dropped into the pool, producing a series of concentric ripples, all emanating from the stone but spreading wider and wider.

These multi-layered readings of a work of literature are, of course, in one sense dependent upon the work, but the wider they range, the more dependent they are also upon schema imposed upon the work from outside. They are as likely to tunnel under the work as to build upon it, to interpolate as to extrapolate, to hypothesize its necessary causes as its likely effects. Eventually, the purpose of interpretation is to convince an audience that a reading is justifiable. Of course, the only audience may be an internalized community, the voice of society or our community that we hear within our minds. But interpretation always assumes a public audience that requires data and logical analysis before it can accept one's commentary.

Criticism considers the values of the text, its adequacy in representing the perspectives of a particular community of readers. Scholes calls this 'text against text', but we would broaden it, especially with younger students, to include ways in which the text itself provides a critique of one's society. The purpose of such criticism is to examine assumptions embedded in the text in relation to our constructs of the world outside the text. Hence, we might call this 'text outside text'.

In Louise Rosenblatt's terms, the latter two activities are not so much a part of the aesthetic, lived-through experience as they are efferent activities directed toward the communication of clarified ideas. However, they may be brought to bear on further experiences of the text, clarifying and enhancing one's subsequent lived-through experience. The pleasure one takes in seeing yet another production of *Hamlet*, or in once again reading an Emily Dickinson poem, incorporates all that we have learned about them.

In Mrs B's class sequence, the pre-reading talk, the oral readings of the poem, and the acting out are all ways to help the text find its voice in the students' minds. The initial written responses, the talk about them, and the students' collaboration in raising and answering questions are all ways to facilitate conversation with the text. Though the students share and modify these responses, they do so in an atmosphere of mutual trust and camaraderie, a setting as intimate as can be provided in a public classroom. The culminating discussion and the consideration of the question of the significance of the poem are ways to introduce interpretation – abstracting, generalizing, thematicizing, as a matter of public discourse. The brief consideration of the applicability of the insights derived from the poem to the students' own experience and the concern for the author's reliability in contrasting the 'fantasy' world of the child and the 'realistic' world of the adults are very brief, very tentative forays into criticism.

What is more important for these students is that the 'study' of literature grows out of and reflects back upon the 'experience' of literature, and the 'experience' of literature is neither abrogated nor superseded by a premature concern for public interpretation and criticism. The 'lived-through' aesthetic experience is not short-circuited by the academic application of a formulaic approach to the derivation of meaning and value. For students to 'cast their own strand of thought and text into this network', those strands of thought and text must be derived from an authentic encounter with the text, not simply an encounter with the teacher's (or some other adult's) text about (around, upon, against, outside) the text.

For the teachers-in-training at the start of this paper and for Mrs B's fifteen-year-olds, public commentary can represent empty verbalism if it does not grow from a personal commitment to the text. If students are to move from private, inner experience to public, outer communication, they must have some intermediate experience of a reading community – a community in which the 'texts' they produce are as important as the texts they experience.

Toward a resolution of the tension

One of the important concepts to emerge from reader response theory is what Stanley Fish (1980) and others have called 'interpretive communities'. Loosely defined, an interpretive community is any group who share enough assumptions, practices, goals and knowledge to make talking and writing about literature with one another a meaningful enterprise. It is an important concept for teachers because perhaps the best available model of an interpretive community is a literature classroom. But it is also a problematic concept, because most of us spent much of our education in literature classrooms that were characterized by neither a sense of community nor opportunities to respond, and because one of the shortcomings of much of the writing on reader-response theory is a lack of a clear picture of what a response-centred classroom might look like, and, especially, what the teacher's role in such a classroom might be.

The problem of deriving a workable pedagogy from reader-response theory is particularly acute for beginning teachers. Fish's (1980, p. 343) following remark spells out the importance of how teachers perceive their authority:

> In a classroom whose authority figures include David Bleich and Norman Holland, a student might very well relate a text to her memories of a favorite aunt, while in other classrooms, dominated by the spirit of Brooks and Warren, any such activity would immediately be dismissed as nonliterary, something that wouldn't be done.

It was interest in what literary 'spirits' influenced juniors and seniors in English education that led us to ask five of them to allow us to conduct interviews about their perceptions of 'literature' – their beliefs about literature in general, their attitudes toward different kinds of literature, their ways of approaching texts, and what role literature played in their lives. What we were interested in getting was a global sense of their beliefs about reading and teaching literature as well as some more specific sense of their ways of going about reading and how they thought they would go about teaching. To quote Fish (1980, p. 364) again, 'not only does one believe what one believes, but one teaches what one believes, even if it would be easier and safer and more satisfying to teach something else'. Mrs B's experience provides evidence for both parts of that statement. She says: 'I have colleagues who consider my use of dramatics, free writing, and student involvement to be "play", an intrusion or distraction from real teaching. The internal conflict your student teachers feel often becomes an external one in high school English departments.'

Though we started out thinking of these weekly sessions as interviews, they soon became more like conversations. Sometimes we asked the students to read a story or poem and they talked about their response to it, and at other times they talked about reading literature or teaching literature in a more general way – about their literature studies in high school perhaps, or about what authors or genres they liked or disliked and why.

Much of what they told us was what you would expect from any group of English education students: that they loved literature and could not wait to try their hand teaching it, or that literature played an important part in their lives but that they were not always sure what that part was. When we asked them to read a story or poem, their responses were predictably diverse, but all were thoughtful and literarily sophisticated in ways that the responses of a group of non-English majors probably would not be.

Other things they told us, however, were less predictable and more troubling.

For example, three of the five students expressed feelings of conflict about differences between their reading preferences and the works they felt made up the accepted canon of quality literature and, by extension, of literature that teachers should teach. One student talked about how much she liked reading the books she read in her adolescent literature class, novels by Sue Ellen Bridgers and Katherine Paterson, and wondered if that meant she was 'not cut out for teaching high school and ought to aim for junior high'. Another named as a favourite Stephen King and described her system of alternating between books she liked and books she felt she ought to read, which she called 'the classics'. Would such a system work with high school students, she wondered, or would other teachers find her lacking sufficiently high standards?

Equally troubling were the feelings of conflict the students felt about why they read fiction – about what it is that makes the reading of a novel or story pleasurable or worthwhile. Four out of five said the main reason they read fiction was to experience the vicarious pleasure of 'living in the text', of identifying with characters. At the same time, they all acknowledged that such pleasure was seldom if ever part of literature classes and that such a response would be viewed, in Fish's words, as something 'nonliterary', something not to be done. One student who had just finished reading Kathryn Lasky's *Beyond the Divide* said, 'I *was* that girl, I stood out there on the prairie with the wind blowing, but I don't know how I'd ever bring that up in any class I was in. Or any class I'll teach, for that matter, except maybe as a lead-in to something more important.' All of the students spoke at some point about the possibility of living other lives through literature, of times and places and experiences to which only literature could provide access – but that was a way of thinking they associated with the reading and talking about reading they did away from the classroom.

Another conflict or tension the students felt centred on differences between how they read – their specific reading process – when reading for a literature class and when reading for pleasure. 'I read for detail when I read for school', one said. 'I try to focus on all the little things I know we'll talk about in class. When I read for myself, I just kick back and let the story sort of swallow me up.'

These tensions or 'conflicts' seem to be specific examples of larger conflicts in the study and teaching of literature – between the ideas of the New Critics and the ideas of reader-response theorists; between wanting students to read 'good' literature and simply wanting them to read; between what Rosenblatt calls efferent readings and aesthetic readings – literature as information or literature as exploration. For these pre-service teachers, however, we think all of these can best be summed up as a tension or conflict between their perceptions of themselves as readers and their perceptions of literature in the institution. It is a tension which is very important to them because they see the move from student/reader to teacher/reader as a move into the institution which will force a reconciliation of their own attitudes and beliefs about literature with the attitudes, beliefs and expectations of some larger community. They were a little apologetic about not thinking about literature in the way that they thought English teachers ought to think about literature, and wondered how they would deal with that discrepancy when they entered their own classrooms. This is not to imply that all English education students are lying in dorm rooms paralysed by a lack of conceptual unity between theory and practice. But we believe the remarks these students made are evidence of unspoken conflicts that have always been with us, but that are just now being driven to the surface as we think more about readers and their responses in our classrooms.

As this basic theme in their discussions emerged, we began to wonder how we might help these particular students come to terms with these conflicts. One possibility we dismissed was that these future teachers needed more education or literary sophistication. The one who spoke of liking Stephen King was a straight-A student who occasionally showed us the insightful essays she wrote for her nineteenth-century novel course. All of them could 'read' their literature teachers' expectations and respond and would no doubt be able to mimic them when they at last found themselves before a class. By the same token, none of them believed that vicariously living in the text was necessarily the best or most important kind of response or that Stephen King was somehow 'better' than Mark Twain, or that they would replace the old critical authority with some new critical authority based on their own approach to literature. In short, they were ambivalent or confused, feeling the existence of conflict, but assuming that such conflicts were normal, probably unimportant, and finally irreconcilable. We believed that the conflicts they experienced were indeed normal, but definitely not unimportant, not if they were concerned about the role of the teacher in a community of response.

As for reconciliation, an interesting thing happened as they approached the end of the interviews: all five of the students involved began to speak about how significant the interviews had been to them, claiming that they had helped them work through their feelings about literature and teaching. What we had considered a favour to ourselves, a not especially rewarding task that took time out of their busy schedules, they found to be a way of understanding and even resolving the conflicts that we had been carefully documenting. Only in retrospect did we realize that the most interesting thing, maybe the most significant thing about the interviews, was not the nature of the conflicts themselves, but the students' response to those conflicts, their use of the process of inquiry we thought *we* were engaged in as a means of thinking about becoming literature teachers.

Unfortunately, in a teacher-education programme as large and understaffed as ours, there was no chance that we could schedule a series of five intensive conversations about literature and teaching with all our teachers-in-training. Though the literature courses they enrol in may gradually come to reflect a responsive mode, we do not foresee much change there soon. What we have devised is a way to let our students collaborate with one another to achieve basically the same goals.

In our course 'Literature for Adolescents', students are divided into lab groups of seven or eight for micro-teaching and other activities. We now devote the first six to eight lab meetings to the same kinds of interviews/conversations used in this preliminary research and subsequently adapted in a more sophisticated research project. To provide a focus for these interviews, students are assigned partners and asked to prepare a case study of their partners as readers. They are encouraged to use whatever means possible to learn more about each other as readers of literature. The following activities are scheduled for their lab meetings:

1 *The reading interview.* After brainstorming possible questions for such an interview within the group as a whole, partners spend about twenty minutes interviewing one another. They begin by asking each other what they read, when and where they read, why they read, how they read, and how their reading habits differ according to different types of reading matter or different purposes. They ask where they get their books for recreational reading, how they decide whether they want to finish a book they have begun, whether they read the last chapter first, and the like.

2 *The reading history.* Each student brings a list of landmark events in their development as readers – when and how they learned to read, what they liked to read as children and what they hated, how their families figured in their reading, and the like. Using these lists, the partners reconstruct rough reading histories, noting what influences shaped them as the readers they now are.

3 *The reading protocols: I.* Applying basically the same techniques used by James Squire in his now famous study, *Responses of Adolescents to Four Short Stories* (1964), students prepare written protocols on a short story. The story is divided into six natural segments. Readers stop and write their responses after each segment. Then, with their partners, they share their responses, noting comparisons and contrasts.

4 *The reading protocols: II.* Each student selects at least two short stories from the anthologies available for the class. They write before they begin reading each story, noting why they chose the story and what they expect from it. They write again after they get into the story and are certain that it is interesting enough that they will finish it, but before the story really takes shape and the outcome begins to emerge. Finally, they write once again when they finish the story. Again they compare notes with their partners.

5 *The reading protocols: III.* We present a poem in class which the students are not likely to have read before. After two oral readings, students write initial responses as Mrs B's students did. Then in small groups of three or four, they share these responses and compare notes. Finally, they write how their responses were modified, confirmed or rejected as a result of these interactions.

6 *Reading inventories.* Sometimes students participate in forced choice reading inventories or questionnaires. The discussion of the results of this 'test' with one's partner is usually more revealing than the actual results of the 'test'.

7 *Free association and clustering.* Either as the very first activity in this sequence or as a culminating one, students participate in the exercise alluded to at the beginning of this paper, adapted from Linda Shaw Finlay and Valerie Faith

(1987). Basically, it identifies key words within students' experience of literature and provides them an opportunity to discuss the significance of their choice and classification of words.

When the case studies are finished and collected, the tutor reads them carefully and publishes excerpts from each one in a class handout. Again, students read and discuss what they find there and write, reflecting on what they have learned through the project.

What they learn, of course, differs from one class to another, but with all three classes with whom this procedure has been used, there have been some common threads. Almost without exception, students express surprise at the objective portrait they receive of themselves as readers, akin to the dismay one might express upon seeing a photograph of oneself for the first time. Donald's comment is typical:

> When I first read Maria's analysis of me as a reader, the first thing I thought was, 'My God, am I really like that?' But the funny thing was, she was right. I didn't realize she knew that much about me from what I had told her, and I don't think I could have described myself better. (I know I wouldn't have done it honestly.)

Students are equally as surprised at the diversity they discover in what they assumed would be a relatively homogeneous group. Donald continues:

> I realize we are miles apart in our likes and dislikes . . .
>   Not all students read alike, read at the same pace, or read the same things and interpret what they read the same way, and a teacher should constantly be aware of this in the classroom.

There are *academic readers*, those who have most effectively internalized the values of the institutional English major. They usually have adapted some sense of canon, a prescribed set of terms and techniques for analysing literature, a mild contempt for 'popular' genres, and the goal of inducting their students into the academy. There are *ludic readers* who define their reading primarily in terms of personal pleasure and enlightenment. They usually have well-defined reading habits. They are likely to speak with open contempt of 'reading between the lines', of the close analysis encouraged in their English courses, and of the rigid assignments they receive there. There are *efferent readers* – mavericks in this company. They often are social studies or journalism majors, and they describe themselves as reading primarily for information, ideas and solutions to problems. There are *divided readers*, who describe themselves with all these terms but who compartmentalize their reading rather rigidly. They are likely to see no more relationship between academic reading and ludic reading than between working out in the gym to lose weight and develop muscle tone and swimming at the lake to have fun and enjoy the sun. They do both, willingly, but each with no thought of the other. And, finally, there are *balanced readers*, who find pleasure in most of their assigned academic reading by reacting to it personally, sometimes even idiosyncratically, and who seek pleasure in reading that challenges their thinking and exercises their interpretive and critical competence.

These English teachers-in-training find themselves at least as diverse as the four types of student-readers described by Susan Hynds (1989). In fact, they recognize themselves and their peers in all four of her case studies: Jay, who reads just for practice, looking forward to the future; Ken, who reads for mastery, to fulfil an assignment; Cathy, who separates reading for school and reading for herself and who hesitates to express her ideas on school reading, who in fact doubts that any teacher would accept students' ideas; and Hal, who is a closet reader but retreats from school assignments, who does not like 'having to prove your opinion through facts and stuff', and says, 'When I read for fun, I don't think about what they do in English, just for my entertainment, yeah!'

For most of these teachers-in-training, the self-knowledge generated through these exercises results in a more humane and sophisticated handling of subsequent tasks in their course; for example, responding to a set of student reading inventories, listing and discussing goals of the high school literature programme, seeing tensions between such goals as 'cultural literacy' and 'personal literacy', adapting curricular approaches – such as individualized reading, literature response groups, common reading – to these diverse goals, and preparing micro-teaching lessons without relying on lecture and straight recitation. They are not as likely to be subject to the tyranny of teachers' implicit theories and biases. They are more nearly ready to transform their knowledge of literature – gained from three years studying literature and its mechanics – into classroom practice. When they learn about themselves, they learn about teaching. They *become* the students they teach. 'To reason one's way through the act of teaching', Shulman says, 'is to think one's way from the subject matter as understood by the teacher into the minds and motivations of learners'. We might say in our discipline that it is to think one's way from the disciplined study of literature to the spontaneous experience of literature, and gradually back again, from the reflection and analysis to which undergraduate English majors have become accustomed to the pleasure and delight in reading which first attracted them to literature, and then to a balance of the two. As Valerie realized, these feelings (cuddling, hot chocolate, bedtime – enjoyment, enlightenment, recreation) are what got us 'hooked' on literature in the first place. William Carlos Williams said it more epigrammatically: 'If it ain't a pleasure, it ain't a poem.'

5 Reading as framing, writing as reframing

IAN REID

If someone asks us to call to mind, without pause for critical reflection, an image of ideal processes of reading and response, it is likely that these will take shape as contemplative acts performed in private by a 'bookworm'. We often tend to think of printed words as directly engaging the individual imagination with an almost Wordsworthian interiority, seeming to 'flash upon that inward eye which is the bliss of solitude'.

Certainly, much of the theory and criticism that goes under the banner of 'reader response' does have just such an individualist emphasis – and has been criticized accordingly (Culler, 1980). Some forms of post-structuralist criticism are also open to the objection that they posit a solitary reader. For instance, the concept of reading that underlies Paul de Man's essays has come under attack (Saunders, 1988) for its blindness to the institutional assumptions within which it operates. To be sure, each of us sometimes reads when alone, but the important general point made by the critics of many reader-response and post-structuralist practitioners alike is just that every act of reading is shaped by the situation in which it occurs, and ought to take account of that fact.

The need to consider the situatedness of reading should be paramount for those whose concern is with what happens in classrooms. It therefore figures importantly in the theoretical model of interpretive processes that has been developed by the Centre for Studies in Literary Education at Deakin University. Broadly summarized, this model is a schematic representation of ways in which readers make sense of texts by adducing several frames of reference. Some of these framings are drawn from information inherent within the text and some from the circumstances in which the texts are encountered (e.g. pedagogic and curricular structures) or are fetched from further afield with various degrees of pertinence.

How does this concept of 'framing' differ from the concept of 'codes' expounded by Roland Barthes (1970)?

1 The latter virtually assumes an intricate literary text and a ready-made subtle reader of high literary competence, whereas the former can indicate how all

reading occurs and how the particular practices associated with 'literary' reading may be acquired and developed.

2 The emphasis of 'codes' is on a relatively formalistic view of textual properties, whereas 'framing' attends more directly to the occasions and processes through which readings actually occur.

3 The concept of framing allows, in a flexible way, for the importance of interactive factors (e.g. in classrooms) during reading and response, because these themselves may serve to frame what is read.

4 Codes do not in themselves account for durational and retrospective elements in reading and response, but the concept of framing can readily be extended to reframing.

5 'Code' suggests a set of fairly clear-cut constituents, whereas the very notion of 'framing' draws attention to the problematic distinction between what is inside textuality, or inside interpretation, and what is outside them.

This needs fuller exposition. To regard our acts of reading as acts of framing is to recognize that we make a text mean something by both separating it from, and joining it with, a variety of references. The metaphor of 'framing' simply reminds us that in order to perceive and understand anything (say, a poem), we must provisionally distinguish it from other things while also relating it to them – as we distinguish figure from ground, picture from wall, poem from page, foreground from background, here from there. Framing is the process of demarcating phenomena in a double-edged way that simultaneously includes and excludes. What makes it provisional is that neither its terms of reference nor its principles of relevance are fixed. As Jacques Derrida (1978a) remarks in an essay on aesthetics, 'Il y a du cadre, mais le cadre n'existe pas' – which I render as this principle: framing occurs, but there is no frame.

Four kinds of framing can be differentiated – though in practice they are intricately linked. For convenience, I label these circumtextual, extratextual, intratextual and intertextual. Please take these terms with a grain of salt and a willing suspension of distaste.

1 *Circumtextual* framing uses the adjuncts of the text, the tangible details that surround it not only with further words, such as a title, but with additional signs and structures to guide interpretation. In so far as we frame a story circumtextually, we read it in terms of the material borders that can constitute it palpably as a text: details of its physical format, cover and prefatory information, blurbs, dedications, epigraphs, titles, opening and closing formulae, authorial ascriptions, marginalia, footnotes, and other such markers. Contiguously, the term may also refer to certain official and unofficial rubrics that are inscribed in classroom practice: what the blackboard says, what the teacher says, what the curriculum handbook says.

2 *Extratextual* framing includes whatever 'outside' information, unspecified by the text but felt to be presupposed by it, is brought to its understanding, along with the reader's various expectations and preoccupations. The extratextual framing of anyone's engagement with a particular text is always somewhat

arbitrary, depending largely on a personal stock of knowledge and assumptions. Because it encompasses many variable preconceptions as well as different degrees of cultural knowledge, it is responsible for most disagreements between readers. But we should not think of these differences as capriciously individual; they stem from institutionalized reading practices. For instance, extratextual framing may include fixed notions about literary genres, derived mostly from certain educational formations: a set of assumptions, let us say, concerning the supposedly intrinsic qualities of the short story form, linked perhaps with a tenacious attachment to protocols of realism for characters and plots. Or, for another reader, the extratextual framing may be primarily political, as in a feminist commitment to scrutinize the fictional representation of gender. In any case, however, what makes any particular frame of extratextual reference more or less apt is simply the scope it gives a reader to draw meaning from other framing elements in and around the given text – from circumtextual elements, already mentioned, and from intratextual and intertextual, which I shall now define.

3 *Intratextual* framing takes shape directly within the pages themselves (or the equivalent, if it is a non-print text), deriving in particular from whatever subdivisional devices interrupt the flow of words. The most obvious of these are spatially emphatic paragraph breaks, section numbers and typographically marked shifts; but anything that can suddenly alter a reader's mode of apprehending the text, such as an abrupt stylistic change, may count as material for intratextual framing. One form that this takes is the effect of ironic disjunction; another is the tale-within-a-tale, or embedded narrative, which often has the reflexive function of commenting implicitly on the text that encloses it. And, indeed, any part of a text that seems to be set off in some way from the rest (a descriptive set-piece, for instance) has the potential to work like that: to serve as an inset model of the whole. Even a significant phrase that is repeated during a story may have a specular framing effect, very much like the refrain in a song.

4 *Intertextual* framing has to do with links between texts, but should be understood as involving more than just casual allusions or traces of 'influence'. For intertextuality, in the sense proposed by Julia Kristeva (Moi, 1986), works through devices by which a text signals how its very structure of meanings depends on both similarity to and difference from certain other types of text, involving a transposition of one sign system (or more than one) into another.

As I have already mentioned, these four processes should not be thought of as wholly separate frames. In any approach to any text, the shifting relations between different framing possibilities are always paramount. For instance, an extratextual dimension must be invoked; no text is comprehensible apart from what its readers bring to it; but the important thing is not to be locked preclusively into one or two kinds of extratextual framing. While a particular text may signify its generic affiliations through circumtextual, intratextual and intertextual devices, these will remain invisible unless a reader can draw on appropriate extratextual information. Conversely, it may happen sometimes that assumptions imported into the reading will frame a text too rigidly to allow its distinctive contours to be recognized.

The research group at Deakin University has studied these aspects of reading practices in secondary school classrooms. When beginning our investigations, we did not have this elaborate typology. What we did have was a couple of strong hunches: (1) that although textual limits and ostensibly unificatory reference-points for interpretation may often appear to be 'given' and fixed, this is usually because of limited habits of perception, routinized pedagogic practices, or temporary pragmatic constraints; (2) that reading skills can be enhanced by developing strategies of mobile reframing. Nor did we see our task as requiring an 'objective' description, by detached observers, of what readers do with texts. Rather, in attempting to understand what happened to texts within a classroom context, we regarded ourselves as part of that context, intervening in students' reading processes rather than watching them from the sidelines. We paid attention to the assumptions they themselves apparently brought to bear on their reading, and explored ways of increasing their awareness of alternative possibilities. What we did, then, was partly a kind of curriculum development, involving a critique of some current practices in teaching literature and an exploration of strategies to open up dimensions in reading and writing that traditional courses have tended to suppress.

One result of our work has been the production of a cluster of resources for schools based on the materials we devised for our investigations, which include video- and audio-tapes as well as various print texts (Reid *et al.*, 1988). As we went from school to school, teachers and students helped us to realize further the potential of these materials in the classroom. Most of what follows is an account of classroom activities that emerged in response to one small text used in our research and, subsequently, in the published resources:

> when i came here the world shrank i only had a little space to be in i don't want to go to the outside just in one room and small just a little area and cosy scared of the world the sport hall terrified me in the staff room i couldn't find enough corner to hide in i got small and smaller minnie mouse i didn't want to be seen from all sides in the print room i did prints i would do them i would hide them i would hide i was scared of everybody i got smaller and smaller you make me so small and scared i wanted to work as the railway crossing keeper with a little heater and a book i didn't want much i didn't want to go to school i just put up with a small area i wanted to sit in the kitchen everything was enough for me very kind thank you for letting me be here i got to be so small before i was brave and loud before was before i wasn't afraid of the headmaster i wasn't afraid and here and here i got smaller and smaller such a little in rubber shoes such a little everywhere such a good girl such a quiet such a little quiet such a very quiet quiet i wasn't any trouble ever the teacher wrote what pleasure to teach such obedient well behaved it took it out of me to be so afraid to be so small to learn books by heart to come first all the time to get prizes and marks i wanted everyone to be pleased i wanted to please and please and pleasant and let me be alive i was toady and toady and silent in the library and never any trouble and not very lively placid and

placid and such a good girl i had no life in me not much i didn't have any big in me not at all i was small i was small i was small i was so small so small small little mouse mousey i wanted people to like me everybody like me accept me before i used to be nasty and every like anybody else when i came here from another country it took the lively from me it cowered me thank you very much toady for letting me live stay in the country i wanted people to like me too much i lost my lively and big i got to be so meek so meek so teacher please so sorry sorry such a good girl never any trouble before i could be rude now I was so small this coming broke me in and broke me took it out of my trying to be so good and quiet and never any trouble and such a good girl and such a pleasure to teach i was a teacher too i know what this is such a note i wrote about the little ones that never gave me worry that i didn't even notice that were too nice and toady toady you little frog i didn't like myself i didn't like me like that as if any time someone could tell me to get out get out i was big when i was child then i grew and got so small i came here and i got younger and less i came here and i got to be so small

The students with whom we trialled this during our research work were asked, without any explanatory preamble, to read the unidentified printed text in comparison with a video-tape performance of it. They then recorded individual written responses to questions, discussed these among themselves, and sometimes responded in other ways also, as I shall explain later. The first discussion recorded here was unsupervised: no teacher or observer was present.

Group A: excerpt 1

At the beginning of their discussion, Robert, the self-appointed leader, suggested they each summarize aloud their individual written answers. He himself led off in response to the first question, 'Describe in your own words what you have just seen and heard'.

Robert: I thought it was basically a piece of dramatic monologue of some kind, in which the speaker relates how she is intimidated by the school she went to as a child or taught at, or maybe both; it's not quite clear. She originally comes from another country, that's made apparent, but whether she was as timid in this country as she was in the previous one is not quite clear. It seems somewhat contradictory.

Jan: Hi, I'm Jan. My idea of what the speaker means is vaguely similar to Robert's, but mine's more based on the feelings that I got from what the writer actually said. To me the way she spoke portrays that she was confused and very unhappy but also more not just unhappy with what's happening, but uncontent with how she is, and I found the style of writing showed her similar to how a child would rant and rave when it was very upset, no stops to pause for breath, but just continuously talking, very lost, very lonely, and very threatened I found.

Jill: I was confused with the passage. I thought it was a person coming from another country and how from their new surroundings their personality changed, from being like loud and that in the old country and shy and meek in the new one and her school. And she wants to please everyone but she's a bit confused, and she doesn't know how to go about it.

Max: This passage seems to have been somebody's release of emotions, and it's all sort of disjointed thoughts and feelings, and the lack of punctuation sort of adds to this feeling. The person seems to be very confused and even lonely, and is sort of really uprooted from the other country and now doesn't really know where they're at. The person seems to be very confused and in the viewing later on she seems to have been more angry than confused. They sort of seem very unstable and even rejected by their new country. In the first part of the passage the speaker sort of strikes me as being male when reading it, but later on it's apparent that it's female, and particular usage and emphasis was made on all the words small and relating to small and little, and it just seems to be the thoughts from somebody's deep realms of their memory and that, that they've been hypnotised and asked to release.

Several interesting things that are latent in this conversation can be clarified in terms of framing. Remember, first, that the usual props or prompts for reading and response have been withheld here, just as they were by I. A. Richards (1929) in the work that led sixty years ago to his book *Practical Criticism*. Student readers are accustomed, as we all are, to being guided towards understanding by a variety of explicit *circumtextual* markers: all those items that may surround or accompany a text, such as its title and signature, other material adjuncts such as information on the covers of a book that contains it, and also messages inherent in the situation through which the text is physically encountered, for instance a curriculum requirement mediated by the classroom teacher's injunctions. In the case that we are considering, such things have seemingly been removed – though, as we shall see, their operation remains no less potent for that.

First, although the group has been left 'alone', they are conscious of the tape-recorder's presence as surrogate researcher; Jan shows this in addressing it directly and introducing herself. Similarly, the list of questions which the students were asked to answer has the function of instantiating a familiar form of classroom authority and so provides a dominant point of reference. The particular questions are probably less important than the act of posing them, which serves to establish this text ('so small', by Ania Walwicz; see Reid *et al.*, 1988) as a *set piece* – serves, that is, to frame it circumtextually as the kind of item to which one is expected to pay a certain kind of attention. The general point at issue here has been discussed in a recent article by Gale MacLachlan (1988). Arguing against the pessimistic view expressed in a previous article that classrooms impose an irresistibly homogenizing effect on whatever is read in them so that generic differences are flattened out, MacLachlan contends that in practice circumtextual framing activates other framing operations, and accordingly an institutional set-up such as an English lesson, for which 'analytical' or literary reading is requisite, focuses a student's mind in a particularly conscious way on those other framing features, intratextual and intertextual, which – ironically – are resistant to mere assimilation within the broad genre of the set text. Thus in the present case, Robert takes the question 'Describe in your own words what you have just seen and heard' as an invitation to assign 'so small' intertextually to a literary type ('basically a piece of dramatic monologue'). And Jan, while less inclined to pigeonhole the text, still recognizes that it *is* to be regarded *as a text* –

the 'style of writing', as she puts it, being in her view one that 'portrays powerful feelings'. On the other hand, Jill is evidently quite disoriented, unable to frame the text circumtextually and therefore at a loss to read its own particular structures; confessing her own confusion, she responds to the passage as if it were a direct expression of someone else's. Max seems at times to share that same assumption about the outpouring of a real person's emotion, and yet at other times is observant about textual features (the lack of punctuation and the repetition of key words).

One would not want to claim, of course, that any brief analysis of a passage such as this in terms of framing can be spectacularly revealing in itself. The value of the procedure is largely in indicating areas that should be examined further in class, and perhaps 'reframed' there. Would Robert, for example, who links 'so small' with a dramatic monologue form, be able to reconcile this generic association with his sense of its 'contradictory' elements? How might that be related to the comment made by each of the other three about the speaker's 'confused' feelings? Could Max's impression that there is something 'unstable' in this speaker be developed to take into account the difficulty Max himself had in finding an appropriate pronoun for 'it . . . they . . . she'? Indeed, Max's explicit remark about the problem of gender identity seems well worth further inquiry. 'In the first part of the passage the speaker sort of strikes me as being male when reading it, but later on it's apparent that it's female . . .'. What lies behind these perceptions? Are they shared by male and female students? Is this an instance of an intratextual element – an ambiguously gendered figure within the text – that has anticipatory relevance to the text's reception? Certainly there is material even in this short transcript for an inquiry into extratextually gendered aspects of the group members' different ways of responding to their reading, and negotiating its significance. Note Robert's use of classic 'male' mentor techniques, for instance, taxonomy, in his presumptive role as viceroy for their male teacher, followed by Jan's statement that her response was 'more based on the feelings' she had experienced. To what extent are different reading practices differently gendered, and differently valued, in the schooling system? To what extent can one generalize about this beyond the particular pattern of interactions in a given classroom, where the teacher's own style of literary response may well be differentially perceived by male and female students, if the class contains both? A new project under way within Deakin's centre for studies in Literary Education is investigating 'these and similar matters.

Group A: excerpt 2

Some of the points just touched on appear in an interesting light in a later exchange:

> *Robert:* The worst question was number six, 'Do you think that what is said is complete in itself?'
> *Jan:* You have to . . . you have to accept it.

Robert: I know, but what does the question *mean?*

Jan: I think it means that . . .

Robert: Yeah, I know – there's a lot of things it could mean though. I reckon the question's vague.

Jan: Well, what did you think? Did you think it is complete in itself?

Robert: Well it depends on how you look at it. As a description it's sort of complete, as an anecdote, which is what it is really, it's complete, and it seems to be a sort of prose poem of a kind and it's a dramatic monologue as well. And as far as that goes, it's probably too long, it tends to drag a bit. But as a story it's fair enough, but it's only in the sense of a story in the real, a story of real life, an anecdote which doesn't really follow the pattern of a story in fiction, at least not often.

Jan: No, but you can't put it into its little box like that.

Robert: No, no, I'm just saying as a story it tends to be a real life story rather than a fiction story, if you see what I mean.

Max: So that sort of question remains in your mind as to what it was. I sort of tend to think you know, why they produce something like this, and you know, to what purpose.

Jan: The purpose of, this woman that needs an outlet for all her . . .

Robert: It wouldn't have been her who wrote it.

Jan: I know, but you're supposed to get the feeling of what she was doing.

Robert: I agree.

Jan: You can't put it in little boxes like that, you've got to accept it for what it is.

Robert: No, but I'm saying that it's a story in the sense that it's something that should happen in real life and as such it's complete, whereas a fiction story, when you have the build-up, then the climax, and the conclusion . . .

Jan: We all know that . . .

Robert: Fine, good.

If the previous excerpt seemed to indicate that Robert's response to his reading was well informed and self-assured, you may think that this second excerpt complicates the picture. Here he expresses impatience not only with the question under discussion but also with his fellow student. 'I know' is his repeated motto, and having declared the question to be a problem he will not allow Jan to deproblematize it. When asked to offer a positive comment, he reaches again for intertextual framing; but this soon gives way to an assertion about the text's non-literary properties. Robert may not be so secure after all when the more explicit forms of circumtextual framing are withdrawn. Jan, in contrast, is dissatisfied with 'little boxes' and seems to be prepared to look more carefully at the distinctive features of the text – though she hardly gets a chance to comment. Again it would have been interesting to follow up some of these remarks with further questions in class – about Jan's mention, for instance, in the context of Robert's bumptiously 'male' behaviour, of the textual speaker's femaleness. Or, perhaps, the interpretation just sketched here should itself be reframed to give a more sympathetic account of Robert's position? Perhaps what he is registering is a clearer perception than the others of the institutional practices that frame their readings circumtextually?

The teacher, normally a predominant circumtextual factor, was absent from this recorded discussion, but his influence remained present. Later in their discussion, these students showed themselves very conscious of their teacher's fondness for framing extratextually whatever they read in class. With the prior (good-humoured) approval of Mr E, we had asked the group to consider among themselves how *he* would probably have gone about presenting the 'so small' material to them.

Group A: excerpt 3

Robert: 'If Mr E had discussed this with you, what sorts of things do you think he would have encouraged you to comment on?' Well for a start, he'd draw a map to show us where she came from and how, after the Second World War, people migrated . . . little arrows everywhere.

Max: I would think the discussion would lead more into the way she felt after moving to countries and the sort of racial type discrimination.

Jan: I think it would be more what brought her to . . . the place she is at the moment, and what was the factors that made her the person she is now, and what she's been through. It's not really in the passage, it's not really clear at all why she became like she is. Was she threatened by the people, or just by the fact that everything's different?

Max: But what about Mr E, what would he have done again?

Jan: Drawn a map.

Max: What sort of lines would the class have talked along, though?

Jan: He probably would have done most of the talking. And he would have said we were above average students . . . I mean, definitely . . .

Robert: He doesn't usually encourage much competition.

Jan: No, but he encourages you to think by what he says, it encourages you to go more in depth, behind what he says . . .

Alerting students to the functions of framings does not, of course, require us to administer theoretical disquisitions in the classroom. God forbid. We can increase their awareness more appropriately by involving them in activities that *reframe* what they read; and we can achieve this in an especially productive way, I shall propose, by bringing their writing into a direct, interrogative and inventive relationship with their reading. But first, it is noteworthy that there are other reframing possibilities. One of these would put readers themselves straight into a circumtextual position, i.e. let them design, and in a sense become, part of the interpretive apparatus. The suggestions made in *Writing with a Difference* about handling this text in class are indebted to the work of several year 11 students in another school who presented the material in their own way to a group of their peers. A few students in one class had been shown 'so small' in the previous year, when their reactions were very similar to those of the group we have just looked at. Part of our interest was in discovering how these students who had already seen the material in year 10 would react to it the second time around.

With this in mind, we made use of two versions of the video-taped performance in conjunction with the printed text; both had been filmed simultaneously, so that the soundtracks were identical, but one ('the medium shot') showed the speaker's face in frontal close-up, whereas the other ('the overhead shot') looked down on her from a height as she stood speaking in that first direction. Attention to these differences tended to denaturalize the text, foregrounding its status as an artefact. The most interesting insights emerged when we invited four of these students to present 'so small' to the other class. They took the invitation seriously, making careful decisions about the sequence of video and print texts, the questions to be posed, and so on. The lesson worked well. During a discussion we had afterwards with this quartet (Group B), they voiced a number of fascinating insights, ranging from matters concerning the interpretation of the text itself to a consideration of what constitutes desirable teaching practice. Here are some snippets of this conversation.

Group B

Jane: We showed the medium shot first because it sort of put them on guard and they had to watch it because it was sort of this girl confronting you with all her problems in a really weird way.

Doug: The first time I saw the video in year 10 it was exactly like that. I thought she was aggressive and bitter about something, and that she was attacking me. And I wanted to stir the students up in the same way.

*   *   *

Doug: We felt we should ask questions because we don't have the same authority as a teacher, and you need to direct the discussion in some way and also we haven't had much experience in directing discussions.

Jane: And it's not much use (for us, at least) just walking in there and throwing something in front of them that says this is what it's about and expecting them to understand. You've got to sort of get around it, you've got to make them think for themselves.

*   *   *

Doug: We wanted to make a lot of the differences between the visual presentation and the written, because it's pretty important. So we wanted to focus on that.

Meredith: Yeah, I thought it was important and seeing how their opinion changed after being exposed to the different versions, because it did change, and that was a little experiment, wasn't it?

Jane: And when we showed the high angle shot they could see how the camera angle had changed their interpretation. They picked up straight away that they didn't feel threatened, they were in the dominant position, she was meek, she has her head bowed and feels guilty and is blaming herself.

Doug: It's funny how the presentation and everything changes. Like because if you read that, it's just a mass of words and you pick up a certain picture, but when you see it she gives it some sort of body. The words are like music that she's performing. I wonder how they would have responded to just the words?

Jane: They would have just tuned out. I don't know. Do you think they might be able to understand it? I've never seen anything like that written down actually. Would our introduction have worked with just the words? What did we say at the beginning?

Meredith: (reading from the lesson notes the group had prepared) . . . The material you are about to see is probably slightly different to anything you have encountered before. (Understatement.) But keep an open mind and be prepared for its unusual presentation. (That's just to say, 'don't worry'.) Because it isn't so straight forward, you need to concentrate on it in a different way, and so don't get caught up in the meaning of each individual phrase. It deviates from the general path quite a bit and it's less important to understand the bits and pieces than the global meaning. Try to keep an idea of what you think is relevant to the total meaning in the back of your mind as you go. And also take note of any recurrent terms, because the repetition is there to direct your attention to certain things, give you clues about what the thematic issues are, and give it a sense of continuity . . .

Evidently, these students have enlarged their own responses to 'so small' by attending to the particulars of its framing and reframing in the classroom. Often, it will be impossible to give students such a magisterially active role. But similar things can be achieved if their own writing is led into a direct engagement with their reading. This procedure, while resembling so called 'process writing' in some respects, would differ from it in rejecting Romantic notions about the 'authenticity' of the individual 'voice' as expressing a supposedly unified self.

Such notions lead to a number of problems for student writers, as Pam Gilbert (1988) has pointed out. And in my view the same notions tend also to frame extratextually some of the least alert and least productive kinds of student reading. It is apparent that students like Jill (in group A) regard texts as expressing a person's feelings with unmediated directness, and this assumption simply disables them as readers. Their reading can, however, be reframed through certain writing requirements.

There are several methods of reframing (Reid, 1987; Reid *et al.*, 1988). A group might initially be asked, before they look at a text like 'so small', to write an autobiographical piece in the first person on a topic such as 'Feeling Alienated'; their writing would then provide one point of entry to their reading. But the next step is the critical one: further writing would be undertaken in order to reframe both that text and their own first writings. This could take the form, for instance, of experimenting with prose poetry, or exploring devices of repetition, or inventing a sliding or dispersed 'I' (which may include, perhaps, shifts – not marked pronominally – between male and female speakers).

The point of this work is in the to-and-fro movement of reflection through which the students learn to read as writers and write as readers. In the course of any such dialectic, other reframings can occur as well. Those gendered responses, for instance, that we considered earlier, will more readily be brought to critical consciousness if the writing task specifies a transposition of the male narrator (let us say) of the text one has read into a female narrator, or if one is required to recast one's own account of some personal experience so that it becomes focalized through the eyes of someone of the opposite sex (Reid, 1988). By such means, students may discover through their own textual practices at least some of the possible subtleties of implicitly gender-restricted readership that

Marie Maclean (1988) analyses in *Narrative as Performance*. At any rate, there is certainly a need for us as teachers and researchers, in our understanding of gendered writing, to go beyond the findings of James Britton and his colleagues (1975) in their work on *The Development of Writing Abilities*. They remark that such gender differences as seem to occur (for example, a tendency for girls to favour the so-called 'audience category' of child-to-trusted-adult and 'function category' of expressive writing) begin to disappear when one compares boys and girls in co-educational schools. But one wants to know much more about the dynamics of interaction between students and teachers within the circumtextual situations that frame what is written. Besides, the writing categories themselves should be critically assessed, as they elide such questions as these: 'Who sets the writing?' 'How is it affected by assessment tasks and other institutional practices?' 'What relation does it bear to the reading practices of male and female students respectively?'

For students, one benefit of writing in direct relation to what they read is that it demonstrates quite practically the role of intertextual and intratextual framing, that is, it acts out the principle that all writing rewrites other writing, and it compels attention to the in-built devices by which texts attempt to control their readers. Let me illustrate these points in conclusion, as it may otherwise seem that I have attached major importance to circumtextual and extratextual framings, as if they were basic, whereas this other pair could be left to the literary connoisseurs.

From the earliest years of schooling onwards, the quality of literary response can be enhanced by an encouragement of reading practices that are alert to intratextual framing. For example in that resonantly plain tale *The Story of Ferdinand* (1937), first published half a century ago, Robert Lawson's superb drawings and Munro Leaf's rhythmic prose comprise the text together. In a sense, the same story is told in parallel versions, visual and verbal; a single set of events could be derived from either sequence. But one of the ways in which the text offers more than a summarizable plot or schema is that through these inner divisions it can offer discreet little visual jokes whose function is to indicate lightly that a reader should not confuse this cheerful fantasy of Ferdinand and what happens to him with animals and events in the real world. We all remember his favourite cork-tree, which is unlike anything in nature; we remember, too, the picture of the other bulls, decorated with bandages and sticking plaster, reading a poster about the stadium in Madrid. Details of that sort constitute inward casements through which the tone can be recognized as whimsical. *Intertextual* framing, also, can be understood fairly simply, as all texts draw on other types of text, and often the signalling is very specific. Ernest Hemingway begins a story like this: 'One time there was a bull, and his name was not Ferdinand and he loved to fight . . .' By this unmistakable allusion, Hemingway's (1951) tale, *The Faithful Bull*, attempts from the outset to transform the genre of sentimental, anthropomorphic fables into something more tough-mindedly macho; the shift of values is intertextually specified.

When all is said and done, the most important thing is not the use of any theoretical terminology of different 'framing' operations, but the need to recognize that meanings depend largely on a delicate adjustment between expectations brought into the reading process and the text's own shaping devices. There is nothing abstruse about this; it can be grasped by the very young and articulated quite concretely by older student readers. In fact, one of the latter, a sixteen-year-old student in a class with which our research group was working, will now have the last word, as I quote from her thoughtful essay on reading children's picture books. In this part of her discussion, she considers the link between what I have called extratextual and circumtextual framings, in particular how these interact at the terminus of a text; and, in addition, she implicitly recognizes the intertextual dimension of reading, whereby one story can be seen as reframing another, and also the intratextual means whereby a story can offer its reader an embedded model of response:

> A very strong focus for any reader's expectations about any story is the way it ends. When we are still quite young we develop set ideas about how stories should work and this depends a lot on how they conclude. The 'happy ever after' convention is almost invariable in books for young readers because writers feel that their readers need reassurance that things will turn out well. In *Where the Wild Things Are* the ending has great importance because it provides a child (who has been encouraged to identify with Max) with a kind of model for self-development. This involves the ability to be independent, up to a point (e.g. of parents), and the ability to turn monsters into mole(hill)s. *The Story of Ferdinand* is basically the same in this respect. He too goes 'home' at the end and is 'sitting there still' very contentedly, having survived the dangers of the bull-ring just by being himself. Conversely, *The Faithful Bull* overturns our expectations of a happy outcome in a way that would be shocking to a young reader. In fact, just as right from its first sentence it is an anti-Ferdinand book; so its breaking of the conventional ending makes it an anti-children's book. This matter of expectations and conventions is therefore closely linked with the matter of audience.

Acknowledgement

I wish to thank the following people: Sneja Gunew for assistance at the conceptual stage; Brenton Doecke who compiled much of the material; Peter Lane and the Australian Research Council for their practical assistance with the research; and Ania Walwicz for allowing us to reproduce her poem.

6 Feminism, Romanticism and the New Literacy in response journals

DEANNE BOGDAN

This chapter explores a conception of literary literacy as 'engaged reflection' through a description and analysis of student response journals, a high school device, applied to a graduate seminar in women's literature and feminist criticism. It explores one intersection between feminist pedagogy, aesthetic theory, and English Studies in higher education, with implications for practice in the high school.

At the 1988 meeting of the American Educational Studies Association, Margaret Means McIntosh concluded her moving lecture, 'Feeling like a fraud', with suggestions for humanizing class assignments in order to develop students' feelings of greater authenticity about their own knowledge. Among the principles underlying the re-visioning of her undergraduate curriculum are the decentred classroom, in which the teacher foregoes the position of 'expert', and the validation of writing as process, in which evidence of student achievement avoids the tyranny of 'soloistic', hierarchical, academic products, such as the formal essay in favour of less externally directed writing, such as student accounts of their own learning experiences. These pedagogical reforms have been increasingly accepted for at least the last ten years inside high schools. They have also become known in English Studies as the 'New Literacy', and in Women's Studies as the attempt to win academic respectability for women's ways of knowing and learning. These ways of knowing are brought about through direct personal experience and celebrating interdependent inquiry. I hope to show how my own efforts to implement these pedagogical principles facilitated my students' learning and to document some rich links between English Studies, Women's Studies and conceptions of literary knowing.

'Ways in': Engagement with the text and reading as a woman

One of North America's most promising movements in promoting literary literacy can be claimed by the Association of Departments of English (ADE) of the Modern Language Association. The ADE has for the last two years been working to break down barriers which separate teachers of English in schools from those in universities. This chapter has grown out of my participation in one of their projects – a session on the teaching of William Wordsworth's poetry at the 1988 Conference of the National Council of Teachers of English. Though not a Romanticist myself, I agreed to prepare a short presentation on some aspect of the topic, 'Engaging literature: Teaching Wordsworth today'.

That 'engaging' should be part of the session's title is not coincidental. As I understand it, 'engagement with the text' has become a given of the New Literacy in English Studies, a given that, in my view, demands fuller theorization. Arising out of the reader-response theories of Louise Rosenblatt (1978) and James Britton (1982), literary engagement in general denotes a state of absorption, involvement, commitment and/or enjoyment in the reading process, which builds on readers' intuitive responses to literary interpretation and aesthetic judgement, in contrast to the intellectualized dissection of literary analysis modelled on New Critical dogma, now anathematized, at least theoretically, in English classrooms.

Within the academic community, literary engagement has been more visible as theory than as practice. Such critics as Wolfgang Iser (1974), Stanley Fish (1980) and Hans Robert Jauss (1982b) are now familiar on college reading lists. But as *praxis*, engagement is beginning to trickle up *from* the schools *to* the universities; and the *response journal*, its major pedagogical tool, has become a promising bridge between the learning and studying of literature, from elementary to graduate school. The assumption that literary meaning resides in the reader is an educational breakthrough potent enough to elicit from its advocates claims that extend far beyond textual interpretation or even beyond verbal communication to that of the efficacy and ownership of learning itself. It is not surprising that such a revolutionary, empowering idea, rooted as it is in the experiential, should be paramount in feminist literary theory and pedagogical practice, and that the response journal should be the vehicle for my own experiment in 'engaging Wordsworth'. What resulted from my classroom exercise served to show that engagement became the link, not just methodologically but substantively, be-tween English Studies and Women's Studies, as we embarked on our inquiry into the feminist critique of Romanticism.

The title of my original paper, 'Joyce, Dorothy, and Willie: Literary literacy as engaged reflection' (Bogdan, 1989), signifies feminist and feminine ways into the issue of 'engaging Wordsworth'. Anyone familiar with the life of Wordsworth would know that Dorothy was William's sister, but who is Joyce? In order to answer *that*, it is necessary to resituate my paper within the larger question of the ADE's agenda. Their interest was not in devising yet another approach to *teaching* Wordsworth's poetry, but in discovering new modes of *learning* it, in finding 'ways in' for contemporary non-specialists whose sensibilities might be out of tune with the major themes of Wordsworthian Romanticism, such as the continuity between the natural and the human, and the transcendence of the poet's moral vision.

The ADE is highly sensitive to ways of learning that might offset a common problem in literature education: students' reluctance to encounter a poem on its own terms, as 'an alien structure of the imagination, set over against us, strange in its conventions and often in its values' (Frye, 1970). All too often students regard it as a 'textoid' (Hunt and Vipond, 1987), the kind of text which is deemed artificial, fragmentary and inane by its readers, totally unrelated to the social context in which it is read. The poetry of William Wordsworth can be as much of a textoid to members of an interdisciplinary graduate class in feminist literary criticism, who have very different ideas about what they want to read and why, as it can to junior or senior high school students. For all of these students, there is the problem of whether the text is 'relevant'. Thus from the outset, the issue of engaging with Wordsworth became a pedagogical problem with exciting possibilities for feminist pedagogy as well as for English Studies. I decided to approach the task by focusing on the relationship between Dorothy Wordsworth, author of journals and 'secondary' poetry of the picturesque, and her brother, William, poet of the sublime and acknowledged architect of Romantic poetics.

The ground for a theoretical inquiry into the relationship between feminism, Romanticism and literary engagement has already been broken by a number of scholars. In *Feminism and Poetry: Language, Experience, Identity in Women's Writing* (1987), Jan Montefiore identifies Wordsworth's poetics, ironically enough, as the 'father' of radical feminist aesthetics, in that Wordsworth's 'Preface to the Lyrical Ballads', with its credo of poetry as the spontaneous overflow of powerful feelings, validates the experiential in literary response, in contrast to the intellectualized aesthetic values of Samuel Johnson and the neo-classicists. Despite the unwitting sexism of Wordsworth's 'definition of the poet as "a man speaking to men"', and of 'the myth of Romantic transcendence', which has posed difficulties for women writers to this very day, Montefiore credits Wordsworthian poetics with forming the basis for two canons of radical feminist aesthetics: the belief that poetry is a way into the poet's own experience and that poetry's capacity for compressing linguistic power is a way into understanding human existence. The poetics of Romanticism is educationally important: its tenets serve as a reference point for the literary conventions and criteria for poetic quality by providing the intellectual context within which poetry is read and studied in classrooms. *Whether* certain poetry engages readers and *how* it does so, then, becomes an educational issue that can be traced back to William Wordsworth.

Whether and how poetry engages readers is also an educational issue in the New Literacy. John Willinsky (1987) has written a persuasive account of the correspondences between the shift in English Studies from a transmission to a transactional model of reading and nineteenth-century Romanticist poetics. He cogently locates current received wisdom about the New Literacy within the history of ideas, positing salient commonalities between the nineteenth century's privileging of a 'theory of organicism and a reverence for the imagination and the self' in reaction to neo-classical literary conventions, and the 'use of express-ive . . . whole language . . . psycholinguistics . . . and interactive, transformative, and constructive models of [reading] comprehension', in reaction to the 'Old Literacy', with its stress on decoding and *explication de texte* in literary interpretation.

My own valuation of literary engagement is ambivalent: I regard the state of total absorption as a form of heightened and lowered consciousness at the same time, thus preventing critical detachment in the same reading act. One of the challenges posed by feminist pedagogy and the New Literacy is to discover reading strategies and pedagogical methods that can overcome the split between emotional and intellectual activity in literary response through what I call 'engaged reflection'. Engaged reflection signifies readers being interested in, committed to and enjoying the process of reading, but not being so enthralled that they remain unaware of what is bringing about their responses.

In *Radical Literary Education* (1987b), Jeffrey Robinson presents an affecting chronicle of his undergraduates' movement from uncritical engagement to engaged reflection throughout an entire term devoted to a single Wordsworth poem, the *Intimations Ode*. By means of class discussion, journal writing and the sequenced study of the literary, historical, biographical, psychoanalytic and compositional contexts of this poem, Robinson led his students to challenge liberal humanist presuppositions of engagement without dismissing its literary or educational value. I intended that my project would add the variable of gender to a similar kind of investigation, in which the main focus was the constructive and constructed nature of a woman's self as reader and writer. Our major objective was to think about the poem and ourselves through journal writing by exploring intertextuality, furthering the integration of literary experience with literary knowledge, increasing awareness of the influence of literary theory on reading and, not least, providing a space for the knitting up of literary and critical reading with personal history as a way of coming to terms with subjectivity. The relationship between Dorothy and William in its many aspects seemed an apt starting point.

The assignment and the journals

Our first assignment consisted of two parts. The first was a 'free response' to two poems, William's* 'I wandered lonely as a cloud' and Joyce Peseroff's 'Adolescent' (1988), a parody of that poem. For the second, the students were asked to write again about the two poems, having read William's 'Preface to the Lyrical Ballads' and the excerpt from Dorothy's journals which is generally regarded as having furnished her brother with the controlling image of his poem. (Both poems and the journal entry are to be found in the Appendix.) The use of the high school device of response journals proved to be a valuable way into the feminist

*To avoid the condescending and implicitly sexist practice of referring to 'Dorothy' and to her brother as 'Wordsworth', and to avoid the stylistic encumberment of 'Dorothy Wordsworth' and 'William Wordsworth', I shall refer throughout to 'Dorothy' and 'William'.

critique of Romanticism and its implications for the educational value of engaging with literature generally.

The more critically innocent responses in the journals tended to focus on 'common sense' interpretation (Belsey, 1980), in which the slide from literature to life is made uncritically. These responses contained reminiscences about the students' own adolescence, which Joyce's* poem allowed them to recollect in Wordsworthian tranquillity. For example, Joyce's opening lines, 'I wandered lonely as a dog / avoiding trouble / and others of her species' evoked only obvious points of contrast between the loneliness of a 'dog' in an urban landscape of alienation and the 'cloud' of Wordsworth's bucolic bliss. As one student put it, 'Peseroff is expressing the decline of William Wordsworth's world almost two hundred years later.' This contrast was recognized by most students as recapitulated in the final invocation to William, 'O William, what common / memories stir our yelps in the dark?', where the reservoir of 'common memories' has been displaced by the cacophonous 'urban music' of a disposable society. The central image of the daffodils, the source of inspiration for William, was seen to have degenerated into the tawdry 'gold stars' of conformist behaviour and the 'civic displays' of bureaucratic control.

The more critically sophisticated journals provided ways into discussions about the relationship between Romanticism, feminism and English studies. These readings centred on three interpretations of Joyce's image of the poem's persona as a 'dog' – as woman, adolescent reader and adolescent writer. For one student, Clare, the phrase 'lonely as a dog' betokened the alienation experienced by man's best friend – woman – and his appropriation of the feminine echoed in the poem's 'phallic clusters' of daffodils. Clare disliked what she saw as the Romantics assuming they had proprietorial rights over the feminine. A fellow student, Marion, was much more positive in her celebration of a woman writer coming into her own. She saw admiringly the poet as a 'real bitch', who, feeling no pain of 'male defined reality', keeps her 'nose to the curb [kerb]'. Marion felt that through looking 'into commonly ignored or misapprehended places – i.e. "the sewer-grate" of her own mind, Joyce finally came out of the broom-closet and into the streets'. For her, the poet spoke 'with poetic authority and distinction', refusing 'to pay obeisance to old forms' (e.g. the stanzaic triplet or metric iambic tetrameter), dropping 'all guise of parody . . . to pose the question directly' in the final invocation 'to a world (albeit dark) where, together, men and women might seek truth'.

These negative and positive perceptions – of woman as victim and woman as exuberant transgressor – were echoed in other journal entries about the poem's persona. Karen, an English teacher, focused on the plight of the typical high school English student as a dog, a hobo, prevented from engaging with Wordsworth directly. Corralled by stultifying pedagogical approaches into traditional interpretations through the 'civic display' of 'policed' meaning that tended to keep Wordsworth untouchable, the student reader 'is forced to wander from the

*In order to preserve stylistic continuity, I will henceforward refer to Joyce Peseroff as 'Joyce'.

experience of the poem'. Jane, however, interpreted the persona's angst in trying to find her voice as that of Joyce herself, who, holding up William's poem as her ideal product, resplendent in its organic unity, can only keep her nose to the curb of process, rebuked by the daffodils of her own muse. As a sociology student who was unaware of Wordsworth's original poem but powerfully aware of the social construction of knowledge, Jane confessed that her interpretation was probably a result of her outsider status in the literary interpretive community; but it was only after she encountered William's theory of poetry in his 'Preface to the Lyrical Ballads' that she could articulate how and why she felt that way.

In the second part of this assignment, students were invited to respond again to both poems as well as to Dorothy's journal entry, with the hindsight of William's critical manifesto, in his 'Preface'. The main aims were to provide a reference point for their initial responses and a means of comparing the poetic values of William's and Dorothy's writing. I have organized my analysis according to three major contexts in which these 'engaged reflections' struck me. The first was the recursive and self-scrutinizing quality of their written thoughts about their initial responses. The second was a preoccupation with engagement as a literary critical issue. The third was a lack of agreement as to whose writing, William's or Dorothy's, was the more successful in achieving the goals stated in William's 'Preface'.

The students enjoyed reconsidering Joyce's and William's poems in the light of the 'Preface'. Their writing was more fluid and bold. Some used William's critical canons to see commonalities in the two poems. Others saw Joyce's poem as directly challenging those canons. Some even saw 'Adolescent' as a better example of William's poetics than his own daffodil poem! The students were more interested in deploying Wordsworth's poetic principles to clarify *their* understanding of *their* reading. Clare subjected the principles of the 'Preface' to Belsey's critique of commonsense theories of language (Belsey, 1980). For Clare, William was operating under the misapprehension that 'poetry reflects the real world', and that 'those who read poetry will respond the same way', thus gaining access to 'universal truth'. She thought that William would probably have classified Joyce's poem as a textoid, as possessing, in his words, '*matter* . . . [that is] contemptible. . . . This wants sense: it is neither interesting in itself, nor can lead to anything interesting.' But for Clare, a city woman, the politicized content of 'Adolescent' was far more exciting than the moment of beauty recaptured, however successfully, in William's poem. By contrast, Jane's examination of William's 'Preface' led her to prefer his poem. While she challenged his assumptions that 'the language of men', 'common life' and transcendent experience produce timeless poetic truth, she nevertheless luxuriated in precisely the kind of aesthetic pleasure that William's poetic method intended to evoke, finding this a welcome relief from self-consciously ferreting out a meaning for 'Adolescent'.

This awareness of self-consciousness brings me to my second and third points: engagement as a poetic value, and who is better at eliciting it, William or Dorothy. Another student, Ruth, cited William's own reference to the poet's 'act of writing in verse' by which he 'makes a formal engagement . . . [to] gratify certain known habits of association'. She noted that both poems 'fly in the face of [Words-worth's] "savage torpor" by calling up images which deny and defy acquiescence to uniformity'. Ruth saw both poems as deliberate intentions by both poets to engage the reader actively. Gayle, on the other hand, complained that 'Words-worth expects his reader to be a mere passive recipient of what is already known to be "true"', while Joyce let her into the text as a collaborator in reconstructing the cityscape. For Gayle, as for Liz, the problem with William was 'that he is a little guilty of the very thing he accuses other "lesser" poets of. He speaks from a "poet's" perspective . . .', rather than translating 'the feelings of us mere mortals'. Liz blamed William's failure to engage her on the self-consciousness he brings to the poet's mandate to engage through the deliberate act of remember-ing. She wrote that perhaps William is correct in his assertion that the poet's task is to bind humankind together by 'passion and knowledge', but, for her, instead of achieving this emotional immediacy, William attenuates the effect through the very philosophical contemplation thought necessary to bring it about. She acknowledged that theoretically 'it may well be that the . . . act of remembering is more significant than the emotions stirred by the memories', but, in the end, instead of dancing with the daffodils, William 'just wrote a poem about it'. This stance, what Marion called the poet as 'magus', the poet as Wordsworth's 'man of "livelier sensibility"', was thought to be counterproductive to the evocation of powerful feeling in the reader, the assumption of the poet's priestly mantle actually working against itself in achieving specific effects. For her, William's credo that a poem has determinate meaning results, paradoxically, in a more diffused poetic effect than Dorothy achieved by her simple description. She saw William's poem as an exhalation, whereas 'Dorothy's daffodils draw air into the lungs; they inspire and conspire to cut cleanly through the persona of the poetic genius looking down at himself as poetic genius.'

It would be a misrepresentation of the students' journals to see them as giving William's poetry and poetics short shrift. On the contrary, William predominated throughout, his centrality as theoretician and supreme practitioner of poetic language and effect incontestable. To look at him directly, backwards at him through Joyce, or obliquely at him through Dorothy, meant inevitably encounter-ing his paramoumcy in generating the very premises upon which a course in personal and creative identity might be structured. When this identity is inter-woven with the reader's poetic engagement as a powerful reception of/connec-tion with powerful feeling, *how* that feeling registers *matters*. Here is where the journal responses to Dorothy's excerpt became invaluable. In having to account for – even merely record – poetic effect (or 'impact', as the students chose to call it), in engaging in reflection about their original response, they necessarily tangled with issues of poetic quality and method.

The journals disclosed a real division among the students on the question of Dorothy and William as 'literary engagers'. The English specialists tended to prefer William, and those who were 'other', Dorothy. I think I can safely say that professional literary conditioning affects how readers are engaged by writers!

This would seem to confirm one of the main presuppositions held by those who criticize the humanist tradition of validating literary engagement itself. Karen, an English specialist, found William's poem more imaginatively satisfying and emotionally intense than Dorothy's 'drawn out and uninspiring' prose, and accounted for her response in terms of Dorothy's distance from nature, her outsider status, as a woman in society and as a poet. She also noted Dorothy's absence from the scene she is describing, an absence, according to William, that is crucial to the communication of powerful feeling. Dorothy's lack of poetic persona was precisely what for Liz, a nonspecialist, rendered Dorothy's daffodils more vivid and immediate. Their specificity was a product of simple memory or direct observation rather than the long reflection recommended by William. Ruth also found Dorothy's multi-layered, nuanced descriptions three-dimensional, all the more active and complex for their being *less* removed, less intentionally poetic; and Clare was prompted to question William's claim in the 'Preface' that poetry *qua* poetry elicits our most passionate responses. Dorothy's directness of perception was for Jennifer paradigmatic of 'a female presence equally as sensitive [as William's] to the world around her'. Ann described this as a presence which expresses through 'the language of [wo]men speaking to [wo]men' the universal vision William longed for 'but failed to convey'.

Ambivalent conclusion

The response journals of these students proved to be a learning tool that extended far beyond the breaking down of potential resistance to William's poetry as a textoid. This part of the assignment loosened their critical categories, integrating literary theory with literary experience, and encouraging reinterpretation of their responses in the first half of the assignment. For instance, some used their insights about William and Dorothy at the end of the process to challenge their own gender stereotyping of, for example, the narrator in Joyce's 'Adolescent'. It also provided the basis for a systematic inquiry into substantive theoretical issues in Wordsworthian criticism itself, which we pursued in subsequent meetings. I believe that the pedagogical project of using Joyce and Dorothy as ways into William via his 'Preface to the Lyrical Ballads' resulted in the students anticipating at a deeply intuitive level the major critical positions embodied in some of the most richly rewarding recent criticism on gender in Romanticism.

I suggested earlier that literary engagement was a phenomenon in need of clearer definition (Rosenblatt, 1978; Harris, 1988; Britton, 1989). I offer here my understanding of engagement as 'engaged reflection' within a larger conception of literary literacy based on the contribution that student response can make so eloquently. Such writing is at the heart of the kind of literary knowing embraced by feminist pedagogy and the New Literacy. It succeeds in overcoming the dissociation of sensibility, that split between the participating and critical responses, between engagement and detachment, which is almost axiomatic in more traditional assignments, such as the externally imposed essay. Such a pedagogical shift has crucial implications for the philosophy of literature education, primarily in terms of revealing the dialectical nature of what it means to come to know anything. The kind of literary knowing these journals disclose freely explores the relationship between intuited knowledge and the continual testing of that knowledge within an intellectual framework or theoretical construct at the same time that the knower authenticates knowledge by taking responsibility for the very process of coming to know. Reader-response journals, a widely used device in junior and senior high schools, are an equally appropriate vehicle at the graduate level. Through them readers can 'come to know', reflecting on literary texts and theory together in an especially fertile discourse, both honouring and interrogating their knowledge as 'experiential realization' (Woodman, 1985). This dialectic can be thought of as 'engaged reflection', in which the knower is both committed to the process of knowing and ambivalent about the certitude or finality of any single act of coming to know.

The importance of being ambivalent – of avoiding closure – has been manifest throughout this project. 'To engage with' is to render natural, transparent and unself-conscious. To be ambivalent is to speak for and against this engagement. To be ambivalent is to engage with language reflectively without having to repress or kill what is signified. To be ambivalent is to be at once accepting and critical. It is to embrace otherness without self-abnegation. This is what my students did in their journals, giving themselves over to a process and a person they did not know but were willing to trust. To be ambivalent is to attempt transcendence without appropriation, to disengage from the spontaneous overflow of powerful feeling long enough to recognize absence in presence, difference in oneness.

The act of reading a text as its co-author has brought about the recognition of difference in oneness: realizing that others' responses to a text contain elements which strike chords in our own. This has been a major contribution of deconstructive criticism to the critique of Western metaphysics. Within English Studies, heightened self-consciousness about reading any text makes a return to a naive assumption about the mimetic adequacy of language to mean precisely what it says impossible. Feminist and Marxist criticism enrich reading as engaged reflection by making the aesthetic joys of 'innocent' reading accountable in terms of gender, class, and race. By insisting on awareness that transparent literary meaning is an illusion, post-structuralist literary theories threaten and promise to unseat the humanist belief in the *intrinsic* educational value of literature with which the language arts curriculum continues to be burdened. Our task now is to help real readers in real classrooms gain aesthetic pleasure, not from naive and passive reception but from an active awareness of the constructedness of a text and the enterprise of author and reader alike. We already know that response journals can be a powerful way into literary experience and reflecting upon it in high schools. What this chapter has argued is that such journals can extend the parameters of literary scholarship and promote the liberating ambivalence that feminist criticism seeks to engender as the process of coming to know.

Appendix

I Wandered Lonely as a Cloud

I wandered lonely as a cloud
That floats on high o'er vales and hills,
When all at once I saw a crowd,
A host, of golden daffodils;
Beside the lake, beneath the trees,
Fluttering and dancing in the breeze.

Continuous as the stars that shine
And twinkle on the milky way,
They stretched in never-ending line
Along the margin of a bay:
Ten thousand saw I at a glance,
Tossing their heads in sprightly dance.

The waves beside them danced; but they
Out-did the sparkling waves in glee:
A poet could not but be gay,
In such a jocund company:
I gazed – and gazed – but little thought
What wealth the show to me had brought:

For oft, when on my couch I lie
In vacant or in pensive mood,
They flash upon that inward eye
Which is the bliss of solitude;
And then my heart with pleasure fills,
And dances with the daffodils.

William Wordsworth

Adolescent

I wandered lonely as a dog
avoiding trouble,
and others of her species,

while daffodils like gold stars
(for good behavior)
rebuked me, and lilac buds

in phallic clusters,
doubling size each day.
I kept my nose to the curb,

never to the grindstone,
like someone looking for money
down a sewer-grate. Depressing,

isn't it, when buses grind past –
not one going where you're going,
the crowd at your back

revving its discontent
as if *you* were leader of the pack.
A Coke bottle tinkles, hurled

rocks ripple the civic
display of daffodils.
You watch Coke drip

into the gutter, livening
a party of ants,
their frenzied dancing –

better to wander, quickly,
away, before the soft
wow of police cars

climbs rapidly up the scale
of urban music . . .
O William, what common

memories stir our yelps in the dark?

Joyce Peseroff

(I would like to thank the author and the *Harvard Magazine* for permission to reproduce this poem which appeared in the July/August 1988 issue of the magazine.)

When we were in the woods beyond Gowbarrow park we saw a few daffodils close to the water side. We fancied that the lake had floated the seeds ashore, and that the little colony had so sprung up. But as we went along there were more and yet more; and at last, under the boughs of the trees, we saw that there was a long belt of them along the shore, about the breadth of a country turnpike road. I never saw daffodils so beautiful. They grew among the mossy stones about and about them; some rested their heads upon these stones, as on a pillow, for weariness; and the rest tossed and reeled and danced, and seemed as if they verily laughed with the wind, that blew upon them over the lake; they looked so gay, ever glancing, ever changing. This wind blew directly over the lake to them. There was here and there a little knot, and a few stragglers a few yards higher up; but they were so few as not to disturb the simplicity and unity and life of that one busy highway. We rested again and again.

Dorothy Wordsworth

7 Safety and danger: close encounters with literature of a second kind

PETER MEDWAY AND ANDREW STIBBS

An opportunity, with dangers, to widen literary study

Although censorship or suppression of literary material used by English teachers has been a relatively occasional or marginal issue in the UK, it is likely to become a more frequent concern in the near future, as the government has taken more control of the curriculum and at the same time given to parents far more say in what is taught. Campaigners who may use this parent power include religious fundamentalists or populist politicians exploiting a backlash against professionals and intellectuals. Progressive teachers are seen as betraying the respectable working and lower-middle classes by espousing just those feckless or bohemian values which the aspiring masses have worked hard to escape (Martin, 1981).

The traditional canon of literary texts could be sustained in the face of such attacks (even though certain novels and plays would need to have their 'heritage' status invoked to counter their depictions of deceit, violence, child neglect and illicit sex). However, at just the same time as there is an anti-liberal reaction, new public examinations in the UK allow teachers to choose the texts which are studied and to draw on a far wider range of literature than comprised the former prescribed lists. So English teachers can expect to be called to account for selecting literary texts which lack the respectability of tradition. They will need to have both a clear rationale for teaching literature and a comprehensible and defensible model of its effects on readers.

We argue that teachers should take current opportunities to widen the range of types of texts they offer and to look outside the realist canons of both children's and adult literature; the teaching approaches suggested by non-realist and openly artefacted material can usefully be applied to traditional realist material. Both these components of a literary pedagogy – the broadening of the canon and the diversification of teaching techniques – can provide useful defences against likely attack.

A realist bias in the canon: A second Golden Age of children's literature

The present staple of literary texts for secondary schools is well established and has two main components. First, there are the successors to the products of the nineteenth-century 'Golden Age of Children's Literature', which some have claimed constitute a second Golden Age (Carpenter, 1985). These are no longer confined to the arcadian classics and fantasies of fixated childhood which made up the first wave. Many have modern settings and some of them are of great delicacy, psychological insight and realism.

Many of these recent fictions written specifically for children and adolescents retain the optimistic liberal-individualist values of the classics of the First Golden Age. Carpenter sees these values as arising originally from a mid-Victorian confluence of the 'improving' and the entertaining in children's books, at a time when children were being romantically idealized and industrial society was being deplored. But their modern successors too rarely have that subversive element which Carpenter identifies in Alice, Pooh and their contemporaries. They tend to privilege a particular identity-type, that of the young person given to sensitive reflection rather than to action. (It may be no coincidence that if young people took such fictional heroes as role models it would make the lives of school-teachers, parents and politicians easier.)

Texts like these are specially open to the charge which Lennard Davis (1987) lays against novels in general: they offer readers a false community with which to console themselves for the loss of real community, and they sustain the myth that what the world really needs is for *individuals* to sort out them*selves*.

Though he sees it more positively (as subverting patriotism), Carpenter (1985, p. 11) also identifies this withdrawal-element in the 'First Golden' canon:

> Its message was that the public world was vindictive and intolerant, and that the man of vision, the true artist, must alienate himself from society and pursue a private dream.

Carpenter characterizes the work of his second, contemporary Golden Age, as being about growing *up* into the *adult* world (rather than about escaping *back* into a *childhood* world), but still in order to be a fulfilled individual.

It might seem that our general claim about the unrelieved individualism of the 'staple of literary texts' is confounded by the popularity of one standard pattern of historical novel for children. In a typical example (for which almost any of Leon Garfield's novels would serve), a child wanders about (or children wander about) surviving vicissitudes in the public domain. But the plots are structured and the comments angled in order to develop or demonstrate the child-hero's individual integrity rather than to explore public domain issues such as the socio-economic origin of the highwaymen, slaves, madhouses, wars or whatever provide and produce the underworlds, underclasses, disruptions and injustices which sensationalize the experiences.

A realist bias in the canon: Social realism and
The Great Tradition

The second component of our 'staple of literary texts for secondary pupils' is aimed at older students, including those taking external examinations. It consists of novels, poems and plays written for adults in the middle third of this century. These texts are not 'modern' in the sense that they have been written in the students' lifetimes, as many of us have found out when we have wished on our students the novels which spoke most directly to us as adolescents only to have them dismissed as irrelevantly 'historical'.

Nor are these texts modern in the sense that they are modernist in conception and style. Recently, parsimony has ensured that texts which English teachers bought in the 1960s (and sometimes had to defend against complaints about the 'bad language' or 'sordidness' in them) have remained in wide use and even been renewed because that is safer and cheaper than replacing them with truly 'contemporary' works. As has already been said, an increasingly oppressive moral and political climate in the UK might exert a pressure to stick to the safe texts at a time when the new examination requirements offer an opportunity to widen the canon.

So schools have hardly been touched by a range of modern texts which might well appeal to adolescent sensibilities: Vonnegut's and other novels influenced by science-fiction; magic realism; contemporary Australian or Caribbean texts; modern European works in translation. It is symptomatic that *To Kill a Mockingbird* (Lee, 1960) is in frequent use, but not *The Colour Purple* (Walker, 1982).

The prevalence of the pre-modern model may owe something to the still surviving influence on English teaching of the Leavis tradition. This is a manifestation of a protestant strand in British culture which emphasizes the authority of the conscience and despises ascribed status and material wealth. In novels of the Cambridge canon, the writing is held to enact the responses of the individual who knows the world through feeling, which is informed by the values of an organic community. What survived of that community in the England of the 1950s and 1960s was held to be found, not in the village, but in the urban working class. Although the heroes of post-war novels which proved acceptable to English teachers certainly agonized about class loyalty as against social mobility, they had little in common with the fragmented or cauterized consciousnesses of modernist fiction of the same period, particularly from overseas. The same protestant ideology, most characteristically manifested in literature as pseudo-biographical novels, informs much of the children's and adolescents' literature we described above as the first strand of the staple. There are not many laughs in secondary school literature after the age of fourteen.

The Leavisite influence in English higher education specially predisposed its products to go into the proselytizing, unglamorous and materially unrewarding professions, such as English teaching in schools. Consequently, the school canon consists largely of realist novels – pseudo-biographies or autobiographies rather than the fabulations and metafictions we think young people could enjoy. But current secondary pupils may well have learned as infants to read on such playful and metatextual picture books as those of the Ahlbergs. They may have learned to 'read' television from sophisticatedly constructed serials and pop videos, and overtly and self-referringly constructed adverts. And their out-of-school reading may be jokey comics, arcane magazines, and cult-fiction of *The Hitch Hiker's Guide to the Galaxy* (Adams, 1979) type.

We asserted above that specially written children's literature for the secondary age range has taken on neither the ideologies nor the narrative devices of modernism. What we have said is even more true of the adult texts which are given the most thorough and prestigious treatment in school. They maintain the Victorian convention of linear single-voice narrative with long passages of description. The hero or narrator is a stable experiencing centre for whom the order in the world, if elusive, is there to be found. One result of this is that students' own writings rarely depart from the conventions of naive realism. The implicit models are rarely those collaged and plurivocal texts, owing more to cinema than to Victorian fiction, which wittily draw attention to, and subvert, their own conventions and coherence. Because students, except for those of a peculiarly literary bent, mainly fail to detect the order of realist fiction in their own lives, and have difficulty turning experience into the sort of writing that is expected, teachers often set them to write their narratives about existing fictional worlds and characters taken from the class texts.

Readings as virtual experiences – or books as things in themselves

This stylistic adherence to realism has social and psychological ramifications relevant to our theme of English teachers' ability to defend the texts they wish to teach. English literature was introduced into the UK school curriculum as a sort of religious study for a secular age by those who thought literature (though not, at first, novels) could do good by representing true states of affairs, good behaviour, or at worst comfortable possibilities affording harmless reflection.

Their argument for literature implicitly concedes its opponents' case, because it invokes the same model of how literature works. Both views treat readings of books as 'virtual experiences', which function as substitutes for the real things they represent because the authors have observed the conventions of reporting in order to trap the reader into suspended disbelief. Just as we can 'grow' and be made better by exposure to the right experiences, so we can by 'virtual' experiences.

But, by the same token, representations of harmful experiences in books can harm us: whether a book does good or harm will simply be a matter of *which* experiences are represented in the work. The implication of this view is that there is nothing specifically literary about selecting a book for a young person. It is the same sort of judgement parents make in exposing children to, or keeping them from, any experience, such as meeting a particular friend or visiting a particular place.

In contrast, our argument – that emphasizing the textuality of the texts we teach provides a defence against the censors – is based on our believing, and on emphasizing in teaching, that the experiences offered by books are not the same as experiences of the sorts of realities they describe. Readers may feel *pity for* a dying character, but they do not feel the same *pain as* the dying character, nor indeed the same pity as for a person who is really dying.

There are other differences between readings of books and 'real' experiences of life. The virtual experience model appears untenable when we remind ourselves that books are objects which we can pick up or lay down, skim or re-read at will. Books are divided into chapters, have neat and usually satisfying endings, and they come in covers with title-pages and the name of the author to remind us they have been invented. Our 'real-life' experience is never determined by others to the extent that our reading is determined by authors. Neither do we have such control over 'real-life' as we can exercise in choosing to shut a book or read it in parts or non-sequentially.

If novels are not represented as informing us, they cannot be represented as telling us lies. They are systems of signs, and they 'refer' only to the extent that we conventionally assign connections between the signs and the rest of reality. In this sense, a novel is neither a window on the world nor a reflection of the world, but another thing in the world.

However, because of the meanings we invest in the signs – the genres, plots, images, 'characters' and words which make up novels – it is not so simple as that. We cannot explain the appeal of the novel – even the non-realist novel – only by what it has in common with ingenious mechanisms or abstract designs or as an artful construction which we recognize as creating an illusion of reality. Reading words is not the same as real experience, but it undoubtedly offers a sort of experience which is not simply of surfaces or codes:

> Even as we claim that literature does not reflect reality . . . we understand that its capacity for engaging the reader in transformation springs from the reader's apprehension of it as something true and real. To deny this is to deny the experience of anyone who has been literally entranced by reading a book (Bogdan and Yeomans, 1986, p. 12).

The powerful metaphors of engagement with fiction – 'immerse', 'lose', 'devour', 'transport', 'identify with' – are too consistent and common to be dismissed. Also, some novels are intended to, and in fact do, have an effect in the real world by creating representations we take as essentially true – *Uncle Tom's Cabin* (Stowe, 1852) and the novels of Dickens did awaken consciences and produce reforms. Something of the realist cause, therefore, has to be conceded. It would show a misunderstanding of the nature of fiction to suppress in ourselves and our students our natural inclination to talk about characters in novels in the same (celebratory, anticipatory, evaluative) ways as we talk about our friends and acquaintances, even though we should want them also to be aware of the constructedness of characters. Denial of that mode of response leads to sterile academicism of the type which bedevilled the teaching of the Greek and Latin classics and, often, English literature until quite recently. The crucial step is to recognize that such responses are legitimate but not sufficient in themselves.

Reading as both engagement and criticism

Deanne Bogdan outlines some of the justifications which have been proposed for literature (Bogdan, 1985) and points out the vulnerability of realist defences of texts (Bogdan and Yeomans, 1986). She claims that a mature reading of a literary (more specifically fictional) text entails an oscillation between two opposed states of relating to the text: an 'engagement' with the text which makes the world it represents matter to us as readers, and an alternating 'detachment' which makes us evaluate it and interpret it as a constructed hypothesis (Bogdan, 1986). Simultaneous realization of both states, in a moment of 'stasis', is rarely to be hoped for.

Bogdan's idea of 'oscillation' helps us to discriminate between engagements which are vulnerable and engagements which serve to power critical readings. Reading by naive readers may seem not far removed from simple absorption in an experience, with far less awareness of the constructedness and the artifice of a book than of its quasi-reality. Such readers may, in a sense, be at the mercy of the representation, and could be harmed in the way the would-be censors fear. For example, there are instances – real and fictional and comic and tragic – of people wastefully or fatally modelling their lives on fictional exemplars, or even of authors modelling their lives on those of their own created characters! (Rose, 1985).

While an ability to switch from engaged to critical reading does not guarantee immunity, readers who have learned – or more to our point been taught – to recognize the constructedness of texts, i.e. to recognize them as sign-systems, games and hypotheses, are better able to resist what Robert Scholes (1985) has called that *Textual Power* which the classics of realist fiction most signally and insidiously exercise.

We make tentative proposals for teaching approaches to reading which would inform students' autonomous reading, in and out of school, encourage an awareness of the textuality of text and promote the sorts of critical readings which prevent the engaged readings with which they oscillate from becoming overwhelming.

Teaching an awareness of the textuality of literature: Widening the canon

To avoid the traps which a realist justification sets for teachers, we propose the use of literature of a second, non-realistic, kind, and the use of a second kind of teaching method which emphasizes the textuality of the realist works now canonic in schools. We also hope to show that this can be done without trivializing literature teaching or undermining its power as a humane education.

First, to teach a recognition of the literary nature of literature, it would help if we introduced students to some texts where, as with the picture books and products of popular culture which we mentioned, the artifice is out in the open – playful texts which feature self-reference, self-parody, self-contradiction, and so on. A novel (not, admittedly, obviously suitable for school use) which we have enjoyed recently, illustrates some of the overtly textual and metatextual features we are thinking of. In Llosa's *Aunt Julia and the Scriptwriter* (1984), we learn over several chapters to distinguish the main narrative, about a boy, his aunt and a writer of soap operas, from the other concurrent narratives which we come to realize are the soaps. The awareness this induces of the constructedness of all the narratives is further heightened when, late in the book, characters and settings in whom we have invested interest and concern start appearing in the wrong stories, as the scriptwriter cracks up. On a micro-level, one of the author's jokes has a corresponding effect: the reader's realization that one sentence describing a character is repeated in several of the plots calls into question the sentence's meaningfulness and finally exposes the 'description' for what it was all along – just a string of verbal signs.

There are *some* texts in use in schools which exhibit some of the modernistic devices we should want to use to indicate the createdness of texts, and which we should ascribe to our literature 'of the second kind'. Robert Cormier, in novels such as *After the First Death* (1979) makes daring use of changing viewpoints and narrative voice and film-like cutting. Jill Paton Walsh, while remaining a moralist, uses stream of consciousness techniques in *Goldengrove* (1972) and *Unleaving* (1976) and pastiche throughout *A Parcel of Patterns* (1983), and in all these texts she interweaves past and present and memory and foreshadowing.

Furthermore, the popularity of play-reading – in groups or classes – with adolescent readers offers a toehold. It is true that in the publishing and purchasing of texts (often based on adaptations of television series) for play-reading in schools, there has been a cult of social realism corresponding to that in novels and stories. But plays are obviously artefactual, even when they are not playful in the sense we have suggested. Such plays as Brecht's (1965) *The Caucasian Chalk Circle* and *The Exception and the Rule*, provide a month's or week's work, respectively, for an adolescent English class. They are easy to produce or semi-produce because of their very artificiality (using narrators, for instance); they offer set pieces easy to stage in classrooms (both those examples culminate in trial scenes, for instance); and they do deal with issues of injustice which appeal in a quasi-documentary manner to young readers.

The plays also offer excellent exemplars of a concept of literature alternative to the realism we have described. Features associated with Brecht's ideas of *epic theatre* and *estrangement* provide disruptions to the narrative through prologues, epilogues, overt and intrusive narration, song and characters' mutual comments on each others' actions. These features draw attention to the artificial nature of the text. Furthermore, Brecht's political purpose is clear in the texts – and available reinforcingly from a study of his life and such poems as *Children's Crusade* (1976) about children wandering about in wartime. His settings of contemporary and universal dilemmas and injustices in mythical and legendary times and places, together with his direct appeal to his audience to change things, represent just that link between the nature of text as artificial sign-system and the power of text to generate relevant hypotheses about possible worlds for which we argue later.

> . . . Observe the conduct of these people closely:
> Find it estranging even if not very strange,
> Hard to explain even if it is the custom,
> Hard to understand even if it is the rule . . .

(from the Prologue to *The Exception and the Rule*, 1965)

Finally, the realist canon could be supplemented by some of the recent texts in which authors deliberately set out to subvert the ideology of classics by representing their events from the points of view of underlings – as in Leeson's *Silver's Revenge* (1985), Needle's *The Wild Wood* (1982) or, for older students, Jean Rhys's *The Wide Sargasso Sea* (1966). These texts represent the pseudo-events of *Treasure Island* (1883), *Wind in the Willows* (1908) and *Jane Eyre* (1847) from the points of view of, respectively, the pirates, the weasels and stoats and ferrets, and the first Mrs Rochester. The comparisons which they provoke ensure that these re-presentations, like the Brecht plays, invite readers to interrogate the values embedded in their plots.

If the texts are translations from foreign languages, so much the better: it gives us the chance to expose their artefactuality by showing passages of the incomprehensible original, or even of showing different translations.

However, even after seeking out such writers as Cormier and Paton Walsh, and looking to translations and alternative versions, we must concede that there is a problem in finding enough playful novels which are suitable for children or adolescents – ones that are not too long, too full of sex, violence and 'bad language', or too concerned with themes of little interest to the young. Perhaps the answer is to appeal to that highly talented plain-clothes arm of English teaching – the writers of juvenile fiction whose major incomes are from purchases of their work as class sets by English Departments – and ask them to read Marquez, Peter Carey, Flann O'Brien and Gunter Grass, and get writing.

Teaching the literariness of literature by a text-centred approach to the realist canon

We also think that there could be significant progress without changing the texts at all. It would help if the approaches to fiction encouraged by the discussion topics or writing we set on novels did not so often implicitly treat the invented worlds and characters of the novels as if they were documentary givens. The theoretical contributions of structuralism, reader-response theories, and post-structuralist criticism (for instance in introducing such notions as 'narrative grammar', Barthes' 'codes', and 'intertextuality') have filtered into British higher education too late to have influenced most schoolteachers of literature. However, insights from them would enhance teachers' repertories of procedures for provoking intelligent engagement with texts.

For instance, the study of 'character' in novels might take the form less of biography or psychology and more of constructing attribute-grids and recognizing stereotypes, so that 'characters' are seen as plot-functions rather than people. Study of plot might take the form less of quasi-history and more of relating it to genre and predictability, so that 'plot' is seen as a rule-governed sequence of motifs. And the novel's language might be studied for its crafty connotations rather than accepted as transparent.

Although realist novels such as *Lord of the Flies* (Golding, 1954) may seem to resist it, they too are susceptible to a reading which deconstructs the text and reconstructs it in different ways to make it do different things. It is not enough to treat it as documentary and invite students to map the island; say what the different responses of the main characters to their maroonings show about their respective temperaments; 'Write Jack's defence of his conduct to his Headmaster'; 'Talk about a time you experienced mass hysteria like that depicted in the novel'; and so on. Teachers can also invite students to recognize the text as an ideologically situated artefact and invite them to rewrite an episode in which they, as authors, exchange the physiques but not the personalities of Piggy and Jack; add two girls to the *dramatis personae*; write in the persona of a female and even feminist author; map the decisive forks in the novel and suggest how the text might have proceeded had some other decisions been taken; insert scenes of cooperation and harmony; consider why the author chose to end the conch at the same time as he finished off Piggy; characterize and explain the differences in the types of language used to describe the hunt, the death of Piggy, and the death of Simon; insert other voices into the text at critical points; read extracts from *The Coral Island* (Ballantyne, 1858), *The Odyssey*, *The Tempest*, Marvell's *Bermudas*, and Tennyson's 'The Lotus-Eaters'; consider what opportunities and difficulties the text would present to a film-maker or compare the film and the book.

Contemporary children may not have read *The Coral Island*, but their TV experience, and maybe their reading of Enid Blyton or Arthur Ransome, or their general knowledge about *Robinson Crusoe* or *The Tempest*, may equip even young readers to recognize in *Lord of the Flies* the use of, and addition to, the genres of stories about children isolated from adults, or about desert islands. Such recognitions could be developed and explicated by students predicting the course of the plot and justifying their predictions by reference both to the internal evidence of the text and their external knowledge of other, comparable, texts.

Some classic statements of pure New Criticism would deny that knowledge of the author might be a resource brought to bear on reading. But students who note the parallelisms between the story and Golding's experiences of the Navy and an all-boys prep school might be better placed to evaluate the text as the invention of a person with preoccupations and purposes. Instead of accepting the 'world' of the novel as an unproblematic given, they might look critically at the values it embodies. Students can list what they think would be the most important cruces or themes of the text to readers (including themselves) of different sex, ethnic or class background, or previous reading experiences. This exposes the part played in a reading of a text by a reader's individuality, culture and political or religious allegiance.

More traditionally, some examination of the language, imagery and symbolism of the text can draw a proper, empowering, attention to the status of the text as an ingenious, but resistible, artefact. So would recognizing the characteristics and purposes it might share with stories in other genres that they recognize – myth, fable, sensationalized true survivors' tales in newspapers.

The same applies to an examination of the manipulation of point of view, selecting and sequencing of events, and the distinction between the time-pattern of the alleged events in history, the time-pattern of the textual narration, and the time-pattern of the reader's reading experience. Readers might be encouraged to ask what possibilities the author avoids having to represent by passing over stretches of 'history'.

The preparation of passages to be read aloud or dramatized can further accent the artefactedness of the text by requiring the readers to recognize and solve problems about dramatizing descriptions, reports of speech, simultaneous events, or the passage of time, or to decide who speaks quoted words on the evidence of forward or backward looking clues in the narration, or of what is said, or of the vocabulary used, or of how the author has laid out the speech.

Hard cases and hypotheses

The approach to literature which we have been proposing enables teachers to deal with the recurrent problem of books which tempt teachers by their 'teachability' but which, they judge, offer distorted or distressing reports of the world. There might be numerous grounds – literary quality, or food for ethical reflection – on which teachers might choose texts that they considered 'untrue'. *Lord of the Flies* might be an example, as might Cormier's (1975b) *The Chocolate War*. There are those novels and plays which distort in a good cause, for instance by presenting in a strong positive light people who have been oppressed and despised by those with power over them, as if women were typically stronger or black people freer than, historically, they have been. And there are those salutarily frightening visions of a world after a nuclear holocaust. How should we deal with these hard cases?

First, we would want our students to appreciate, as part of their routine response to new texts, that all representations of the world, including those we find 'true', are the constructions of somebody who had values and agendas, who made certain choices and could have made different ones. We might then add that novels imaginatively actualize potentialities which their authors find in the world. It helps to see imaginative fiction as hypotheses which can say not only 'The world is like this', but also 'The world *could* be like this'. This characteriz-ation of novels depends on both of their contrasting functions – their referential function, which links fiction to the real world, and their semiotic function, which makes them hypothetical. These hypotheses are not abstract aesthetic constructions: they can move us to desire or hate the states they present. So they can have political effects. Fictions about the past, the present or the future can supply utopian visions of possible futures which may guide our actions and choices.

It follows that we should help our students towards a style of reading which switches not only between an involvement with a pretended reality and a cognitive appreciation of its construction, but also between an involvement with a pretended reality and an evaluation of that pretended reality against their knowledge and experience of the actual. Such an evaluation, made possible by the deconstructive analysis which reveals its pretendedness, would ask: Does the potential for this presented alternative world truly exist in the world as I know it, and would this realization be desirable? Their evaluation needs to be powered by whatever joy, anxiety or indignation the novel's rhetorical force gives to the reader's intellectual engagement. To use a phrase from Bogdan (1986), we need to put our students both 'in and out of love with literature'.

A rationale for literature teaching by expert teachers who choose their texts

We return to our opening theme of defending literature teaching from the censors. If literature offers constructed hypotheses which need both to be recognized as such and to be 'experienced' in the power of their realized quasi-actuality, two things follow.

First, literature is worth studying because young people *need* to consider hypotheses about the world, since it is only from these that they will come to better it. That provides English teachers with a justification for their material, and a defence against the charge that they are exposing children to experiences their parents would rather they did not have. Indeed, if children are to learn about the range of possibilities within human experience as part of their preparation for life, they *need* to read about experiences which a parent or teacher would not expose them to in reality.

The other consequence of the need to teach the passionately critical reading for which we have argued is that literature needs teaching by experts who know how the powerful charms of literature work, for good or ill. That provides English teachers with an argument that they know best how to protect children from the dangers of literature-misunderstood-as-experience, and how to teach the children to be disarmers for themselves of the magical powers of the texts they need to read.

Acknowledgement

An earlier version of the second half of this chapter entitled 'Justifying literature as more and less than life' appears in the forthcoming book compiled by J. Collins (ed.), *Vital Signs*, University of Buffalo Press.

8 Molesting the text: promoting resistant readings

MARNIE O'NEILL

In Western Australia, the personal growth model of curriculum became the dominant model throughout the 1970s and early 1980s, although everything from the Great Tradition through New Criticism to personal growth/response was represented in classrooms. Many teachers experienced conceptual problems in placing literature in the personal growth curriculum model, and seeing what it was (if anything) students learned about literature through personal response approaches. My previous publications (O'Neill, 1984a, 1984b, 1987) addressed the place of literature in education in general, and post-growth model English in particular. Working from an eclectic base of sociology, growth model curriculum thinking and personal response theory, I distilled a set of functions of literature. Perhaps, not surprisingly, the broad dimensions of the set were the development of metaphoric mode perception and thought, aesthetic awareness, the presentation of ideal ways of being, construction and reconstruction of self, social constructions of reality (and escape from it) and the formation of a moral and ethical values system.

The hypothesis that these were functions that literature fulfilled, particularly for adolescents, was tested in two different research studies. In a pilot study (O'Neill, 1983), students were interviewed about their responses to literature, their constructions of literature and what they perceived to be the functions of literature personally and for the community at large. This study was extended with a larger group of students ranging in age from twelve to sixteen years (O'Neill and Reid, 1985). In a second study (Leaper, 1984), adolescent subjects were interviewed about their responses to a taped reading of Ted Hughes' poem 'View of a Pig'. Students' responses in the two different studies confirmed that literature fulfilled the functions described above some of the time, depending on the particular student's motivation in reading the particular work.

On the basis of this theory and research evidence, the problem of what kinds of classroom interactions would maximize the functions of literature for the individual student in the context of growth model approaches to curriculum was explored.

Louise Rosenblatt's proposition that recognition of the individual reader's primary spontaneous response to a literary work was critical to growth of the individual reader seemed plausible. So too did the argument that individual readers come to a text with varying backgrounds and preoccupations that will shape their responses to it. A model of classroom interaction that would allow the students' first contacts with the text to be free from teacher intervention, and would provide an opportunity for their primary spontaneous responses to be articulated and shared with trusted peer group settings was developed.

Theoretically, such an approach should have encouraged students to explore what they found in the text, and begin to modify their primary spontaneous responses with their peers, rather than having a 'right' response imposed or suggested, however tacitly, by the authority of the teacher's perceived greater experience of life and reading.

The middle stages of the model provided opportunities for students to interrogate the text and develop their own maturing response to it in either transactional or poetic modes. It was anticipated that choices in activities and tasks would allow students to learn in their preferred mode, and that the opportunity for poetic mode responses would contribute to the development of metaphoric mode cognition. Only when students felt secure with their own responses to the text, would they be exposed to readings by other critics. In leaving the introduction of other critics so late in the engagement with the text, it was argued that far from disowning their own responses in favour of those of established critics (Britton, 1977), students would have the confidence to engage with readings offered by other critics. The outcomes of such an engagement with the text should have been shifts in the psychological, cognitive and social map/structures of the reader, which would contribute to what they brought to subsequent encounters with literary texts. There are, however, significant hidden factors in this approach to literary texts in the classroom. It is only by discounting or ignoring these factors that one can argue that a primary spontaneous response is possible in the classroom.

Neutrality of classroom setting

Built into the model is an assumption that classrooms are neutral; that the primary personal response of the student readers will *not* be affected by the knowledge that the text has been selected (by a curriculum board, the teacher, from a short list by consensus with peers) for reading, and therefore has some special status; that the students will be expected to 'do work on it'; and that if the text is worthy of classroom time, their response to it ought to be positive.

There are other assumptions, so much a part of the 'given-ness' of classrooms as to be almost invisible. By the time students reach secondary school (where much of my teaching experience took place), they have already established and internalized a set of reading practices that is rarely made explicit or examined in approaching a text. They have also acquired a set of assumptions about literary texts that, again, is rarely 'surfaced' in coming to a new text. Some of these assumptions relate to:

1 *Structure of text:* e.g. if the narrative is not presented sequentially, shifts in chronological order will be clearly signalled and a deliberate part of the writer's design.
2 *Narrative voice:* generally speaking, that the narrative voice will be consistent and reliable. If not, the unreliability will be cued early and an 'explanation' offered.
3 *Characters are unified:* that is, their behaviour is consistent, as is the behaviour of other characters towards them and that their behaviour can be judged on cultural norms. If characters do 'grow' or 'develop', the changes can be attributed logically to their experiences within the narrative.
4 *Positioning of reader:* the text offers a preferred position from which it is to be read and a 'right response' is engendered by accepting that position.
5 *Coherency or consistency of response:* a 'mature' critical response is one which gives a 'unified' reading of the text, explaining any gaps, silences or inconsistencies satisfactorily, rather than highlighting them as problematic.
6 *Compatibility with cultural values:* 'making sense' of a text entails being able to place it within the cultural framework of the reader. If cultural values are held up for scrutiny or question, in the end there will be a rapprochement with, or a minimal modification of, the reader's social construct. Students are rarely expected to take issue or disagree with the values constructed by the text: part of the procedure for selection of texts is that they will promote sound moral (cultural) values.

As long as these assumptions are allowed to remain subliminal, it is unlikely that students will make socially critical readings. Operating on these assumptions ensures perpetuation of the dominant cultural reading, and disenfranchises those students whose cultural experiences and values are different.

Intervention in the reader's experience with the text may make some of these assumptions explicit or overt, make some of the invisible aspects of the text problematic, and open the possibility of readings that challenge the dominant readings.

Students can read the text

Inherent in the value placed on primary spontaneous response is the assumption that students can read the text sufficiently competently to make a primary spontaneous response other than 'Yuk!' or 'It's dumb!' The logical extension of that assumption is that students ought not to be asked to engage with texts that they are unable to read on their own; teachers should choose only those texts which students are 'ready' to read. If we accept such a line of argument, it seems to me that we abrogate our function as teachers in two ways:

1 Because we judge the 'readiness' of individuals (or groups) and thrust an appropriate text at them, reading competence becomes simply a matter of maturational development.
2 Because reading, particularly literature, is a 'natural' activity, students ought to 'make meanings' for themselves, rather than being shown how texts can be constructed and, consequently, how they might be read.

Such a position seems to me to ignore the fact that reading is a learned behaviour, that there are cultural assumptions about texts and certain conventions of text that it helps a developing reader to know about whether they are kept or broken. An episode from my teaching experience might illustrate this point. I was working with a group of competent readers (sixteen to seventeen years old, approximately 'A' level) in a specialist Literature course. They had one year of specialist literary studies behind them and had previously read, discussed and written about (among other things) John Fowles' (1963) *The Collector* before encountering William Faulkner's (1935) *As I Lay Dying*. Taking refuge in the validity of primary spontaneous response, I advised them to read the text, as we would begin work on it in a couple of weeks' time. If a non-reading of the text can have a primary spontaneous response, theirs ranged from 'He's (it's) mad!', 'Yuk!' to 'We can't read it'. Their problems, of course, were not with 'getting the words off the page' but in that the approaches to text acquired by their previous reading practices did not seem applicable to Faulkner's text. They could find no way into it.

Taking hurried advice from a friend, I engaged the group in some pre-reading activities. The students were provided with a modernized synopsis of 'Little Red Riding Hood' and a set of character cards, including an upwardly mobile businessman, his 'arty' wife and nubile daughter (the R. R. Hood family), a heroic young forest ranger (Horatio Oak) and a de-jacketed Hell's Angel (Timba Wolfe). This was, of course, a text in itself, constructing particular cultural values and stereotypes, especially in relation to gender and class; the students had to decide to what extent they would take them up or write against them. Working in groups of two or three in the role of one of the characters, the students produced two or three chapters from the beginning, middle and end of the narrative frame. A small group ordered the chapters, which were published so that each student had a copy of 'As I kept trying' or 'My grandmother was a wolf'. A class reading (apart from producing much laughter and an over-inflated opinion of their own wit and cleverness) made the structure of Faulkner's text accessible to the students, and raised for them questions of sequence, reliability of the narrator, perception and 'reality', and cultural stereotyping. From there, reading Faulkner's text became an exciting challenge rather than a task that they saw as beyond their competence, and opened up other questions about character, interrelationships and cultural norms for them.

If, as a group, we had persisted with attempts to read the text (even in chunks, rather than as a whole) and I had encouraged the students to articulate their responses, puzzles and confusion with the text, given sufficient time, some of them may have developed sufficient engagement with the text to move from their negative primary response to a mature critical response. Many of the students would not have read the text, and as a consequence might have been convinced of their own incompetence, or resentful because of their suspicion that, as a teacher, I was withholding from them the key to the text. If texts teach us how to read, what would my students have learned? Perhaps more to the point, what would they *not* have learned about the construction of text?

Cultural assumptions

A tension exists between the idiosyncratic quality of personal response and the impact of the cultural framework in which the personal response is shaped. Berger and Luckman's (1967) position, that for a society to legitimate itself every child must be told the same story, and that the collection of stories which constitutes the literary heritage of a society has its place in developing and perpetuating the society's view of itself, carries with it the corollary that every reader's response must fall within acceptable boundaries; there is a 'right response'. Rosenblatt's (1938) proposition that literature offers readers socially favoured types of adjustment and compelling images of life which readers verify against their own experience, modifying or rejecting them as seems necessary, suggests a greal deal more idiosyncracy than is likely to be available to a reader constructed within a particular linguistic and cultural context. For either of these positions to be tenable in the arena of classrooms, it must be assumed that classrooms are monocultural, that cultural convergence is the norm, and that cultural values are so internalized or commonsensical as to not require surfacing.

In the classroom, such assumptions paper over differences of race, class and gender, and coerce readers into accepting the dominant cultural position on them. For instance, in the early 1970s, texts like *To Kill a Mockingbird* (Lee, 1960), 'The Test' (Gibbs, 1970), and 'After You My Dear Alphonse' (Jackson, 1970), were in common use in Australian secondary school classrooms. In predominantly white classrooms of my acquaintance, the question of how these texts might be read by a black American reader simply did not arise. The dominant reading given was from a (more or less) sympathetic white middle-class perspective. Similarly, if texts such as *Coonardoo* (Pritchard, 1972) or *The Fringe Dwellers* (Gare, 1966), which offered versions of the impact of white Australian culture on Aborigines, were taken into classrooms, generally speaking, they were read from a white Australian position. Even if aboriginal students were present in the classroom, the discourse did not permit a challenge to a white Australian reading.

The same period saw the advent of British working-class literature, such as *A Kind Of Loving* (Barstow, 1960), and *The Loneliness of the Long Distance Runner* (Sillitoe, 1959) in Australian secondary classrooms. While the encounters may have raised students' awareness of class issues, the sexism inherent in the texts passed unremarked. The combination of a strong reading position offered by the text, and the dominance of expressive realism as a classroom discourse offered few opportunities for a resistant reading. Sixteen- and seventeen-year-old girls in co-educational classes simply had little opportunity (or felt it unacceptable) to challenge the marginalization of female characters or the attitudes to women portrayed through the narrative stance of, for example, Victor in *A Kind of Loving*.

If the classroom discourse does not make explicit assumptions about the constructedness of texts and the cultural values that texts might endorse, then the personal growth model will validate the primary spontaneous response which has the greatest degree of 'fit' with the dominant culture. Readers whose primary spontaneous response diverges from the dominant reading will gradually have their response 'modified', undermining rather than strengthening their perception of themselves as competent readers. At the same time, the classroom discourse is likely to marginalize the relevance of their life experience to literary readings. They will always get it wrong unless they subordinate their experience to the dominant cultural reading.

Whose culture?

Shifts in the constitution or structure of a society do not guarantee that literary readings will also shift. In 1988, the Tim Winton story, 'Neighbours', formed part of the Tertiary Entrance Examination paper in English. In the story, a young couple moved from the expensive outer suburbs to an inner-city neighbourhood full of European migrants. The young woman works to support them while her husband finishes his thesis on the development of the twentieth-century novel. At first, the young couple find the behaviour and customs of their neighbours (specified as Polish and Macedonian) offensive. The young couple are remarkably incompetent at growing vegetables and building hen houses, but succeed with help, advice and supervision from their neighbours. Eventually, they find themselves participating in and contributing to the community life of the neighbourhood, unlike their parents who cast shocked glances over the fence when they come to visit.

How is the reader to fill the gap about the cultural and ethnic background of the young couple? The consensus of the marking panel (comprised mostly of secondary and tertiary teachers of English) was that the young couple in the story were middle-class Australians of Anglo-Saxon origin. Most candidates produced a similar reading, but many assumed the young couple were Asian immigrants. In retrospect, explanations can be offered for this particular reading, but they were not offered by the students. Those who produced the dominant reading did not account for their readings either. This may be because they were unaware that alternative readings were possible. Perhaps their reading practices simply did not make it possible for many candidates to contemplate members of a dominant cultural group placed in a minority situation. Some of those who did, and were able to read the young couple as Australians, then gave a reading of the assimilation of the young couple into their multicultural neighbourhood as a dreadful lowering of their standards. Those who read the couple as Asian immigrants seemed not to find it problematic in terms of the rest of the text.

If students after five years of secondary education in which personal response theory has been the dominant English curriculum model make responses like those, then perhaps something has gone wrong. Maybe reading activities in secondary classrooms rarely go beyond sharing the primary spontaneous response, or using literature as a stimulus for poetic mode writing by students. Perhaps students are not encouraged to re-read texts sufficiently closely to problematize their own primary spontaneous responses. This is not simply a call for more academic rigour or a cry of despair that students do not read properly any more. I think that it raises a genuine question about what we are and/or should be teaching students about the nature of text. If they are not aware of the constructedness of text, but see stories as 'natural' or 'true', then certain questions will not arise. For example, why has the young couple in 'Neighbours' not been assigned a nationality when all the other characters have? What are the possible ways of filling the gap? Are any of the alternatives more supportable than others, in terms of the structure of the text? What other assumptions (about text or culture, for instance) do we draw upon to support our readings?

Resistant readings

An assumption underpinning growth model approaches to text is that the texts themselves are neutral and that readers make meanings from them. Some texts, however, are constructed in such a way that avenues of meaning are progressively closed off, sometimes without the readers being aware either that it is happening, or how it is happening. Such 'tough' or closed texts make it very difficult for a young, immature, inexperienced or unsophisticated reader to see how they have been positioned to arrive at a particular response to the text. One way to distance the reader from the process is by intervening between the text and the reader. In approaching Stan Barstow's (1969) story 'The Fury' with Diploma of Education students, the title of the story and the name of the author were withheld. The students were provided with a synopsis, and asked to work in small groups constructing their own stories.

Scenario

A couple have been married for a number of years. The woman seems to have little in her life to compensate for the lack of children. The man has kept a large number of rabbits, but now keeps only a few with which he hopes to win prizes at the shows. Before he sets out for one such show, the woman specifically asks him to come home early enough to go together to a film that she wants very much to see. He comes home much too late for that. A neighbour later tells the woman that she saw the man with another woman on the evening that he was so late.

Writing Activity

Using the synopsis as a basis, write your own story, filling in the details and developing the situation. You may choose to do this activity individually or in small groups. As you shape your story, consider:

• how you will construct the characters

- with whom you will want the reader's sympathy to lie
- how the other woman became involved with the man. Does she know that he is married? If so, what has he said to her about it? What does she think his wife is like?

Frequently, these students (suspecting a trap had been laid) sought to disrupt the conventional triangular story by writing against it. Irrespective of this, sharing the stories and asking the students to articulate the cultural and/or literary assumptions from which they had been working, made those assumptions explicit before the students engaged with Barstow's version of the story. Following the discussion, the students were provided with the title of the story, and various sources and allusions were explored before they predicted the kind of story that Barstow might have written.

The first groups with which this work was done were provided with the Barstow story and four alternative endings:

Mrs Fletcher breaks the news to Fletcher that the husband of the woman with whom Fletcher was having an affair has murdered her. Fletcher says disbelievingly, 'She meant nowt to me', and seems to comprehend the impact of his behaviour for the first time.

Fletcher attempts a reconciliation but in a display of female solidarity Mrs Fletcher rejects him and demands that he leave for good.

Fletcher and Mrs Fletcher do have a reconciliation, but Mrs Fletcher is conscious the whole time that there is no future because she has slaughtered all of the rabbits in their hutches.

There is a full reconciliation between Fletcher and Mrs Fletcher and they decide to work together to show the rabbits and win all of the prizes.

The students were then asked:

(a) Which ending do you think is the one that Stan Barstow wrote? Be prepared to give reasons for your choice.
(b) Are there any endings which you would discount as being impossible? Why is that?
(c) How does each of the endings affect:
    (i) the tone of the story?
    (ii) your attitude to the characters?

Almost without exception, students were able to identify the Barstow ending.

Other groups were provided with the endings (including the Barstow ending), but not the story. These groups were just as successful in selecting the correct ending. Perhaps none of this is surprising; the students were, after all, sophisticated readers with a wide experience of text. Interrupting the text did allow them to see how they were being positioned as readers, what assumptions were operating in the text, and how their experience of other texts contributed to their reading of this one.

Interfering with the text in other ways further unhinged the tendency to closure. For instance, when 'ferrets' replaced 'rabbits' as Fletcher's pets in the synopsis, students laughed spontaneously. In Australia, at least, there are very different sets of responses and values associated with rabbits and ferrets. A man who keeps Angora rabbits must be 'all right' if a bit soft; a woman who could slaughter them in their hutches must be beyond redemption. On the other hand, a man who has kept a large number of ferrets for the purpose of showing them could justifiably be viewed with deep suspicion and probably deserves anything he gets. A woman who had to live with such a man might be considered to have had due provocation if she slaughtered the ferrets. The substitution of ferrets for rabbits affected the readings of both characters, but also made it possible to discuss why the students responded differently.

Intervening in the text and defusing the ending made other things in the text problematic as well. For instance, it was possible to go back into the text and examine the ways in which Fletcher was presented, how the character of Mrs Fletcher was constructed, and how other women in the story were portrayed. In these ways, an examination of the sex roles within the story could be explored. If the text remained unassaulted, the students had little or no resistance to the reading that 'this is a moral tale of how a jealous woman ruined her marriage' (offered by a student teacher to a group of fourteen to fifteen year olds in an all boys school). Beyond this reading, which the boys seemed happy to accept, little interrogation of the text is possible.

Conclusion

Where does all this take us? Not necessarily to a denial that literature might fulfil the functions summarized earlier in this chapter, but perhaps to the position that personal response approaches to literature, embedded in personal growth curriculum models, might not be the best way to promote those functions. The exemplars offered in this chapter are anecdotal, and therefore scarcely conclusive. However, the personal response approach seems not to encourage a critical awareness of the ways in which texts can be constructed, nor of the practices by which readings are arrived at. Furthermore, if reading a text is treated as a predominantly idiosyncratic process, while the reader may gradually develop tacit understandings about the structure of text, these understandings are not readily transferred from one reading experience to the next.

The assumption that texts are neutral or inanimate objects from which the reader is free to make meanings seems untenable. Texts read in classrooms are in double jeopardy – they have been selected by someone, with some motivation, whether or not it is made explicit. Thus I would argue that a student reader's response in a classroom is never likely to be 'spontaneous'. The process of sharing and modifying response opens the possibility (probability?) that the dominant reading will prevail; alternative readings, rather than supplying space for exploration and consideration, may be dismissed. Classroom strategies which foreground the ways in which texts and readings are constructed may be more helpful to students learning to read, than promoting a notion that response to text is fundamentally idiosyncratically grounded in personal experience.

What should we do instead? I would argue that we should encourage students to see the following:

1 A text is a *construction*, not a *reflection* of reality that is 'true'.
2 Texts have constructed in them assumptions about, for example, race, gender or class, which a reader might challenge rather than accept.
3 Gaps or silences in a text might be treated as problematic; filling them in different ways produces different readings.
4 The ways in which readers fill gaps may not be *idiosyncratic* but arise from cultural or social values.
5 While texts may offer the reader a particular position from which to read, the reader does not necessarily have to accept that position.
6 Texts are sites for conflicting or competing meanings rather than consensual responses.
7 Resistant or culturally critical readings offer more opportunity for *equity* of participation.

To achieve the above objectives may mean disrupting the reading, 'molesting' the texts to make their problematic nature evident, rather than presenting them as things of beauty to be enjoyed forever.

9 What do students learn from literature teaching?

TANJA JANSSEN AND
GERT RIJLAARSDAM

The project

This chapter is based on a project that is now in progress to determine the results of literature teaching in schools in the Netherlands. As a general rule, Dutch children receive no formal teaching of literature until the fourth year of secondary school. The main emphasis on literature teaching comes in the fifth and sixth years, when the students are sixteen to eighteen years old. What is the use of teaching literature? What do students actually learn from it? Despite the fact that teachers put a great deal of time into teaching literature (it takes up about a third of all the time spent on teaching Dutch), next to nothing is known about what the students derive from this process.

It was this state of affairs that led us to set up a small-scale project to examine the field of literature teaching. Our chief aim was to develop an instrument with which the benefits of literature lessons could be charted. We used 'learner reports' in order to collect the learning experiences of students and a similar instrument to determine teachers' objectives and their estimates of the product of their teaching of literature.

The instrument for obtaining learning experiences from the students was divided into four sections.

Section A

'I have learnt from my literature lessons that/how . . .'

You may have learnt things so that you know general rules, facts, techniques. You know how something should be done, how something is constructed.

Introductory phrases

- I have learnt/noticed/discovered/now know that . . .
  because/then/in those days/for example . . .
- I have learnt/noticed/discovered/now know how . . .
  because/then/in those days/for example . . .

Write below and on the next sheet as many learning sentences that apply to you as possible.
(. . . . . . .)

Section B

'I have learnt from my literature lessons that it is not the case that . . .'

You may have learnt or discovered that there are exceptions: things have sometimes turned out differently from what you had expected.

Introductory phrases

- I have learnt/noticed/discovered/now know that
  it is not true that . . .
  it is not the case that . . .
  there are also . . .
  not all . . .
  whereas I used to think that . . .

Write below and on the next sheet as many learning sentences that apply to you as possible.
(. . . . . . .)

Section C

'I have learnt from my literature lessons that I . . .'

You may have learnt or discovered things about yourself. About what kind of person you are, how you react to things, how you work best, what you like, what you dislike.

Introductory phrases

- I have learnt/discovered/noticed/now know
  that I think . . .
  that I am good/bad at . . .
  that I like/hate . . .
  that the best way I can do . . . is to . . .
  because/then/for example . . .

Write below and on the next sheet as many learning sentences that apply to you as possible.
(. . . . . . .)

Section D

'I have learnt from my literature lessons that I do not . . .'

You may have found out some exceptions about yourself. Everything you have discovered by way of exceptions about yourself: that you are not always as you thought you were, that you thought you were always like this or that, or that you always acted in such and such a manner, but that it has turned out that this is not always the case. That you like other things than you thought you did, that you react to things differently from the way you thought you did, that you work differently from the way you thought you did. What kind of exceptions about yourself have you learnt from your literature lessons?

Introductory phrases

- I have learnt/discovered/noticed/now know that it is not true/not the case that . . .
  I always . . .
  I never . . .
  I always like/dislike . . .
  I am good/bad at . . .
  I always have to tackle . . . by . . ., but that I can also . . . whereas I used to think that I . . .

Write below and on the next sheet as many learning sentences that apply to you as possible.

(. . . . . . .)

We also asked nine teachers who were known to teach literature in a non-average way for their collaboration in completing three questionnaires:

1 *What they offered in their teaching of literature.* This questionnaire consisted of a series of multiple-choice questions about the content and form of their literature lessons: the number of hours devoted to literature, the method used, the kind of work the students did, and so on. We also used this questionnaire to collect certain background information on the teachers: age, experience, etc.
2 *Their expectations regarding the benefits of their teaching of literature.* We asked teachers to put themselves in their students' shoes and write down the learning experiences that they expected of them. The questionnaire was divided into the same four sections we used in the students' report. We also asked the teachers to write down their negative expectations: possible learning experiences of their students that the teachers disliked.
3 *Desired learning effects.* We asked them to write down learning effects that they considered desirable, without regarding the constraints they experienced in their daily practice, and any that they considered undesirable. This questionnaire was also divided into the same four sections.

We also gave the learner report instrument to the students of these nine teachers, confining ourselves to the top two forms in grammar schools. For each teacher, fifteen students were selected at random, except that over the whole sample we ensured that the numbers of boys and girls were equal. The data we collected consisted of 267 statements by teachers on the expected benefits, and 1278 learning sentences from students on the actual benefits.

When analysing the learning experiences reported by both the teachers and students in their reports, we modified the classification scheme for the objectives of literature teaching drawn up by Purves (1971). Purves's scheme has two axes: along one of these lies the content, on the other various behaviours that are required. The content falls into four general categories: Literary Works, Contextual Information, Literary Theory and Cultural Information. Literary works, the texts being used, are differentiated by Purves according to genre and period or chronology, which results in no fewer than nineteen subcategories. Contextual information includes authors' biographies and all kinds of history (cultural, social, political, intellectual). Literary theory refers to literary terms, and to critical systems. Cultural information embraces such items as mythology and the Bible.

Purves distinguishes between five types of behaviour: to know, to apply knowledge, to respond, to express response and to participate, each of which can be subdivided. 'To know' consists of recognition and recall, and is required, for example, when students have to learn a poem by heart or to remember items of contextual information. 'Application of knowledge' is when the student 'matches some concept that he already possesses with the phenomenon he is considering' and is required if students are asked to relate their knowledge about an author to a particular literary work, or to compare two literary works. 'Response' includes reading, thinking, feeling and acting in some relation to the stimulus of the literary work. Response, as Purves observes, cannot be taught or measured directly. 'Expressed response' *can* be taught and measured, as it is the articulation of response in such forms as re-creation and talking and writing. Re-creation means things like putting on a play or producing illustrations for a poem. Purves divides talking and writing about response into eight subcategories, distinguishing among other things, expressing engagement, analysis, interpretation and evaluation. 'Participation' embraces being willing to respond, taking satisfaction in responding and accepting the importance of a literary work.

We have gone into Purves's classification scheme because we used it as the basis for our analysis of the learner reports by teachers and students. However, the scheme does have limitations:

- Some of the distinctions drawn by Purves proved to have little relevance. For example, the Cultural Information content category, and in particular mythology and the Bible, played no significant role in teaching literature in the Netherlands.
- Purves was looking at curricula as defined on paper by teachers or schools, which tend to contain clearly formulated objectives. Our material, statements by teachers and students, is rather less amenable. In particular, students were inclined to use a large number of vague and abstract words, so that their statements are difficult to place in one of Purves's general categories or subcategories.
- Purves's scheme is too narrowly aimed at objectives that have a bearing on instruction in literature and nothing else. Goals that may fall within the scope of teaching literature and other subjects, such as learning to work together, correct spelling, essay writing and critical thinking, are ignored. This was a major problem for us, because the students and teachers in our study made many statements that were of a more general nature.

These considerations led us to make a number of changes (see Fig. 9.1). First, we changed the categories of behaviour by distinguishing between 'knowledge', 'skills' and 'attitudes'. Secondly, we increased the number of content categories. The main changes were:

BEHAVIOUR

CONTENT	1 Knowledge	2 Skill	3 Positive attitude	4 Negative attitude	5 Display other activities
1 Literary works					
2 Literary contextual information					
3 Non-literary contextual information					
4 Literary theory, analysis, interpretation					
5 Relationship literary work/reader					
6 Use of literary language					
7 General use of language					
8 Obtaining of information					
9 Literature lesson					
10 Other contents					

Figure 9.1   Classification scheme

- A distinction between 'literary' and 'non-literary' contextual information. Literary contextual information embraces *inter alia* biographical information and literary history. Into this category fall such statements as 'I have learned how literature developed from the Middle Ages up to the present' and 'I have learned what the features are of classicism'. Into the category of non-literary, cultural and social contextual information we placed such statements as 'I have gained a picture of how people used to live'.
- The addition of 'relationship of literary work to reader'. By this we mean all learning experiences in which the student says that he has learned something about his own reading behaviour or that of others. For example: 'I have learnt that others look for more in a poem than I do', and 'I have noticed that I tend to give up if I don't like a book right at the start'. This is also where we put

discoveries about the reporter's own taste. For example: 'I have noticed that I now like reading real literature: I have stopped reading romantic love stories'.

- The addition of 'use of literary language', which relates to writing, reading, speaking, listening and looking in relation to literature. For example: 'I now know how to write a poem', 'I have learnt how to write a resumé of a literary work', and 'I have learnt how to prepare and deliver a talk on a book'.
- The addition of 'general use of language', which relates to learning to write, read, speak, listen and observe in general, without special reference to literature. For example: 'I have learned to organize my writings', and 'I know now how to compose a paragraph'.
- The addition of 'literature lesson'. Students quite often made evaluative statements about the teaching of literature, particularly about the obligatory reading list. For example: 'The reading list makes me allergic to literature'.

Results

Our first question was related to the validity of the learner report as an instrument: 'Do different goals and contents in the teaching of literature reflect different learning experiences for students or are the outcomes of different approaches more or less the same?' To answer this question, we looked among the teachers to find representatives of three rhetorically distinct approaches: the literary history approach, the structural analysis approach and the textual experience approach. In practice, we are unlikely to come across them in any pure form, but it is possible to identify teachers whose answers show that they tend more strongly to one of these three approaches. We also found the opposite: teachers whose answers showed that, explicitly or implicitly, they rejected one of the three approaches. We give portraits of the three representatives and their opposite numbers and describe differences in the learning experiences reported by their students.

The literary history approach

Teacher A was the only one to indicate that he devoted more than half his literature lessons (between 60 and 80%) to literary history. He is a highly experienced teacher of Dutch who is interested in literature and keeps up with the specialist literature on the subject. Of the literary texts that he discusses in class, about half date from before 1880. This is a large proportion, compared with the other teachers in our study, most of whom take no more than 20% of their texts from before 1880.

When discussing texts in class, A says he pays a lot of attention to the literary historical and cultural historical background. He also deals with a number of concepts from the theory of genres and from the structural analysis of narratives or novels. The actual form that his lessons take he describes as 'always or almost always from the front of the class': students seldom work individually or in groups.

According to A, cultural education is the most important aim of his literature teaching. Alongside this he attaches some weight to the literary and aesthetic education of his students and to increasing the enjoyment they gain from reading. He does not see his literature lessons as contributing to the students' self-knowledge or individual development.

The learning effects that he expects to achieve reflect the emphasis on cognitive objectives, ignoring the more affective goals. The learning experiences that he expects his students to have lie mainly in the area of factual knowledge. He does not expect his students to have learned much about themselves, but he does expect them to have learned something about interpreting literary texts, the way in which literature is created, and non-literary backgrounds. He also expects his students to be capable of applying their knowledge of non-literary backgrounds to literature of any period.

The negative effects that A expects lie mainly in attitudes towards literature and reading. He thinks that many students have a negative view of reading literature and of what literature can mean to them. He also thinks that some students learn nothing but facts, not always important ones, about the lives of the writers they study.

As the opposite of A we chose teacher F. She too has considerable experience and is interested in literature, but the works she discusses with her students are mainly modern, and matters of literary history constitute only a small part of her curriculum. Instead, she stresses the social reality of the world experienced by the student, and the evaluation of texts. She gives her lessons from the front of the class but often makes the students work in small groups.

Her main aim is to teach her students how to enjoy reading, how to make enjoyment last, and how to increase it. Cultural, literary and aesthetic education are subsidiary. Unlike A, she tries to add to the students' self-knowledge and individual development.

The learning effects that F expects to find are evenly divided between 'knowledge of the world' and 'knowledge of yourself'. She expects her students to know how to approach a literary text and to know that there is no one right interpretation, but several. By the time they leave school, her students will also have been introduced to poetry and they may have discovered that some poems are fun to read. F predicts that her students will be moderately positive in their attitude to her literature lessons and the obligatory reading list. Possible negative effects, she thinks, might be that some students will have acquired an aversion to reading, particularly poetry. Another negative expectation is that students will find her lessons too easy and that they will have failed to appreciate the usefulness of the literary terminology they have learned.

Did the students of these two teachers report different learning experiences? An analysis of the learner reports revealed that they did. The main differences are:

- Teacher A's literary history teaching elicits more learning sentences relating to the 'reproduction of knowledge' than the non-literary history oriented approach taken by teacher F (37% of all learning sentences compared with 25%).

- There is also a difference as regards the content. For A's students, stress is placed on the literary and literary historical background: 23% of all their learning sentences can be placed in this category as opposed to 14% in the case of F's students. A's students report that they have learned about non-literary, social or cultural backgrounds (7%), whereas this barely receives a mention from F's students.
- A's students write fewer learning sentences to do with 'attitudes': 37% compared with 51% for F's students. This is consonant with the emphasis that A places on cognitive goals at the expense of the more affective goals of literature teaching. Not only do A's students express a positive attitude to literature and literature teaching less often, but they are also less likely to express a negative one. Thus it is not the case that, across the board, A's students score lower on reading enjoyment than F's students.
- A's students refer to fewer different skills and contents than the students of F. In other words, the learning effects achieved by F are slightly more varied.

The chief differences point in the direction one might have expected. The difference between 'literary historical' and 'not literary historical' teaching is clearly reflected in the learner reports. A's literary historical approach went together with more cognitive learning effects, particularly in the area of literary history, and fewer affective learning effects (i.e. attitudes to literature). The learning effects achieved by A were broadly in line with his objectives.

The structural analysis approach

As a representative of the structural analysis approach, we chose teacher G, who, instead of conventional teaching, uses a home-made 'story analysis' syllabus in his lessons. Most of the literary texts that G uses are modern. Most of the teaching is done from the front of the class, but G also often gives his students the opportunity to work on their own. He devotes most attention to the structure and style of the work, its content or message, and where it stands in relation to the literary historical context. In class, he discusses a number of important concepts of structural analysis: perspective, characterization, theme, motif, and so on.

G stresses two objectives: cultural education and literary and aesthetic education. He attaches less importance to increasing the enjoyment of reading, individual development and social awareness. He expects that his students will acquire demonstrable knowledge and that they will be capable of applying it. For example, by the time they leave school, they will be expected to have learned how to analyse a book and to know that careful reading is necessary to do a book justice. He also stresses that they have to put a lot of time into a book if they are to penetrate its deeper meanings.

The negative learning effects that G expects lie in attitudes to literature and its teaching. He expects students to find reading boring and not to appreciate the point of learning about literature. He also expects to find a negative attitude to analysing and interpreting books.

G's opposite number, teacher B, indicated that he did not use any kind of structural analysis approach. He was also the only teacher to say that he hardly ever raised matters of literary theory in his lessons. The works that he reads and discusses with his students he groups largely by their chronology. When discussing them in class, he stresses the content or message in the text, paying less attention to structure and style. His chief objective is to give his students some knowledge about the valuable things that Dutch culture has to offer. Education in literary aesthetics is a secondary consideration. (Unfortunately, as regards B's expectations concerning the effects of his teaching of literature, we know nothing, because he was the only teacher not to complete the questionnaires.)

We found that the learning experiences of the students of G and B did differ, although the differences were not particularly large. In the case of G, 17% of the learning experiences related to analysis activities, whereas for teacher B it was 13%. To judge by students' comments, G's teaching is the most oriented towards structural analysis. His students also reported slightly more often than the others that they found analysing and interpreting literature difficult.

The textual experience approach

Our questionnaire showed that teacher D's teaching is characterized by a high level of attention to the connection between the book read, the students' world of experience and social reality, and to the evaluation and assessment of literary texts. When it comes to literary history, D does relatively little. The texts that she reads and discusses with her students are mainly modern and do not come from textbooks. She teaches from the front of the class but often gets the students to work in groups.

D's main objective is to let the students learn from experience that reading can be enjoyable, in the hope that they will continue to read or will start to read more. She also tries to use her literature lessons to aid the students' acquisition of self-knowledge and social awareness. Cultural, literary and aesthetic education have third place in her order of priorities.

D expects to achieve a more positive attitude to reading. In particular, she expects students to learn from experience that they are capable of becoming deeply involved emotionally with a book or poem, that there is rarely a single right answer and that to enjoy literature there is no need for them really to 'learn' anything at all.

The negative effects that she expects are that students will discover that they do not like reading and that literature lessons are vague and pointless.

D's opposite number is teacher A, who we have already described as an exponent of the literary history approach. Unlike D, he pays little or no attention to the connection between the text and the world in which the students live and which they experience. Nor does he pay much attention to current social reality or the evaluation of texts. 'Self-knowledge' is not one of his objectives, and increasing the enjoyment of reading also scores pretty low. His teaching is chiefly designed to serve cultural education.

If the learner report is a valid instrument for describing the learning effects of teaching, we would expect the reports of the students to reflect the differences between D and A. The students of D would be more likely to make attitude-oriented statements about literary works and indicate that they enjoyed reading, or at least did not consider it a chore. We would expect D's students to report more learning effects of a personal character, with a higher proportion of references to 'learning about yourself' (as opposed to learning about the world) than would A's students.

Our analysis confirmed these differences. A total of 59% of the learning experiences reported by D's students referred to attitudes to literature, compared with 37% for A's students. D's students also scored higher on positive attitude and reading enjoyment: 34% as opposed to 24%. The statements made by D's students are more personal across the board. In other words, they are more likely to say that they have learned things about themselves from their literature lessons than are A's students.

All in all, the instrument of learner reports proved to be sensitive enough to reveal differences in learning experiences or perceived benefits from different approaches to literature teaching.

Our next question concerned how perceptive the teachers were about the outcomes of their teaching. We were interested to know how far our results would reveal discrepancies between the learning experiences predicted by teachers and those reported by students. We refer to a discrepancy (1) if a learning experience predicted by a teacher fails to be reported by a single student; (2) if there are students who report a learning experience that the teacher regards as negative; (3) when students report learning experiences not predicted by the teachers.

Of the teachers' goals, between 38 and 82% were not reflected in students' learning experiences. But there is also another way in which the teachers got it wrong: of the learning effects that they expected to find in the students' reports and which they regarded as negative, between 0 and 86% fail to turn up in the students' reports. In other words, in 40% of cases, teachers' fears about negative learning experiences are without foundation. The discrepancy between teachers' objectives and the benefits in the eyes of the students is also apparent from the following: on average, 75% of students' learning experiences were not predicted by teachers at all. Presumably, our data support the idea that there is very little certainty about the benefits of teaching literature: even highly experienced teachers are not very good at estimating the learning effects.

The next question is which classes of goals were not reflected by outcomes and which outcomes were unpredicted. We confine our comparison to those categories of learning sentences that were used frequently by the teachers and cover 80% of all the teacher sentences; the categories are ranked according to the frequency with which they were mentioned by teachers.

Table 9.1 The 'outcomes' of the teachers' curriculum

Type of benefit in terms of content and behaviour	Teachers' expectations (%)	Students' benefits (%)
1 Literary works/negative attitude	99	71
2 Other contents/knowledge	74	13
3 Relationship between literary work–reader/knowledge	70	32
4 Literary works/positive attitude	66	118
5 Other contents/skills	66	2
6 Non-literary contextual information/knowledge	62	29
7 Relationship between literary work–reader/negative attitude	62	14
8 Literary contextual information/knowledge	58	117
9 Literature lesson/negative attitude	45	41
10 Relationship between literary work–reader/positive attitude	41	25
11 Literary theory/negative attitude	33	14
12 Other contents/other activities	33	28
13 Use of literary language/skill	29	30
14 Literary theory/skill	29	40
15 Literary works/knowledge	25	65
Total	79	64

Table 9.1 shows the teachers' 'core curriculum', covered by the fifteen categories that contain 80% of the expected learning effects. A total of 81% of the expected benefits were achieved. In other words, it looks as if teachers' expectations as a whole are adequate. But there are a few interesting under- and overestimations by teachers. Certainly as regards the knowledge about non-literary contextual information (6) and about the relationship of the literary work and the reader (3) we can say that education does not appear to be achieving what teachers think they ought to be making it achieve. Teachers exaggerate the outcome of a negative attitude to the relationship of work and reader (7), but they also underestimate positive attitudes to literary works (4), and knowledge about literary contextual information (8) and literary works (15). It seems that the pattern of under- and overestimations can be related to the discussions in the field about literature lessons; teachers' estimations seem to be influenced by those discussions. They are too negative about the attitudes, influenced by those who state that literature lessons make students dislike literature, and they underestimate the knowledge categories, maybe because it is less sophisticated in practice to achieve knowledge about books and literary context instead of knowledge about the relationship between the work and the reader.

We can also make another comparison, by looking at the extent to which teachers correctly predict what students have learned from their literature lessons, using the core of what students reported by way of learning experiences. It is interesting to compare the top of the teachers' curriculum with the top of the students' curriculum.

Table 9.2 shows that teachers predicted 75% (60: 80) of the students' core curriculum well. It is conspicuous that teachers expect less knowledge of literary history than students reported: these learning experiences are probably less desirable. Teachers' fears of negative attitudes to the teaching of literature are well founded but slightly exaggerated: while it is true that students more frequently report negative attitudes than positive ones, teachers overestimate the number of negative statements and underestimate the number of positive ones. Some remarkable results are seen in the items about language skills. In 9% of their learning experiences, students reported that their literature lessons have

Table 9.2 The students' curriculum

Type of benefit in terms of content and behaviour	Benefit reported by students (%)	Benefit expected by teachers (%)
1 Literary works/positive attitude	118	66
2 Literary contextual information/ knowledge	117	58
3 Literary works/negative attitude	71	99
4 Literary works/knowledge	65	25
5 Literary lesson/negative attitude	41	45
6 Literary theory/skill	40	29
7 Literary theory/knowledge	35	16
8 Relationship between work–reader/ knowledge	32	70
9 Use of literary language/positive attitude	32	4
10 Literary lesson/positive attitude	32	8
11 Literary contextual information/ positive attitude	30	0
12 Use of literary language/skill	30	29
13 Non-literary contextual information/ knowledge	29	62
14 Other contents/other activities	28	33
15 Literary works/other activities	26	0
16 General use of language/skill	25	4
17 Relationship between work– reader/positive attitude	25	41
18 Literary contextual information/ negative attitude	23	16
Total	80	60

taught them language skills. Teachers are evidently not aware of the fact that the writing of referential texts – projects, essays, appreciations and reviews – is regarded by students much less as a teaching method than as an end in itself.

Conclusion

We started out with a desire to demonstrate that the use of learner reports can be a valid instrument for charting the product of teaching, i.e. the learning experiences of students. The instrument is sensitive enough to reveal differences in the perceived benefits from very different forms of literature teaching. By asking teachers to predict what their pupils would write, and comparing these predictions with the students' learning reports, we obtain indications of the degree to which the teaching concerned is achieving its objectives. On the basis of such an evaluation, individual teachers can adjust their teaching.

Such an evaluation might also have the effect of making people's view of literature teaching less gloomy than at present. There is nothing worse than teaching something without knowing exactly what good your teaching is doing, especially if you have the impression that the negative effects are great. We have seen that teachers are worried about negative attitudes caused by their teaching of literature. We also saw this in another way. We asked teachers to report what learning experiences they expected to find in their students' learner reports that they themselves considered negative. What emerged was that teachers fear negative statements about attitudes to the reading of literature (17%), to literature itself (12%), to the teaching of literature (6%), to cultural phenomena in general, interpreting texts, and acquiring self-knowledge, and an antipathy to particular writers (each of these categories scored 4%). Of the expected but feared teaching/learning effects, 50% relate to a negative attitude, but pupils report a negative attitude much less often than teachers fear. And they mention 1001 things that teachers miss as possible learning effects.

Are teachers so uncertain about the effects of their teaching that they not only fail to predict them correctly but also have excessively negative expectations about the attitudes that students form as a result of them? We hope that with this instrument and its progeny we will be giving teachers a clearer insight into what their pupils get out of literature teaching.

Acknowledgements

We would like to thank Milja Vels and Bieneke Verheyke for their part in collecting data and coding in this project.

10 Children's books: always back of the queue?

STEPHANIE NETTELL

For me, as a journalist, a children's books editor and reviewer, the idea of 'response' applies not only to the young reader but also to professional colleagues and, on a wider scale, to society as a whole, whose response to children's reading is so often puzzling and distressing.

There is, for instance, a curious atmosphere about any discussion of literary awards and prizes: anyone involved with an award is always forced into a kind of defensive defiance, such that you are really quite pathetically grateful if someone ever goes so far as to admire your choice of winner. There is no reason why the different awards should feel in competition with each other, nor why librarians, teachers, and so on, should almost invariably be critical of a winning choice, except, it seems to me, for an anxious insecurity that we all share. I have seen how enormously worrying it can be to plump for one book above all others, presumably because we all feel a little threatened about our critical abilities when others make a different choice. Strangely, this seems to apply to those looking on as interested spectators as well as to those who are actively involved. We really ought to remind ourselves every so often that anyone who goes through the whole process of struggling to select an award cares deeply about books, and is, therefore, when it comes down to it, on the same side as ourselves.

As one of the longest established literary awards, the Guardian Award for children's books is twenty-two years old. And with its fairly impressive list of winners (see Table 10.1), I think it is true to say that it is one of the most prestigious: all but one winner is still writing. John Rowe Townsend, my predecessor on *The Guardian* and Bill Webb, then the paper's literary editor, founded the award, setting as its standard one of 'literary excellence', its main criterion being that it is a tribute paid to a writer by his or her peers – the four judges must themselves be children's authors. They serve on a rota of roughly four years. I choose them, and I suppose what is in my mind is not just their critical ability to recognize good writing, plotting, etc., but whether they can see themselves as both adult judge and child audience. They are often previous winners for the obvious reason that this means they will no longer have hopes of winning it themselves – previous winners are excluded. This is one aspect that

Table 10.1   Winners of the Guardian Children's Fiction Award[a]

Year	Author	Title	Publisher
1967	Leon Garfield	*Devil in the Fog*	Kestrel
1968	Alan Garner	*The Owl Service*	Collins
1969	Joan Aiken	*The Whispering Mountain*	Cape
1970	K. M. Peyton	*Flambards*	Oxford University Press
1971	John Christopher	*The Guardians*	Hamish Hamilton
1972	Gillian Avery	*A Likely Lad*	Collins
1973	Richard Adams	*Watership Down*	Rex Collings
1974	Barbara Willard	*The Iron Lily*	Kestrel
1975	Winifred Cawley	*Gran at Colegate*	Oxford University Press
1976	Nina Bawden	*The Peppermint Pig*	Gollancz
1977	Peter Dickinson	*The Blue Hawk*	Gollancz
1978	Diana Wynne Jones	*Charmed Life*	Macmillan
1979	Andrew Davies	*Conrad's War*	Blackie
1980	Ann Schlee	*The Vandal*	Macmillan
1981	Peter Carter	*The Sentinels*	Oxford University Press
1982	Michelle Magorian	*Goodnight Mister Tom*	Kestrel
1983	Anita Desai	*The Village By the Sea*	Heinemann
1984	Dick King-Smith	*The Sheep-Pig*	Gollancz
1985	Ted Hughes	*What Is the Truth?*	Faber
1986	Ann Pilling	*Henry's Leg*	Viking Kestrel
1987	James Aldridge	*The True Story of Spit MacPhee*	Viking Kestrel
1988	Ruth Thomas	*The Runaways*	Hutchinson
1989	Geraldine McCaughrean	*A Pack of Lies*	Oxford University Press

[a] In all instances, the date of publication is the year previous to the award.

has quite an influence on the award, because good writers often go on producing good books, and excluding those books can tilt the final result. On the other hand, not giving the award twice does broaden the field, which is part of the aim of the award, and also nudges us occasionally towards a new writer. In practice, the award has been given only three times to a first novel – *Watership Down* (1973), *Goodnight Mister Tom* (1982) and *The Runaways* (1988).

There is a certain amount of ambiguity about whether we are recognizing a book (which is what we always do, in fact), or an author, as our rules apply to the authors as much as to the books. What we never claim to do, because it is obviously invidious given the fact that every book is different in its intent, appeal and style, is claim to be awarding the *best* book of the year. We are, John Rowe Townsend once said, allowed to award the *body* of an author's work, but the danger of that is, that unless one is psychic, hitting the right book and not what later proves to have been a particularly weak specimen is far too tricky. If it is the book in the context of that year that is being recognized, not the author, then it does not matter so much if the writer fails to write again, while if you hang back waiting for a better example from someone promising, then the right moment somehow never seems to come again.

But let us return to the concept of 'literary excellence'. I stoutly defend the Guardian Award against those who like to say that all award-winning books are actually unread by children. However, I do think it is essential that our award should go to a book that is special, that is pushing at the frontiers of children's literature, expanding young imaginations, widening their world, allowing them to explore new ideas, emotions, language and experiences, and perhaps in doing so demanding something from its readers in return. An award winner, by definition, must stand out from the crowd. And that means it must, inevitably, appeal primarily to the good reader. But that does *not* mean it is inaccessible to the majority of children, and an unreadable book must never *never* win an award just because it strikes adult judges as clever. I really cannot emphasize this too much – it is something the panel discusses and worries over endlessly. And speaking personally, I have the least patience with the clever 'sixth-form' type of novel, whose authors I suspect get far more favourable treatment than they would if they took the plunge and dived into the adult end of the pool, where they really belong if they had the courage to try. But that we are élitist is still a criticism we have to face regularly. And therefore it is very encouraging and satisfying when you get a call or a letter from someone, especially a child, who has enjoyed a book, and seen on the jacket that it has won the Guardian Award, and wants to know which other winners they can read. However, it does tend to be the same three titles that crop up each time – *Conrad's War* (1979), *Goodnight Mister Tom* (1982) and *The Sheep-Pig* (1984).

It has often been said that children, and not adults, should be the proper judges of their own reading matter. I believe that there should be at least one award which is indeed of their choosing, but because children are as varied in their tastes, development and opinions as anyone else, I do not see that a better choice will necessarily emerge, and judging by the Young Critics' award at Bologna and that of our own Federation of Children's Books Groups, the result is likely to be as open to argument as all the others. Also, because such enterprises are impossible to organize without a lot of adult intervention of one kind and another, they are probably no more representative of unadulterated young opinion than those phoney Top Teenage Reading lists that come from the Book Marketing Council. Someone, somewhere, gives the kids the books in the first place. Therefore, although I am not against the idea, I do not think it is any less flawed than any other method.

During the initial selection process, although literary quality is the first criterion, linked to enjoyment, I must also admit that I could never be happy with a winner that contradicted those principles – putting it pompously, I suppose I mean the social, political and moral principles – *The Guardian* and I myself believe are important.

Though I imagine that the librarians involved in selecting the Carnegie Award would say the selection process is horrendously dictatorial, I believe choosing a winner is *benevolently* dictatorial, and that the final result seems not to differ so tremendously from the results of other methods – I think our record proves that it cannot be going too far wrong. The tradition for *The Guardian*'s adult fiction award is for the literary editor to ask his regular reviewers for their choice, but such an avenue is not open to me for two reasons: first, with only four pages a year, none of my reviewers could be expected to have a sufficient overview to make a responsible choice; and, secondly, it is laid down that my judges must be writers for children, and because one of my quirks is to dislike too many authors reviewing each other, few of my reviewers could fulfil that qualification.

Because our judges are unpaid, we do not ask them to plough through a hundred books in order to make a shortlist. I do it instead. Therefore, we do not publish an official shortlist like other awards, nor do I even encourage publishers to tell their authors they are on a shortlist – although afterwards it can be a boost to someone, especially an unknown, to say so on a jacket or whatever.

During the month of January I read through the produce of the previous year – and I have the advantage of having seen most of the books already, even though I may not have read them all, though I have to re-read them anyway – and try to select about a dozen titles that seem to me to represent the best of various genres and age groups.

Picture books are excluded because there is no way one can compare a picture book and a teenage novel. The lower age limit is established at about seven, and even then, young books have a hard time when compared directly with older fiction. More often than not, the judges cannot help feeling that such books are too slight to be outright winners. Though the 1989 runner-up, Magdalen Nabb's *Josie Smith*, about a super little rising-six, and as suitable for reading aloud as it is for newly independent readers, is probably the youngest book to make it into the winning class, it could not, as things stand, hope to beat a book aimed at older children like Geraldine McCaughrean's *A Pack of Lies* (1989).

The process begins when, in November, I send out a letter through the Book Marketing Council's children's book group and put a notice in the trade journal *The Bookseller*. After receiving many titles through the post, I ring those publishers who have not responded, and ask for any titles I think necessary. However, authors can send in their own titles and the judges can make suggestions – as long as the book in question is fiction, has been published in the UK in the previous calendar year, and is by a British or Commonwealth writer. On average, I receive one copy of about 125 titles from twenty-three imprints. After drawing up my shortlist, a copy is then sent to each judge in February.

Early in March the four judges and I meet to decide a winner. However, it is rare indeed for the judges to be unanimous from the outset: often a compromise has to be made. This does not mean that the award is given to a second-rate book, but that though people differ as regards their first choice, they often agree on their second choice. However, we never choose a book that any member of the panel would hate to see win: hence the compromise. We have often been surprised by our choice – I worry when it faces hostility, but in retrospect I think that is all to the good – and I believe it demonstrates a certain liveliness and open-mindedness on the part of our judges. They do go for what they themselves want, not what they believe the world would want. I think our list shows a spirit of independence, some shrewd judgements, and a good range of subject matter, style and ages.

I then interview the winner and present him or her with a cheque for £500 at a celebration lunch. The runner-up (who gets nothing but a morale-boost), their publishers, the judges, past judges and general friends of the award are also invited. And, despite everyone's efforts to the contrary, that is probably the last the world hears of it all. Which leads to the question: 'What was it all for?'

I think everyone who sets up a prize has two motives. The first, and most important, is the desire to draw the attention of an uncaring world to the best of children's books, and to what the world of children's reading can offer. I believe there is a genuine altruism in the motivation, because the returns otherwise are so small. Although *The Guardian* realizes that every time the phrase 'Guardian Award' is heard or seen, it is an advertisement for the paper, and that the reputation of the paper as one that cares about the arts, or the young, is enhanced, anyone who has tried to get publicity for anything to do with children's book awards will know that self-seeking is not a likely motive. In the case of the *The Guardian*, no other national paper is going to give it a plug, and only the local press and radio, and specialist journals like *Books for Keeps*, are realistic possibilities for interest. We had an item on 'Treasure Islands' recently, the BBC radio programme about children's books, and that was seen as quite a coup.

Does anyone, then, get anything other than £500 from it all? I believe winning affects the author's next book and the review coverage it might expect, that the words 'Guardian Award' – which can be printed on the paperback cover – are a 'come on' for some people, and, most of all, that it makes the author feel that someone out there is taking notice – that it is, after all, worthwhile. All of the winners I have met said it gave them a tremendous boost, encouraged them to go on, and cheered them through the next book. And all the publishers and authors who say they despise awards, are thrilled when they themselves come through to win.

I believe that this is all we can hope to do in this country: draw the public's attention to the fact that children's books – good children's books – exist at all, and give a simple morale-boost to a lucky writer every year. In the USA, the equivalent of the librarians' Carnegie Award, the Newbery, puts extra thousands on to the sales of a title: here some would have us believe it is practically a death knell, even among the librarians who theoretically chose it. Why on earth is this so? Everyone agrees books are a good thing. Everyone these days gets very worked up about children being able to read, so presumably *children's* books are a good thing. Why, then, are children's books always at the back of the queue?

I am convinced that the reason lies deep in the psyche of our society and its attitude to the young. The apathy with which children's literary awards are regarded is merely part of the apathy with which children's books are regarded, which is itself merely part of the way children, their education and their interests, are regarded. This is why, for instance, although children's books are the main growth area of the publishing industry, involving 10% of turnover and 20% of sales, they get less than 4% of the review space – and that is in *The Guardian*. Most newspapers give them even less than that. For reviewing purposes, children's books are a sub-genre, like crime or science fiction, to be given quick, brief notices every so often (and not, indeed, as often as crime and science fiction!). There is not one adult literary editor on a major newspaper or book journal who genuinely cares about children's books, knows anything about them, or is willing to give decent space to them. Children's books remain the poor relations of the literary world. Their authors are not considered interesting enough in their own right to warrant media attention. It is not enough just to write a good book (this, actually, is increasingly true of adult writers, too, in today's press), but there has to be some controversial hook, or the fact that the author's made a million – money talks to journalists. There can surely be nothing left to say about Dahl, and yet there they go each time children's books are mentioned – you would think he was the only writer we have ever produced.

The world pricks up its ears when a children's author writes an adult book – people like Jane Gardam, Penelope Lively and Nina Bawden. When Ann Schlee was shortlisted for the Booker Prize, *Rhine Journey* (1981) was described by everyone – including her publisher Macmillan on the jacket – as her first novel, despite her having won our Guardian Award. Both she and Anne Fine, when they produced adult books, were treated as miraculous examples of new-sprung novelists, as if their many excellent children's books were sorts of embryos. Andrew Davies won the first Guardian Award I handled, and there were a lot of raised eyebrows at the time: *Conrad's War* (1979), which I still think is a brilliant book, had not had one single review until then, though it went on to win the Boston Globe/Horn Book Award. The *Marmalade Atkins* series (1979–88) followed, not in the same class but tremendously popular with kids themselves, both as books and on television, but it was only when his successful *adult* television plays arrived that the press recognized him in a big way.

This apathy is why, given the financial and commercial importance of the young lists to their publishers, their authors are paid less (often their editors too) and their advertising and promotion budgets are so low. I may add that for the first time in the memory of our Award, both the winning publishers of 1988 and 1989, Hutchinson and Oxford, declined to take an advertisement to support their author on our page – a matter of £200 or so. Although we felt this to be rather tacky at the time, it is more than that – it is important. In newspapers like *The Guardian*, and I am sure in most quality papers, the adult literary pages are guaranteed (unless the climate changes catastrophically); they are regarded as a public service, a cultural obligation that will appear each week unfailingly, contributing to the reputation of the paper as much as anything else. But I must earn my space. There is in theory a proportion of three columns of advertisements to pay for five of editorial. Now, because publishers will not or cannot come up with that, despite being given special rates below any other advertising in the entire paper, I regularly go through the irritating business of, if not actually being *threatened* with having no page, then at least having to be grateful for being *allowed* a page. Publishers, of course, would much rather have a review than an advertisement anyway, regardless of cost, but I wonder if they realize that they may wake up one day to find *all* review space has died because they refused to support it.

And this apathy is also why, at the retail end of the business, bookshops hate the small return on children's books, their awkward sizes, the fiercer demands made on the knowledge of the bookseller by the customers. Only the committed booksellers, the honourable few, battle on. Let us hope the small independents survive the tactics of the big chains.

Finally, this apathy is why, when a skilled, well-qualified school librarian's role in our children's education is so obvious it does not need spelling out, it should be one of the first to be cut back. This is why, in a world where every emerging democracy, no matter how embattled by poverty and debt, recognizes that educating its people so they can read and think for themselves is a priority, we in our First World smugness are unable to find the money for teachers and librarians, far less books. Instead, we seem to be sinking deeper and deeper into an increasingly philistine world. It is in this world that I think book awards have a useful role to play.

When I look at the tastes and preferences of the great British public, I cannot help thinking it is over-optimistic to assume, as many of my colleagues do, that a child will automatically move on from *Sweet Valley High* or *Fighting Fantasies* or *The Famous Five* to something meatier if you just leave them alone. Which newspapers have the largest sales? Which adult paperbacks are the real bestsellers? Which television programmes get the highest viewing figures? How many adults, indeed, ever do move on from pulp to 'decent' books? I am not totally at ease with the philosophy that it does not matter what children read as long as they are reading. While I would never *stop* a child from reading a book, any book – and the more the merrier – I do believe in positive guidance towards more demanding and perhaps fulfilling books. I would not ban or remove titles, but I would take positive action to *add* something, to suggest alternatives. And this is what book awards and prizes can do very well: they are suggestions and pointers for readers to discover something new that is rewarding, challenging and exciting – something they may not otherwise have known about.

Far from literary awards becoming less sensible or necessary, it seems to me that in the current climate – where philistinism is not only accepted but is becoming actually respectable; where books as *books*, not material for reading tests, scarcely matter; where everything, from hospitals to classrooms, research departments to libraries, must show results by measurable profits; where 'intelligentsia' is as much a dirty word as it would be in some totalitarian state (for proof of this I need only quote the report of the Lords' debate over Clause 29, which made it an offence for local government bodies to appear to 'promote' homosexuality: 'Lord Beloff, supporting the Government, claimed that concern about the clause was reserved only for the intelligentsia' – note the contempt in this dismissal) – awards are a lively, cheering way of remembering what ought to be blindingly self-evident: that books are essential for society, for its education, its leisure, and its standards of tolerance and decency. The continuing and alarming response to *The Satanic Verses* should remind us that writing is, after all, where all the *real* intellectual risks are taken, and any event that celebrates what writers, and I should add artists, are trying honourably to achieve, at whatever level, is worth our support and encouragement. And so I call on all of you concerned with the young – who are the only hope we have for the future – it's time you pushed your way to the front of the queue!

11 US censorship: an increasing fact of life

JOHN S. SIMMONS

Since the mid-1970s, censorship cases in US schools have increased dramatically. Public school teachers in several regions of the country, and at all grade levels, have found themselves the targets of individuals and groups who demand that they remove from their classroom libraries and their recommended reading lists the titles of books which those would-be book banners feel to be inappropriate for consideration in the classroom. These citizen activists are, by and large, uncompromising. Many teachers and school administrators have caved in peremptorily to the challenges. Others have stood their ground and, when they have done so, litigation has frequently taken place. What follows is a brief summary of some of the more notorious cases which have occurred in the past (roughly) fifteen years.

In 1976, the Island Trees School Board, representing a group of Long Island, New York communities, had a number of books, mostly modern fiction, removed from the library shelves of the high school in Leavittown. The Board charged that the books were 'anti-American, anti-Christian, anti-Semitic, and just plain filthy'. Among them were Kurt Vonnegut's *Slaughterhouse Five*, Desmond Morris' *The Naked Ape*, and Alice Childress' *A Hero Ain't Nothin But a Sandwich*. Backed by the American Civil Liberties Union, a group of parents sued the school board under the first Amendment to the US Constitution. The case wound its way through the federal court system, ending up in the US Supreme Court in 1983. It is a significant case for three reasons:

1 It was the first school censorship case to reach the Supreme Court in modern times.
2 It occurred in an affluent northeastern suburb generally regarded as politically 'liberal'.
3 It pitted two fundamental American rights against each other: the right of freedom of expression versus the right of local communities to control their schools.

The fall of 1978 saw a significant nationwide Republican victory. A few months later, the US Congress passed, as part of an omnibus education bill, an amendment sponsored by Senator Orrin Hatch, which made mandatory the granting of a request by any parent to examine – and possibly challenge – 'all instructional materials used in any research or experimentation program supported by federal funds'. While the expressed scope was directed towards those materials used for psychological testing in public schools, its implications were seized on by a number of recently formed – late 1970s to early 1980s – conservative pressure groups which were beginning their assault on several areas of public school programmes. The Hatch Amendment opened the door for those groups to scrutinize and often demand the removal of a number of curricular materials, a procedure they were still implementing when this chapter was being written.

Some of the more prominent investigative organizations are:

1 The Educational Research Analysis Corporation.
2 The Liberty Forum.
3 The Eagle Forum.
4 The Concerned Women of America.
5 The National Legal Foundation.
6 The Citizens United for Responsible Education.
7 The Association of Christian Educators. (The goals of this organization are interesting ones. Among them are to bring public education back under the control of Christians, to take control of all local school boards, and to take control of all counter-productive, secular humanist curricula from local schools.)

These and other less well-known groups have provided the impetus for much of the book-banning effort of the 1980s.

In 1980, the Arkansas legislature passed a law providing that 'creation science' based on fundamentalist interpretations of the Earth's creation, should be given equal time with evolutionary theory in biology and other science courses. Shortly after its passage, a group of Arkansas parents filed suit, claiming that the law was unconstitutional. (The parents' suit was upheld in the US District Court in 1984, and the law was abolished.) One year later, President Ronald Reagan successfully nominated Mrs Sandra Day O'Connor, an arch conservative, to replace a moderate on the Supreme Court. This nomination marked the beginning of the end of a body which had been generally supportive of civil liberties adjudication.

In 1982, the Louisiana legislature passed a 'creation science' bill which was essentially the same as the one passed in Arkansas two years earlier. The law was declared unconstitutional by the US District Court in 1985, a verdict which was upheld by the Circuit Court of Appeals in 1986. And in Mobile, Alabama, Judge W. Brevard Hand, US District Court, ruled that a law passed by the 1981 Alabama legislature authorizing prayer in public schools was constitutional. Judge Hand also stated in his decision that the First Amendment did not apply to individual states in such cases. His decision was reversed by the Circuit Court in 1985.

However, 1983 proved to be a big year in the progression of censorship issues in the USA. In April, the Supreme Court ruled, in a 5:4 vote, that the Island Trees School Board had been wrong in taking books off the shelves at Leavittown High School. The Court warned, however, that their decision applied only to school libraries. Writing for the majority, Justice William Brennan stated, 'This case is about a library, not a school's curriculum . . . we freely concede that the school board has the right and duty to supervise the general content of a school's course of study.' Justice Brennan's statement was indeed a prophetic one as later events will verify.

Earlier in 1983, a few members of the Alabama State Textbook Commission filed a minority report asking that 100 books be removed from the state-approved list. Among them were *The Diary of Anne Frank* ('a real bummer'), Ibsen's play *A Doll's House* ('feminist propaganda') and Maya Angelou's novel, *I Know Why the Caged Bird Sings* ('promotes hatred and bitterness against whites'). The books were in fact removed from school classrooms and libraries for a short time but were replaced when a group of parents wrote to their legislators demanding that a new anti-censorship law be drafted. At about the same time, in Hazelwood, Missouri, an affluent suburb of St Louis, a high school principal removed two articles from the student-written school newspaper: one was on teenage pregnancy; the other on the effects of divorce on young people. The parents of the student editors brought suit against the principal and the school board, which supported the action on the grounds that the action violated the students' First Amendment rights. Thus another censorship case began its litigious trek.

There was no more ominous event in 1983, however, than the publication by a joint commission of the Association of Supervision and Curriculum Development and the American Library Association (1983) of a five-year study on censorship events in public school classrooms and libraries. The following represent some of the more significant findings in that survey:

1 A dramatic increase in censorship cases reported, particularly in the first three years of the decade.
2 In more than one-third of the cases reported, the books in question were removed, most without any review procedure.
3 In 56% of those cases which represented a second challenge to a particular school, the chief administrator removed the book(s) without due process.
4 In slightly more than 30% of the cases reported, the original complaint about a book came from a member of the faculty or staff of that school.
5 Only about 15% of the cases of library censorship uncovered by the study were reported in the media.
6 A considerably larger number of challenges (more than twice as many) came from organized groups rather than from individuals.

It can readily be seen that the first three full years of the Reagan administration witnessed a dramatic growth in book-banning activity in the USA. There was more to come.

In 1984, People for the American Way, a non-profit organization dedicated to the protection and preservation of freedom of expression, revealed that sixty-nine challenges to school text materials were reported in the previous year (People For the American Way, 1984). Removals of these materials from classrooms or libraries took place twenty-three times. At the same time, another kind of censorship, one well known to experienced secondary school teachers, made news throughout the country. Almost simultaneously in Vienna, Virginia and Minneapolis, Minnesota, two high school students found certain irregularities in the anthology texts of two Shakespearean plays, *Hamlet* and *Romeo and Juliet*, published by Scott-Foresman. They found that, when comparing the Scott-Foresman school text with one they found in their home libraries, 100 lines had been deleted from *Hamlet*, and 320 were missing from *Romeo and Juliet*. While acknowledging these deletions, the publishing firm refused to reinstate the lines. In November of that year, at the business meeting of its annual convention, the National Council of Teachers of English (NCTE) unanimously passed a resolution against the 'wilful adaptation or abridgement of literary texts by commercial publishers of curricular material' (NCTE, 1985). (For the record, that resolution has gone largely unheeded if recently published or revised literature anthologies and individual texts are any criterion.) Another form of curricular meddling became an issue under national scrutiny: 'proactive censorship'. This is when various individuals and pressure groups try to coerce publishers into excluding parts of textbooks *before* they are published for use in schools.

Of all the years catalogued in this chapter, 1986 must stand out as one of dramatic confrontation between public school curricular leaders and those who wish to control their initiatives. In Hawkins County, a small rural area in east Tennessee, eleven fundamentalist parents objected to the fact that their children were being required to read certain state-approved basal and supplementary text materials. They were supported in their opposition by the Concerned Women of America. Included on the list of 'objectionable' texts were: *The Stories of Hans Christian Andersen, Cinderella, The Wizard of Oz, The Diary of Anne Frank*, and several others. The parents claimed that these selections contained 'occultism, evolution, secular humanism, pacificism, feminism, and disobedience to parents'. They sued for the right to have their children placed in separate classes in which texts were used whose contents were more compatible with their beliefs. Their case was turned down in the District and Circuit Courts in 1988 and, in January 1989, the Supreme Court refused to hear the case.

Meanwhile, back in Mobile, Alabama, 624 parents, supported by the National Legal Foundation, sued to have removed from schools a large number of materials at all curricular levels. The parents' main indictment against the books was that they promoted secular humanism which, the parents claimed, was a religion, thus violating their children's First Amendment rights concerning freedom of speech and other expression of personal conviction. This proved to be the premier case of 'secular humanism' as a point of contention in the struggle to remove objectionable materials from public school classrooms. About a year later, the previously mentioned District Court Judge, W. Brevard Hand, ruled in favour of the parents and ordered that forty-four state-approved materials be removed from all Alabama classrooms. Thrown into virtual hysteria, the State Board of Education voted 5:4 to appeal Judge Hand's decision. In April 1988, the Circuit Court of Appeals reversed it, and the forty-four materials were returned to the classrooms.

At about the same time, a fundamentalist minister in Lake City, Florida, enjoined the Columbia County School Board to remove the book *The Humanities: Cultural Roots and Continuities*, a state-approved text used in an elective twelfth grade humanities course. His reason lay in the fact that the text contained Aristophanes' play *Lysistrata* and 'The Miller's Tale' from Chaucer's *Canterbury Tales*, both deemed lewd and lascivious. The text was immediately removed when the school board gave the Columbia County High School principal the authority to remove peremptorily any text which he felt to be 'objectionable'. A group of parents, led by a Lake City Junior College English instructor, sued the school board after making an unsuccessful attempt to have the text restored to the classroom. The American Civil Liberties Union, which to date had maintained an unblemished record of success in school censorship cases, entered in support of the parents.

Late in the spring of 1986, a fundamentalist parent entered Mowat Junior High School in Panama City, Florida, to complain about her daughter's having to read *I Am the Cheese*, a novel by Robert Cormier (1975a). Although over 90% of the parents polled by the school had given their consent to the all-class use of the book, the parent refused the teacher's offer of an alternative selection for her daughter. She demanded, instead, that all copies of the book be removed from the school. The English department, chosen that year by NCTE as a 'center for excellence', refused that demand. The parent went to the (elected) county superintendent and reiterated her demand. An active member of a local Assembly of God church, the superintendent ordered that book, plus two other 'young adult' novels (*About David* by Susan Pfeffer and *Never Cry Wolf* by Farley Mowat) to be removed immediately. The county school board backed his decision. The teachers resisted, groups supporting both sides of the issue organized, and the school board dealt with the petitions late that summer.

The confrontation swelled and exploded early in 1987. A group of teachers and parents had filed suit in the US District Court. Rigid guidelines for book selection and retention were imposed unilaterally by the superintendent. In April, he threw out sixty-four books in current use in the high school English courses, noting that there was 'some profanity' in each one. All of Shakespeare's plays were removed; so were such classic works as *Oedipus Rex, Wuthering Heights, Animal Farm, Call of the Wild* and *The Red Badge of Courage*. The community was thrown into an uproar. Two weeks later, the school board overruled the superintendent and restored all of the books. The board retained its original guidelines, however, and in the fall refused the Mowat teachers' request to restore *I Am the Cheese*. By the end of the calendar year, the beleaguered but prayerful superintendent announced that he would not run for re-election in 1988.

In a review titled *Attacks on the Freedom To Learn*, People for the American Way (1986) reported 153 cases of school censorship in 1986, up 18% from 1985. In 37% of these cases the materials were retained. The remaining cases were still under some form of deliberation as that report went to press. The report further indicated that organized groups were more often responsible for challenges than were individuals, by a ratio of more than two to one.

The Supreme Court took another turn to the right in 1988. Justice Lewis Powell, whose even-handed decisions had made him the pivotal court member during the decade, retired and was replaced by yet another conservative.

The long, frustrating dialogue over the seating of Justice Powell's successor created an extended vacancy on the nine-member court. Thus, when the Hazelwood, Missouri case, speaking to the issue of student journalistic rights of expression, finally came before the Supreme Court in January, only eight members took part in the deliberations. Their decision, however, was a profoundly significant one. By a 5:3 margin, they found for the Hazelwood School Board and the high school principal. Writing for the majority, Justice Byron White stated that 'A school need not tolerate student speech that is inconsistent with its basic educational mission.' In February, this decision was used as legal precedent by US District Judge Susan Black in Jacksonville, Florida, in determining that the Columbia County School Board had not violated anybody's First Amendment rights in removing the humanities text which contained the offensive selections by Aristophanes and Chaucer, as described earlier. To some observers, the one-to-one relating of such articles appearing in a student newspaper with works written by ancient and medieval masters seemed somewhat quaint and curious. The plaintiffs took a different view, appealing the decisions to the 11th Circuit Court in Atlanta, Georgia (reported in People for the American Way, 1989).

In July, US District Court Justice Roger Vinson of Pensacola, Florida ruled for the school board in the Panama City *I Am the Cheese* case. He stated that 'local school officials do not violate the First Amendment by making curricular decisions with legitimate pedagogical goals.' The case has since moved on to the 11th Circuit Court where it was under deliberation as this chapter was being written. For the record, Judges Vinson, Black and Hand had been appointed by President Reagan. During his presidency, he was able to appoint over 50% of the currently seated federal judges – and they are on the bench for life.

The International Convention on Reading and Response at the University of East Anglia took place as 1989 entered its fourth month. Even in that short period, however, some significant events in the book-banning crusade had taken place. In January, the 11th Circuit Court upheld Judge Black's decision in the Columbia County Aristophanes–Chaucer case. This represented a first-ever defeat for the American Civil Liberties Union (ACLU) in school censorship cases which had reached that level of the federal judiciary. The ACLU then pulled out of the case entirely, leaving the Lake City parents on their own as they wrestled with the decision as to a subsequent appeal to the Supreme Court. The judge making this latter decision commented, 'Common sense indicates that the overall curriculum offered by a school not only includes the core . . . but also such elective courses as school officials design and offer.'

The first half of 1989 saw many incidents regarding book-banning that are worthy of note. The Texas State Board of Education rejected demands by a conservative group of citizens, led by the Gablers, to eliminate 100 literary works contained in current anthologies which had already been approved by the State Textbook Adoption Commission: all stories by Poe and Melville ('depressing'), *Romeo and Juliet* ('teen suicide'), 'The Sniper' ('in war, no side really wins'), and *all* works of John Steinbeck ('his name has been associated with liberal causes') (reported in People for the American Way, 1989).

On a more optimistic note, the California Board of Education's Curriculum council has put into effect a recommendation made by the 1988 State Assembly that 'real literature' replace the currently used graded reading materials with their highly sanitized content, phonics emphases, and carefully conceived readability levels. The edict also requires publishers to label all selections which have been abridged or adopted (a first hopeful response to the proactive censorship strategy of educational publishers described earlier). On the other hand, Phyllis Schlafly made a public statement that the major goal of the Eagle Forum for 1989 was to purge all journal writing activity from US public school classrooms.

Regarding this summary of events, I interviewed Talbot D'Alemberte, Dean of the Florida State University Law School and President of the American Bar Association. Dean D'Alemberte's area of expertise is constitutional law with a particular interest in First Amendment adjudication, which states that Congress shall make no law which will restrict a citizen's freedom of speech or other expression of personal conviction. What follows is a summary of his responses to my questions.

Students' and teachers' First Amendment rights are threatened by the current censorship movement. The trial court application of the Hazelwood, Missouri case to the one in Lake City is 'disturbing': that particular application is like comparing apples and oranges. Many materials currently found in classrooms and libraries at all curricular levels are now at risk, books once routinely added to the curriculum now being sharply questioned. The number and intensity of the challenges made in the past ten years have come as a surprise. In regard to the attitude of the Supreme Court, he is sceptical.

The challenges brought about in school censorship cases will continue into the foreseeable future. The focus of current ones has been on ideology rather than on profane language and explicit sexual and scatological descriptions. This change concerns him a great deal. The challengers are a manifestation of a deeper problem: that of parents' desire to control their children. This problem is further evident in the emergence of increasing numbers of 'Christian' schools in which faculties have no input into the philosophy of the curriculum. The desire of these schools is to seek state accreditation and then to remove students from public schools at all levels in order to save them from secular humanist study and to place them under the guidance of doctrinaire teachers.

The ACLU has *not* lost its will to fight the censorship movement. The group

t that the Lake City case would meet defeat at Supreme Court level and that
is would act as a signal to several states to enact repressive legislation. Thus
ney dropped out of the case at the Circuit Court level. They were also waiting to
see how two particular Justices would behave in cases involving civil liberties.

The results of recent challenges and court decisions will almost inevitably have
an impact on the willingness, and even eagerness, of administrators in some
school districts to deny the introduction of new books into the curriculum and
even remove some which are in current use. The main worry is that the temper of
the times will discourage teachers from choosing 'new' books for their courses of
study, especially contemporary selections. This concern is reflected in an essay I
wrote (Simmons, 1986) – 'The young adult novel: Looking down the road' –
which appeared in the *ALAN Review*:

> In the days to come, the pressure will be intense on teachers to justify their use of
> young adult novels in terms of their literary quality. This will be particularly true of
> those who teach in middle schools and junior high schools, who teach average and
> above average students, and who would use YA novels for all-class reading and
> study. Unlike their senior high counterparts, they don't have the literary scholarship
> of the centuries to fall back on when the buzzards descend.

Some prominent conclusions from this long chronology are as follows:

1 The conflict between First Amendment rights and local control of the schools
  has, for the moment, been resolved. The Hazelwood and Lake City cases
  strongly imply that students and teachers surrender at least some of their rights
  at the schoolhouse door.
2 A clearly defined transition has taken place in the nature of censorship
  challenges: from profanity and explicit sex/scatology to 'radical' ideological
  themes, i.e. those which differ from fundamentalist, orthodox Christian and
  super-patriotic values. Thus books are threatened at *all* levels, kindergarten
  through college.
3 There has been an unprecedented amount of litigation resulting from the
  challenges of recent years, and more is likely to follow, largely due to the
  pressure groups now zeroing in on the school curricula.
4 The increasing activism of the pressure groups named earlier and the
  increasing capitulation of school administrators to their demands is likely to
  continue, especially in the light of recent decisions made by Reagan-appointed
  judges.
5 There will be increased confrontation on the issue of proactive censorship.
  The power of fundamentalist pressure groups *et al.* is already being pitted
  against the 'real literature' advocates, as in the 1989 California Assembly
  decision.
6 There will be continued debate over the secular humanist issue. The defeats
  suffered by fundamentalists in the Mobile and Hawkins County cases have not
  weakened their resolve. Thus the *separation of church and state* is clearly present
  in current censorship dialogue.
7 Increased power in choosing and retaining books has been placed firmly in the

hands of building administrators – a chilling fact given the widespread and deep-seated curricular ignorance of the great majority of such individuals.

8 At the moment, the fate of young adult fiction, as used in today's schools, is in great jeopardy. Only time will tell as to the status therein of the Great Books of the Western World.

12 Home stories

NICHOLAS TUCKER

Scholars such as Walter Ong (1982) and Eric Havelock (1986) have had much to say recently about the general twentieth-century takeover of storytelling by print. This is described as inexorable and in some ways regrettable. The warmth of the oral tradition and its genius for engaging personally with individuals or groups is contrasted with the comparative coldness of print as a storytelling medium. Print cannot make special allowances for the listener's special needs or moods of the moment; nor can it include those listening to it or anything about them in the stories it narrates. Such coldness may be partly responsible for many children's lack of interest in learning to read or in persevering with it once taught, given that many still may be looking for something more personally immediate in the world of fiction.

Print is also accused of persistent bias towards the establishment values of those who control it. Children have not been the only minority required to fit into its often rigid patterns or else often find themselves branded as reluctant readers. Women, ethnic communities, the physically handicapped and political or social out-groups could all argue that it has often been easier to make sense of their particular experience not by reading what happens to be available about them in print, but by listening to what others have to say in the same situation. Print may offer only a travesty of the realities known to many without particular power or prestige in society. Unlike oral storytellers, it is not dependent on holding the interest of every group of consumers it happens to be addressing, nor in altering its perceptions in common with those listening at that moment.

Such are some of the arguments against the general supremacy of print. But rather than discuss these any further, I would like to make a different point too often ignored in this controversy. Oral stories are still told every day all over the world. Yet, apart from the performances of a few professional storytellers, oral stories at least in the Western world generally exist at so self-effacing a level that any organized discussion of them is almost unheard of. I am talking here about the stories we tell our own children on walks, in the car, or at other odd moments of the day. I refer to these stories as 'home stories', not because they always involve characters drawn from the home, although this is often the case, but because they are normally told for home consumption only. Such stories tend to fade away when strangers approach, only resuming when any dangers of eavesdropping are past.

Reasons for this protective embarrassment are easy to find. Home stories are usually narrated without much prior thought. Unsurprisingly, they are often heavily plagiarized. Oral stories have always been able to get away with this sort of pilfering without fear of legal repercussions. Older siblings, parents, grandparents or whoever else, can therefore happily borrow from books they are reading or have read long ago, television plays, films or stories told to them by others. Young audiences seldom spot the theft unless it is done too blatantly from a source they already know. Those adults better equipped to draw scornful comparisons as a story gets under way are not usually given the chance to do so in the first place.

Another potentially embarrassing feature of home stories is their frequently rambling nature. Driving a car while telling a story lends itself more to free-association than to rigorous plotting. Sometimes a story hardly gets off the ground; elsewhere it might flower in a direction no-one, least of all the narrator, really expects. There may also be abrupt changes of mood, for example from the would-be moralistic to black humour as storyteller and audience tire of one effect and start experimenting with another. If very young audiences are involved, repetitive slogans or situations may pile up in so mercilessly inexorable a way that even an Enid Blyton or Roger Hargreaves might have hesitated about trying to do the same thing in print. Sub-plots by the nature of things are generally absent, as it usually takes all the narrator's concentration to keep one storyline going, let alone two.

A third reason for this protective privacy lies in the stories' often highly personal nature. Their vocabulary may abound in special family words, indecipherable to others without extra explanation. They may also deal with particular family myths, featuring relatives, friends, or enemies, now sometimes transformed into grotesque figures amusing to those who know them while satisfying to the narrator happy to discharge a certain amount of mild aggression this way. At other times, family myths may turn into collective fantasies of wish-fulfilment, with each listener and the narrator duly rewarded with one of their dearest dreams. Scraps of conversation overheard that day, odd figures encountered on the beach or in shops, particular sights still fresh in everyone's memory may also be woven into these tales, meaningfully for those who are listening but often only puzzling for anyone joining the family at that moment. Elsewhere the narrator may reach into memory, recalling family stories told by another generation but still highly dependent on a detailed knowledge of who's who.

A last cause for shyness is that home stories can sometimes be just that little bit risqué. Lavatorial humour may occasionally intrude to the delight of a young audience along with a vague feeling that such things should not really be spoken out loud. The end effect is often a combination of mild shock and explosive laughter. These are the jokes that family outsiders are rarely allowed to hear and which are often totally denied by the adult who uttered them should he or she be challenged in company about their existence. The same coarse humour may be in evidence when it comes to describing unfortunate physical appearances or mimicking unusual modes of speech. Not that such stories are always slightly naughty; they can be as fiercely moralistic as any Victorian tract, inveighing against misguided children who fail to eat their greens, prefer watching television to going on walks, or anything else that is currently irritating the adult narrator.

None of this is the type of material that will one day lead to a new *Alice*, *Wind in the Willows*, *Hobbit* or any other classic that started out as a story told to children. Perhaps this literary barrenness is why home stories are usually ignored in any wider discussion of children and the fictional process. Yet children often enjoy them very much, remembering them long after many 'proper' stories by famous authors have been forgotten. I shall now argue that the very weaknesses of home stories as already outlined could often turn out to be strengths so far as children are concerned. This argument has nothing to do with attempting to rehabilitate home stories as lost works of art, because almost all of them clearly are not. But I do believe their popularity has something to teach all of us, and that discussion of them has a legitimate place in any overview of the developing interaction between children and fiction.

Take the issue of plagiarism as a possible strength rather than weakness. Once common in all literature as a form of literary obeisance from one author to another, any suspicion of plagiarism today is a matter for severe sanction. Yet children can greatly benefit from the plagiarizing skills of their elders. Classics like *Beowulf*, *Robinson Crusoe* or *Gulliver's Travels* are accessible to younger readers only when cut-down and re-told in a contemporary manner. Modern classics too, like William Golding's (1954) *Lord of the Flies*, can hold a younger child audience entranced in an oral version long after attention would have wandered from reading the original or hearing others read. As it is, most home stories will probably not reach towards such literary masterpieces for inspiration. Yet, occasionally, adults may find themselves dredging up a bit of this or that from one when searching for a good plot, and even if what follows gives only the smallest flavour of the original this can still act as a positive gain in the imagination.

The rambling, repetitive structure of many home stories can also be seen as a strength as well as a weakness. If a story seems to be going badly, it is never too difficult to change its direction in mid-stream, swapping minor characters for major ones perhaps, or building up on one fortuitously popular detail to the exclusion of all others. Such changes are often highly sensitive to the audience concerned, either overtly by way of responding to specific requests or else implicitly through an awareness that if there is any more in the same vein everyone will soon get well and truly bored.

It is also possible for narrators to include details from the immediate here and now in their stories. Most fiction in print has to be about the past, from long ago right up to the time when the book was written before being sent off to a publisher. A book that attempts to be ultra-contemporary in any one area often comes a cropper with children in that nothing for them is ever quite so out of date as last year's styles or 'in' topics. This is quite reasonable: one year in an eight-year-old's life represents a comparatively huge proportion of his or her experience. Last year's slang, for example, can seem very far away indeed – this is one reason why canny children's authors often provide young characters with an invented argot that does not date since it has never been current in the first place.

Narrators, on the other hand, may if they wish live much more in the present. Their stories can refer to things experienced that very day, even that particular minute. An American visitor to A. S. Neill's experimental school Summerhill described how Neill, when telling younger pupils a story in her presence, brought in not only herself but also the fantasy that she was the bearer of some vitally important papers certain villains were out to steal. Later that evening, two little girls asked her in private whether the papers were now safely hidden in her room (quoted in Croall, 1983). Narrators can also tell stories where the children who are listening are allowed to meet usually unattainable contemporaries such as favourite pop stars, footballers or television idols normally absent from the world of fiction. No wonder such stories often prove so popular compared with the more impersonal fare on bookshelves. They are also usually told in language intuitively edited for words or references that the narrator suspects the children may have difficulty in understanding. If possibly obscure material of this sort is included, the narrator can always weave any explanation into the story immediately this seems necessary, using audience feedback to expand a story rather than interrupt it for the sort of explanation often necessary with a written text.

The deeply personal nature of many home stories can be another factor in making them so immediately interesting to the young. Some may involve the very boys and girls listening to them. While it can sometimes be difficult for such children to identify with the more remote young heroes or heroines of children's fiction, there can be few problems when it is your own self that is involved. The power of this type of instant appeal has been known ever since the first minstrels made a habit of tactfully inserting the names of their current hosts and protectors into the heroic ballads they used to sing for their suppers. Centuries later, A. S. Neill also told stories to his pupils where they themselves were the main characters: 'He assigned roles to the children which he intended would touch on their fantasy life. If they were shy or withdrawn, he would give them the most horrendous or courageous exploits to perform' (Croall, 1983). During these stories, he would encourage his pupils to comment, criticize or interrupt. Another adult witness recalls the effect on one, typical five-year-old:

> As Neill went on with the story, this boy got up, and very slowly took a step forward, his eyes fixed on Neill all the time. And then he did it again. And again. At last he was right up against Neill, staring at him entranced (Croall, 1983).

This type of instant identification can also occur when home stories incorporate friends, neighbours or other locals, including occasional authority figures such as teachers, doctors or dentists. If these are already held in some awe, featuring them in a story can be an excellent way of helping them seem more approachable, at least in the imagination. Incorporating local scenery can also make any heard story easier to visualize. As it is, on those occasions when any of us reads a story set in scenery we already know, the effect on the mind's eye is usually greatly enhanced. In place of the normal, rather fuzzy background that gradually forms in the imagination as authors strive to describe the various settings for their stories, suddenly everything may seem much more vivid. It can be the difference, say, between reading Wordsworth just after rather than before a first visit to the Lake District. For adult readers, such additional clarity in the imagination may be little more than a pleasant bonus. For children, it can sometimes make all the difference between a story that quickly takes off and one which obstinately refuses to leave the launching-pad because nothing within it is immediate enough to fire that first, all important act of imaginative reconstruction in the young reader's mind.

Other home stories use personal factors in a different way when recounting true or semi-true stories drawn from the family's past. Telling children stories about 'When you were little' can prove as narcissistically satisfying to them as any gloating over old family photographs. Other stories about their parents' or grandparents' own past can also be popular, with ease of identification sometimes making even the most banal account interesting simply because it concerns someone that the listening child already knows well and can therefore easily visualize. Grandfather being evacuated in the last war or Auntie surviving her first day at infant school can be of riveting interest to children already able to superimpose such well-known faces on to imagined, incongruously younger bodies wearing the strange fashions of the time. Such stories eventually suffer if repeated too often or for the sake of any extra moralistic or admonitory effect. But in the early days they always start with certain advantages, and as a result are often remembered long into adulthood, sometimes to be passed on to other generations.

The last characteristic of home stories that can sometimes make them seem unsuitable for public consumption is their occasional dives into mildly sexual or scatological humour. Such stories with their occasional slightly naughty words or ideas can have a distinct edge over the literature a child is otherwise surrounded with, whose prim contents may stand in contrast to the earthy world of the school playground. If visiting adults ever happened to hear some of my grandfather's stories of this sort there might be mock-disapproving tut-tuts or shakes of the head: another welcome change from the more usual, blander adult responses to children's fiction in print. He told many stories, all of which mixed the childish and the adult in a charming way. Had he ever gone in for a more vicious type of talking dirty this would have been a different matter, but there was never any question of this, and his stories remain one of my favourite childhood memories.

This is not to deny how grateful I am to the books I came across at the time as well. Home stories can be very comfortable, but books inevitably offer a wider view, carrying its own particular form of excitement. Their vocabulary may be harder but always worth persevering with, given that from an early age family words must speedily be replaced by a common vocabulary once out of doors in order to avoid incomprehension or patronizing laughter. Books can also be more easily shared with friends than can home stories, which often seem to evoke yawns rather than interest when enthusiastically re-told to a third party. If based on true happenings, good home stories are also apt to be somewhat limited in quantity, lending themselves to unwanted repetition if demanded too frequently.

Home stories based on imagination can also seem repetitive over time as each narrator's particular form of free association and inner fantasy life becomes more familiar. In Christina Stead's (1970) brilliant and profound autobiographical novel, *The Man who Loved Children*, the devouring father of the title takes this process to extremes by using home stories and a private language to bind his children into a continually exclusive relationship with himself. Any other possibly competing adults outside the family are always traduced in his stories. While his smaller children readily enter into his resentful, sometimes mildly paranoid tales, these gradually come to seem more like prisons than playgrounds to his oldest daughter, around whom the novel is written. Instead, she longs for stories describing young adults leaving home and parents far behind in search of wider experience.

The Man who Loved Children stands as an eloquent warning to any parent attempting to force home stories on children after they have ceased to enjoy them. Before this time, home stories have many good things going for them; yet, while parents are frequently encouraged to read to their children at the earliest opportunity, there is much less addressed to them over the desirability of telling home stories as well. This may not matter very much: the best home stories usually get told whatever educational pundits may or may not advise, simply because everyone enjoys them – storyteller and audience. Yet for those parents or grandparents who may feel somewhat shame-faced about spinning such stories at all, there is no harm in pointing out that they are doing an excellent job for the development of all story appreciation. Getting children to love fiction has nothing to do with rushing them on to print to the exclusion of every other type of narrative. At a young age, *all* stories that are popular from whatever source are important.

This point is also worth stressing to teachers, especially those taking younger forms. It has always struck me as absurd that teachers may sometimes find in the book cupboard something of dubious quality to read to pupils when they could often so much more profitably *tell* them a story instead. This was powerfully brought home to me during a course for schoolteachers I taught recently with Dr Lissa Paul at the University of New Brunswick. The teachers were motivated and hard-working, yet when asked to bring a specimen story book suitable for reading aloud, most of the literature was arch, wooden or heavily moralistic, as uninspiring to listen to as it must have been to write.

As these teachers were a mature group, often having come to Canada years ago from different parts of the world, we felt sure they could probably do better by drawing on private memories instead. So for our next session, we asked them to think of one story popular in their own family that they were prepared to share with everyone else. It could be sad or funny, fact or fantasy, so long as it was a tried family favourite from the past or of more recent vintage. After all, we pointed out, fairy stories and legends now in print also started as stories told in the home.

The results were most encouraging. One teacher originally from Holland told how her family was forced to eat tulip bulbs during the Dutch famine of 1944. As an infant at the time she had such red cheeks that neighbours used to joke that she must have eaten only the red bulbs. Another from Ireland told about a wooden door she had preserved in her house. It came from the ship on which her brother was wrecked during the war. For two days he had clung on to this door, but sadly both he and it were eventually washed up with the young man only having a few hours to live. By retaining the door, his sister felt she was still keeping in touch with the brother she had lost.

A third story concerned an obstinate old grandfather in Britain during the blitz. One evening while he was making the family soup, the air-raid warning sounded and bombs began to fall. 'But Guy went on stirring the soup, as if nothing had happened.' More bombs, nearer this time, causing a saucepan lid to crash to the floor. 'But Guy went on stirring the soup, as if nothing had happened.' And so the story continued, each bomb closer, each impact causing more damage, but the old man still at the stove, determined never to surrender in what had become his private war. It was told slowly, the natural rhythms of the refrain obviously the product of many repetitions in the past.

Not all the stories were about the last war. Younger participants chose other topics, one recalling her first day as a nervous student-teacher – a story she had previously tried out on her pupils and which had so captivated them it had become the object of numerous requests. Like all the stories chosen, it was closely based on what had actually happened. Favourite *fictional* home stories did not feature, and it would probably have taken more time and confidence before these too could be shared easily around a group. But the stories that were told were greatly superior to those that had been read out the day before. For one thing, they often touched on important topics like death, fear and hunger, omitted from the more anodyne texts the teachers had selected previously. Children can sense when a story is really meaningful to those choosing it, not least from the way it is narrated. In several cases, the teachers telling their stories had tears in their eyes. Few classes could resist this type of appeal, or easily forget the story that occasioned it. As the teachers were usually characters within their own stories, once again this would make it easier for pupils to visualize the story and to share the feelings of a narrator they have already got to know well.

Other positive points came up in subsequent discussion. Teachers who had sometimes recounted personal stories to their classes maintained this often helped free the tongues of pupils with their own home stories to tell. Other teachers became more positive about other people's stories once their own had been listened to. This is hardly surprising, yet I wondered subsequently whether there may be an important point to be made here about the way that many teachers become disenchanted with children's literature in general as they spend more time in the classroom. Perpetually being forced to live through the imagination or memories of others by reading only their stories out aloud may well lead to frustration in those who feel they have their own stories to tell. Allowing a teacher's own storytelling creativity the chance of an occasional break might do wonders for everyone's morale, with written stories prompting oral stories afterwards and vice versa to the ultimate benefit of literature, the teacher and the class.

There are obviously dangers inherent in telling home stories in the classroom. Books are public property and can be checked for content; home stories are more unpredictable, and there may be occasions when parents would not wish for stories involving, say, superstition, religious indoctrination or prejudice to be inflicted on their children. Other home stories may sometimes release pupils' stories that deal with family matters better not discussed in public. Should certain home stories based on the truth come over as too disturbing for children, it is impossible to console them afterwards with the idea that 'It's all only a story.' Unlike the African tribe whose storyteller temporarily kills off each character every night lest they return to disturb the dreams of his audience, teachers may occasionally have to live with various upset reactions from some home stories. When a book is involved, it is always possible, should complaints arise, to pass some of the blame on to publishers, authors or library staff. With home stories, teachers are more on their own.

But one of the attractions of teaching is the freedom it gives for the pleasures of reminiscing or storytelling. Most of us can remember many of the personal stories teachers used to enjoy telling long after we have forgotten the lessons in which they occurred. My teachers often used to apologize after these episodes, referring to them as mere 'digressions' unworthy of inclusion in any proper lesson. Yet many of these remain fresh in my memory forty years on, with my French master continuing to drink water from a dirty river after fighting for three days in the trenches, or a much younger teacher still rowing twice across a river with muffled oars at night in order to rescue a friend from under the noses of the Gestapo. ('Wasn't that brave of me?' he used to enquire at the end, just in case his not always deferential class might somehow still have missed the point.)

Home stories like these are the stuff of history, sometimes on a large scale, more often where the local, intimate history of a family or an individual is concerned. Such stories about things that have actually happened should wherever possible be shared with children, who have a right to know what has gone on in the past and how it has affected those they now know as older people. Other stories that arise from a teacher's imagination may be equally memorable. Storytelling creativity is not something owned only by children's authors. It is a skill most of us can and should claim for our own from time to time. We often do this confidently and intimately within our own families. I suggest it is something teachers could certainly try more frequently with the outwardly more formal but inwardly often just as receptive audience of a classroom of pupil-listeners.

13 Reading, re-reading, resistance: versions of reader response

BILL CORCORAN

The clear lesson of history is that conceptions of what it means to read well are far from fixed. Just as there is no timeless, universal and undistorted meaning buried in *Macbeth*, so each of us inevitably presents a view of reading bound by a historicity which is our only way of getting at an understanding of the self in the present. My project will be to clear a path through Culler's (1983) various 'stories of reading', with the specific purpose of exposing a series of residual questions and curricular possibilities raised by particular conceptions of 'literature', texts and textuality, and an associated set of constructed roles for the student reader and the teacher. What I will unearth in the historical spaces where reading, re-reading and resistance meet are a series of *almost* stratified zones of reading, which, when penetrated, reveal that the fissures which traverse the text and problematize meaning belong as much to its context of production as to its various historical moments of reception.

What is at stake for me in this process is as much an attempt to reaffirm the positive contribution that reader-response theory has made to an understanding of the phenomenology and psychology of a skilled act, as it is a rejection of the notion that the term 'reader' denotes merely some solitary physical or psychic existence. Like Giroux (1983a, 1983b), Bakhtin (1981) and Donald (1985), I want to move the reading subject a little left of centre in order to see what part the developing, historical individual is required to play when the dialectic between structure and agency, initial reading and re-reading, allows for intentional stances of refusal, opposition or resistance.

The problem is that the *active* readers posited in many versions of reader-response theory are not, by definition, *strong* or *resistant* readers until they can read 'against the grain' of a text's dominant ideology. This deliberate attempt to read from alternative perspectives of class, race, religion or gender demands that the reader be sited in a discourse which acknowledges the social construction of the self and its inevitable positioning within a set of wider cultural formations and categories. That is, the self, or reading subject, must be seen as a hybrid sum of institutional and discursive practices involving family, class, gender, race, generation and locale. Ideological development, in these terms, results from an internal struggle for hegemony among competing points of view, directions and values.

On the way to outlining a pedagogy based on zones of reading, re-reading and resistance, I will rehearse very briefly some moments from literary history, move on to a more detailed account of how readers, writers, texts and contexts have been re-theorized, and highlight some of the discontinuities between active and resistant practice. The critical benchmarks in this enterprise will come in the form of assumptions about language, and perspectives from a radical, resistant pedagogy.

Texts, readers and teachers: Six historicized relationships

Each of the numbered possibilities at the apex of the triangle in Fig. 13.1 represents a particular conception of text, which prescribes in turn parallel sets of roles for the teacher and the student reader. There are, in fact, six loosely disguised critical stances, providing an immediate set of reference points, each of which is far from discrete, because it exists in a different dialectical relationship with each of the others. The clear danger in the brevity of the following accounts is that the whole enterprise may slide too easily into parody:

1 The 'cultural heritage' position, associated primarily with Arnold and Leavis, casts the teacher in the role of custodian and transmitter of the literary culture, and reduces the student to a cultural *tabula rasa*.
2 The New Critical artistic text – Wimsatt's (1970) 'verbal icon' – elevates the teacher to the status of certified explicator and patriarchal keeper of the textual code, and reduces the student to a passive consumer of expert explanations.
3 Subjective and psychoanalytic versions of reader-response theory (Holland, 1975; Bleich, 1975; Slatoff, 1970; Bettelheim, 1978) see the text as potential embodiments or blueprints of the reader's 'identity theme' or 'existential predicament', the teacher as facilitator of these intensely personal and idiosyncratic responses, and the student as provider of unique response statements.
4 In the transactional versions of reader-response theory offered by Iser (1978) and Rosenblatt (1978), the text is variously seen as a norm or template which contains within itself sets of instructions for its own realization. Since the emphasis falls on the lived-through transactions between readers and texts and the ways in which textual features such as gaps or indeterminacies thwart the reader's attempt to create a *gestalt*, the teacher must be skilled in the task of setting the reader's repertoire of literary and life experience to work on a range of appropriate texts.
5 In certain structuralist and semiotic accounts, the text is described as a 'readerly/writerly' (Barthes, 1970) or as a 'closed/open' (Eco, 1979) document. A writerly/open text uses a range of structures to force the reader to take an active role in textualization; by contrast, the repetitive structures of a

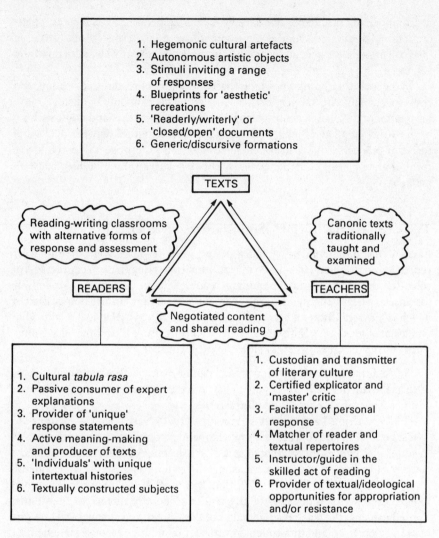

Figure 13.1 Readers, texts, teachers: The possibilities in a literature classroom

readerly/closed text constrain the reader's possible interpretive role. When planning a sequential curriculum of varied texts, the teacher necessarily becomes an instructor/guide in the skilled act of reading, who recognizes that students are 'individuals' with unique intertextual histories.

6 At the broadest cultural level, the text must be seen as coterminous with a wider pattern of generic/discursive formations, with embedded ideologies, and teachers and students as subjects constructed in the very processes of the reading and writing they have already done (Althusser, 1984; Derrida, 1978b; Lacan, 1977). Since much reader-response theory gestures towards an opening up of a dialogue with students, and a problematizing of questions of

authority, the significant stance taken by the teacher here is a recognition of the text's potential opportunity for 'appropriation' or 'resistance'.

The 'trailing clouds of glory' on each side of the triangle represent sketchy forms of possible curricula which emerge when the classroom site takes as its primary focus one or other of the interactions among texts, readers and teachers. With the emphasis, for example, on the line that connects texts and teachers, we could expect a classroom filled with 'classic' texts from the canon, traditionally taught and examined, and with considerable use made of the literary critical essay. Where there is some consultation between teachers and students there is at least the likelihood of a negotiated range of texts, and some shared reading from the popular culture. If the focus is more squarely on the transaction between reader and text, then the classroom may take on the form of a reading-writing community which uses a range of texts and alternative forms of response and assessment. It is to this element of the framing and contextualizing of readers and writers, and to the emergence of a political agenda around the notions of text, genre, discourse, textuality, structure and subjectivity that we must now turn.

Texts, readers and discursive formations

The major shifts in the modern theoretical enterprise – from work to text, from author to writer, and from the personal/aesthetic to the cultural/pragmatic – are clear enough, even in this foreshortened account. What Figs 13.2 and 13.3 set out are the grounds of an answer to a question posed by Robinson (1987a), whose diagrams I have adapted to my purposes:

> What, besides the code, the language used by the writer of the text, does a reader need to know in order to read a text successfully – to comprehend or construct a reading that is reasonably consistent with meanings constructed by other readers of the text and the meanings intended by the writer?

If we can set aside for the moment, as Barthes (1970), Foucault (1977) and Derrida (1978) would do, the imputation of authorial intentionality in the last part of the question, we can see that Fig. 13.2 sets out five elements for the concept of text: *code, writer-in-text, reader-in-text, text-as-ideology* and *text-as-structured-language*. All five of these elements are mutually constitutive, and interact both as textual elements and as reader constructs. According to Eco (1979), the semiotic grounds for this set of relationships is that the reader is 'strictly defined by the lexical and syntactic organization of the text', and the text is seen in turn as 'nothing else but the production of its own Model Reader'. Even more pointedly, the symbiotic relationship between reading and writing is established when the Model Reader is seen to be able to deal 'interpretatively with the expression in the same way as the author deals generatively with (it)'.

Whereas much reader-response theory adopts a psychologistic perspective which stresses the cognitive strategies and skills of individual readers, cultural theorists use the idea of *codes* to argue that the making of meaning is not merely a

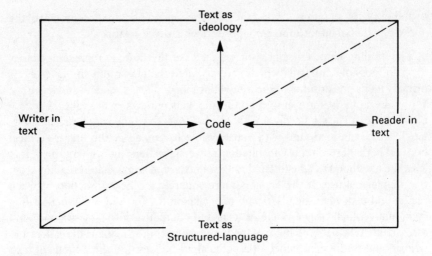

Figure 13.2   Five components of text

subjective or individual experience, as both readers and texts are inevitably shaped in specific sociocultural contexts. Barthes' (1970) codes, embedded in language and textual conventions, and applied largely to the analysis of narrative, account for five generic features of narrative: (1) the element of mystery and surprise (the hermeneutic code), (2) patterns of action and behaviour (the proairetic code), (3) the way characters are constructed in language (the semic code), (4) the code of theme and representation (the symbolic code), and (5) the code of reference or culture (the cultural code). Conceived in these terms, the notion of code is truly central, as it allows the process of signification itself to be investigated by referring to the shared knowledge which enables both writer and reader to be inscribed within the text. The broken line in Fig. 13.2 indicates how code acts as a thread to stitch together textual structure and ideology.

The constructs of *writer-in-text* and *reader-in-text* are features deriving from various sources – text grammars, narratology, reader-response theory and semiotics. According to Rimmon-Kenan (1983), for example, the reader is 'both an image of a certain competence brought to the text and a structuring of such a competence within the text'. Apart from Eco's (1979) model reader, whom we have already met, there is a plethora of other candidates variously qualified to fill the reader-in-text position: the 'actual reader' (Van Dijk, 1977), the 'historical reader' (Jauss, 1982b), the 'informed reader' (Fish, 1980), the 'implied reader' (Booth, 1961; Iser, 1978; Chatman, 1978), the 'ideal reader' (Culler, 1975) and the 'superreader' (Riffaterre, 1978). Undoubtedly, each of these living beings or encoded constructs will have their textual or 'real' uses, and some compelling cases have been made for the ways in which adolescent or child readers are constructed in fiction.

The last two elements, *text-as-ideology* and *text-as-structured-language*, are as intertwined as the relationship between *writer-* and *reader-in-text*, although they could bear some initial, separate scrutiny. The text-as-ideology argument abjures, as we shall see, mimetic assumptions of literature, arguing instead that ideology materially and inevitably inheres in texts. In Althusser's (1971) terms, ideology *interpellates* (calls into existence by naming) the individual within a superstructure riven with contradictions and conflict. The importance of the text-as-ideology argument is that it acknowledges texts as intratextual sites for struggle, rupture, inconsistency and instability. Neither the self, nor the characters in texts are coherent, consistent or unified, though as Belsey (1980) suggests, what classic realist fiction does is to interpellate or insert the reader into a specific 'position from which the text is most "obviously" intelligible, the position of the subject in (and of) ideology'. So it is that commonsense readings are themselves ideologically constructed, often in the form of an idealized and comfortable humanism.

Arguing respectively from the standpoints of semiotics and radical pedagogy, Eco (1979) and Giroux (1983b) propose three stances that readers and students can take when confronted with the ideology of text or the hegemonic structure of the school. First, *accommodation*, to apply one part of Giroux's larger argument, involves students in learning to accept the requirements of particular discourse conventions, without necessarily questioning how those conventions privilege some forms of knowledge at the expense of others. In Eco's (1979) parallel formulation, if readers 'share the ideological judgments expressed by the text at the level of discursive structures', they are unlikely to probe the 'underlying ideological scaffolding at a more abstract level'. The second of Giroux's stances involves *opposition*, with specifically disruptive behaviour often leading to a refusal to learn the patterns and conventions of a particular discourse community. Here, in Eco's terms, readers may ignore the text's ideology completely and superimpose their own 'aberrant' readings. The third, and most productive possibility, according to Giroux, is *resistance*, the dialectical value of which he explains in these terms:

> The pedagogical value of resistance lies, in part, in the connections it makes between structure and human agency on the one hand and the process of self-formulation on the other. Resistance theory rejects the idea that schools are simply instructional sites by not only politicizing the notion of culture, but also by analyzing school cultures within the shifting terrains of struggle and contestation (Giroux, 1983a).

Eco recognizes, as well, that open texts in particular are sites where conflicting discourses struggle for existence, definition and attention. So the resistant reader, after challenging the text's explicit value systems, goes 'further with an ideological analysis so as to "unmask" the hidden catechization performed at more profound levels'.

On its own, the notion of text-as-structured-language takes on board story grammars (Mandler and Johnson, 1977), schema theoretic views of language (Anderson and Pearson, 1984), structuralist views of literature (Propp, 1968; Todorov, 1975), and some of the analogues between literary theory and reading process pedagogy outlined by Harker (1987). The proposition that there is something learnable and therefore teachable about the structure of text has been argued most persuasively by Culler (1981):

> The whole institution of literary education depends on the assumption . . . that one can learn to become a more competent reader and there is something (a series of techniques and procedures) to be learned. We do not judge students simply on what they know about a given work; we presume to evaluate their skill and progress as readers and that presumption ought to indicate our confidence in the existence of public and generalizable operations of reading.

The last part of this chapter seeks to illustrate how this largely unanswered challenge can be approached through the mastery of embedded zones of reading operations.

For the moment I need to restore the all-important nexus between text-as-structured-language and text-as-ideology, and to illustrate its operation in the social-semiotic tasks that Meek (1988) and Eco (1979) set themselves. For Meek, the broad question has always been how 'real' texts, mainstream children's literature as opposed to artificial reading schemes, teach what readers learn. Her re-reading of texts like Hutchins' (1968) *Rosie's Walk*, Burningham's (1977) *Come Away from the Water, Shirley*, the Ahlbergs' (1986) *The Jolly Postman, or Other People's Letters*, Hughes' (1986) *The Iron Man*, and Jan Mark's (1980) 'William's version', always in the company of young readers, underlines the structural oppositions of print and picture, the semiotics of innovative and stylized drawings, and the discursive overlays of texts which abound with intertextual echoes. Above all, Meek (1987) argues, what children learn is the 'nature of the possible . . . how to use language for subversion, for reordering things in their heads if not in fact'.

For Eco, the focus is on the ways that certain kinds of closed texts structurally induce a limited and predetermined response. Be they Superman comics, James Bond novels, TV soap operas or Mills and Boon romances, these texts depend on established formulae of redundancy and repetition. They rely on 'the constancy of the same narrative scheme', on 'the same sentiments and the same psychological attitudes' on the part of the characters, and they become stylistically 'a museum of deja vu, a recital of overcoded literary commonplaces'. Though the products of skilled craft, closed texts create a 'hunger for redundance'. Through 'ideological overcoding' the closed text delimits and constrains the role of the reader, who becomes an uncritical consumer of unambiguous ideological messages.

The additional boundaries in Fig. 13.3 indicate not only the range of knowledge and experience that readers and writers bring to texts, but the extent to which particular subjectivities constitute, and are constituted by, the notions of genre, discourse and intertextuality. Such considerations give the lie to notions of the 'free' reader (Scholes, 1985) or the 'free' response (Purves *et al.*, 1973). Texts come into existence, as much for individual writers as for individual readers, in the context of similar texts locked away in a storehouse of personal and cultural memory (Kress, 1986). As intertextual sites, genres are subject to cultural

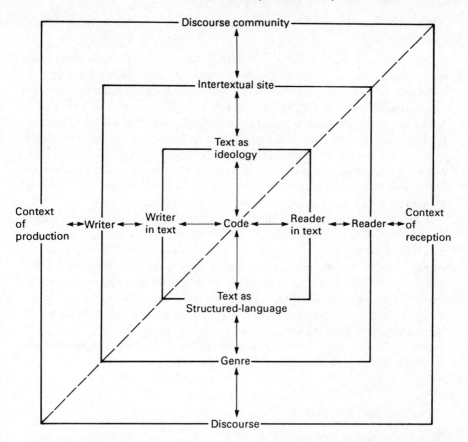

Figure 13.3   Text, reader and writer in the contexts of genre and discourse

framing, so that the very sameness of their defining structures is constantly threatened by a series of situated, cultural negotiations. 'There is no single generic pattern', Reid (1987) argues (and Zipes, 1983, abundantly illustrates), for *Little Red Riding Hood*, or for any other fairy tale, because 'there is no firm constancy of orientation, complication or resolution; there is no authentic original plot, theme or whatever; each retelling resituates the tale . . . remixing and reshaping its generic affiliations'. Yet our successful classroom writers, the ones who play on the margins of a genre, recognize at once how stereotype and parody are organically interdependent. Learning genres as both reader and writer is, therefore, a fundamental way of understanding particular versions of the world. The force of this connection has been captured by Scholes (1982):

> We read as we have been taught to read and until we have been taught to look for certain things we will not see them. And we write – always and inevitably – on the basis of models of writing we have already encountered. The ability to be creative . . . is not given to the novice but is earned by mastering the conventions to the point

where improvisation becomes possible, and power finally is exchanged for freedom once again.

The outer rectangle in Fig. 13.3, through its stipulation of the historically distanced contexts of reception and production, addresses the question of how particular subjectivities constitute a particular discourse community and are constituted by a particular discourse. We can understand, for example, how a particular form of gendered subjectivity both allows and disallows a feminist reading, and even the difficulties faced by teachers wanting to escape from or even reconsider the various discourses in which they have been constructed. The reader, the writer and the text are produced in and through social and discursive formations, so that the individual psyche is seen to be part of the symbolic order of the culture within which it is formed and operated (Donald, 1985).

To understand how writers and readers are implicated in pre-existent genres and discourses is to understand the historical, social and political processes which produce and sustain ideology and power relationships. The possibility of constructing alternative histories out of alternative genres and discourses is not guaranteed by the mere knowledge of our prior construction and positioning in particular genres and discourses. Witness, for example, the difficulty experienced by teachers who attempt to escape from the romantic discourse of 'personal growth' teaching with its illusory promise of the individual's freedom to act, or the student writer's difficulty with the ideological coding of stories that are inevitably distinguished along gender, race and class axes.

A range of active and resistant practice

What Iser (1978), Rosenblatt (1978), Bleich (1978), Fish (1980) and others have offered is a clearer understanding of the phenomenology and cognitive operations of reading. Their general focus is on the dynamics of a transactional event that sees active readers bringing particular personal and literary repertoires to bear on a text which contains within itself some necessary structures and perspectives (of plot, character, narrator, or implied reader) which are intended to guarantee an aesthetic reading.

Other writers, seeking a more immediate classroom praxis, like Jackson (1982, 1983), Benton and Fox (1985), Corcoran and Evans (1987), Hayhoe and Parker (1984, 1988), Thomson (1987), Protherough (1983, 1986) and Probst (1988), have suggested various forms of teacher intervention which are intended to heighten students' awareness of the ways texts instruct their readers on how to read them. Representative strategies include: interrupted readings that allow processes of anticipation and retrospection to be brought into play; the sequencing of a scrambled text so that the logic of temporal and causal order can be seen in its relationship to the use of narrative transitions and cohesive ties; the application of cloze deletions at the level of the word, sentence or paragraph so that these artificial gaps can serve to heighten the reader's awareness of the processes involved in filling out the 'real' gaps involved in the text's construction.

Jackson (1982) is acutely aware of the problems involved in using strategies such as these, which deliberately slow down the onward flow of temporal processes or which tamper with an intact text:

> So before we cut up and divide material to improve children's reflective habits about what they read, perhaps we ought to consider more carefully exactly how children make sense of what they read through their expectations meeting and being modified by the claims of the print, and also allow the story as story to fulfil its carefully prepared logic before using it as a vehicle for reading development.

When Jackson's students work through a group prediction based on Saroyan's 'The Great Leapfrog Contest', they focus on the story's 'carefully prepared logic', on the working out of a single, stable and determinate meaning put there by the author and extractable by any reader with a sufficiently well-developed sense of the 'moral logic' of a story. By contrast, when Mellor *et al.* (1987) turn to the same story, and delete its ending, their particular purpose is to draw attention to the gendered roles set up in the story. How do students react when they discover that Saroyan proposes a future for the rebellious young girl who had been the undisputed and even sadistic winner of the 'great leapfrog contest' in terms such as these?

> It was probably the woman in her, which, less than five years later came out to such an extent that she became one of the most beautiful girls in town, gave up tomboy activities and married one of the wealthiest young men in King's County, a college man named, if memory serves, Wallace Hadington Finlay VI.

In the end, Mellor *et al.* are more interested in provoking a reading which is both resistant and symptomatic. That is, they draw the student reader's attention to those gaps or silences in the story which might have given some indication of why a young working-class girl should suddenly stop rebelling. Further on they ask whether Saroyan's intention was 'to suggest that questioning gender and class role expectations is something that girls grow out of', and they wonder whether Saroyan was simply 'unaware of this possible reading'.

With respect to another of their selected stories, Ray Bradbury's 'The Whole Town's Sleeping', Mellor *et al.* provide an elaborate edifice of textual framing aimed at directing students' attention to an alternative reading of a story hitherto approached only as an exemplary suspense mystery. The alternative reading, based it must be said on their own historically placed re-readings, suggests that the story *must* be given a feminist reading because of its unexamined assumptions that 'women are the "natural targets" of male violence' and that the story presents an 'unsympathetic presentation of the heroine-victim'.

What interests me most about this argument is not so much the story's claim for an alternative, resistant reading as the anthologists' tacit admission that to get beyond a set of constructed expectations they would need to interfere so drastically with the student's initial encounter with the text. How far will teachers go to manipulate or frame a particular reading? How far will they *require* an alternative set of reading practices? How far will they choose to ignore the kind of compelling evidence that writers provide about their own intentions and contexts of production? Certainly, as Giroux (1983b) has argued, there are a number of 'structured silences' in literacy practices that fail to recognize the explicit connections among language, knowledge, ideology and power. Instrumental and interactionist ideologies, for example, both ignore the class, race and gender histories of significant numbers of students. Language is reduced to a vehicle for the organization and expression of ideas and emotions, and power (in the interactionist view) becomes a mere exercise of 'cognitive problem-solving or . . . journeying into the self'. At the very least, then, students need to be taught how to locate and analyse the culture-specific significances involved in textual ideology. That is to say, they must learn the *constitutive* rules, the premises of successful play that allow them to move beyond subjective responses to the surface of the text to an understanding and critique of the related patterns of events, environments, attitudes, behaviours and ideas coded in the text.

Re-reading, rewriting and resistance

This chapter has been moving towards a pedagogy based on the relationships among reading, re-reading, rewriting and resistance. I want to end, therefore, by endorsing the claims made by Lunzer and Gardner (1979), Thomson (1987), Dias and Hayhoe (1988) and others that the most successful reading is marked by reflexivity, a sort of metatextual awareness of one's own reading processes. But I want to go further, with Johnson (1988), McCormick *et al.* (1987) and Giroux (1983a, 1983b), all of whom see the new pedagogy as marked by a particular kind of emancipatory resistance which allows students 'to read in opposition to and then beyond the hypnotic transparency of the language that imprisons them (to) read its contradictions and incorporate them into a richer, more self-conscious, and perhaps more homeodynamically controlled text-world' (Johnson, 1988). In yet another rejection of the reductionist, encyclopaedic view of literacy enshrined in Hirsch's (1987) minimalist list or the demands of a National Curriculum, Johnson explains the minimal reading requirements of cultural literacy as 'a thoroughgoing engagement with and enjoyment of the multiplex workings of language, textuality itself'.

I will conclude by arguing that classroom reading events, as much as local and national curricula, need to be based on an acknowledgment of certain zones of reading such as those indicated in Table 13.1. Unlike the psychological categories which underpin developmental or stage models of response (Applebee, 1978; Protherough, 1983; Thomson, 1987), or the naming or counting systems of content analysis used in early critiques of sexism and racism (Zimet, 1979; Lorimer and Long, 1979), the unstable and overlapping zones of Table 13.1 acknowledge the cultural positioning of the reader, and are not tied to reflective categories or presuppositions held by a teacher or researcher. The overarching argument is that reading that simply goes along *with the grain* does little to emancipate readers, and even less to enfranchise them as writers. What is needed are not only strong readings *against the grain*, which challenge textual structures

Table 13.1   Zones of reading

passive	active	resistant
reading	interpretation	criticism
objective	subjective	intersubjective
univocal	equivocal	dialogic
with the grain	against the grain	redefines the grain
monocultural	bicultural	multicultural
readerly	re-readerly	re-writerly
immanent meanings	constructed meanings	contested meanings
textual	circumtextual	intertextual

and ideology, but also more resistant readings which *redefine the grain*, in the process constituting radical rewritings of the text and of the world of the reader/writer.

The *passive*, *active* and *resistant* dimensions of reading have been an overarching theme of this chapter, especially in the light of an argument which proposes the constructed nature of both readers and texts. Certainly, there are immediate contradictions with any notion of a passive reader, unless, as Nelms (1988) points out, we are recalling Iser's (1974) stance of passive synthesis. Classrooms which acknowledge all three zones of reading open up a potential space where a range of cultural codes will be both displayed and contested. Vigilance may still be needed to see whether the teacher continues to send subtle but firm messages about whose readings and which reading strategies or heuristics are valued and supported. As various critics of personal growth teaching and reader-response theory have argued (Belsey, 1980; Meares, 1988; West, 1987), commitment to a plurality of readings is no guarantee that the classroom remains unmarked by privileged modes of analysis, privileged values and privileged ways of reading the world. In Barthes' (1982) words, 'what remains oppressive in our teaching is not finally the knowledge or culture it conveys – but the discursive forms through which we propose them'.

More attention needs to be paid, therefore, to the issue of the cultural framing of the reader, the text and the teacher. Which aspects of the perspective and construction of the reader (sex, family and class background, race, age differences or historical placement) *help* the reading, and which *hinder* the reading? How are perceptions and emotional reactions related to a range of specific, constructed cultural factors as much as to clinically conceived sets of temperamental or egocentric dispositions? How, above all, does the text seek to position the reader in a cultural space from which images, descriptions and narrative ploys all appear transparent and natural? To address such questions is to understand that both active and resistant levels of interrogation are involved in the progression from *immanent*, to *constructed*, and *contested* sets of meanings.

These sorts of considerations also mark out the possibilities for *monocultural*, *bicultural* and *multicultural* classrooms. Again, to get beyond mere tokenism we must foreground the reading practices sanctioned in the multicultural classroom as much as, or more than, the range of texts admitted to that classroom. As Taxel (1988) argues, we still know very little about how factors such as ethnicity, gender and socio-economic status influence response. How, for example, would the responses of a middle-class black child differ from those of a white child to books like Taylor's (1977) *Roll of Thunder, Hear My Cry* and Sebestyen's (1979) *Words by Heart*?

The progression from *reading* (through response) to *interpretation* and *criticism* as reconceptualized by Scholes (1985), is a timely reminder of how teachers can stop teaching literature and start helping students to 'come into their own powers of textualization'. As indicated earlier, the value of semiotic accounts of reading is that they avoid infecting students with forms of exegetical paralysis transmitted by constant exposure to the question 'What are the hidden meanings in this text?' Alternative invitations to consider the constitutive rules for generic coding and the cultural codes embedded in character, action and situation enable students to move beyond personal or 'literary' grounds of judgement to forms of criticism that allow them to 'speak for a group or class on issues of importance to that class'. Exactly to what extent students in the later years of secondary school should be taught the regulative rules of particular critical games, such as structuralism, feminism or Marxism is a difficult question. In the end, as Scholes and the teachers in Nelms' (1988) collection would argue, our task as literature teachers is to help students identify the underlying patterns in textual features that render them culturally significant.

This is the sort of direction suggested by the *univocal, equivocal, dialogic* dimension. Univocal interpretations close down rather than open out the opportunity to apprehend and evoke a text's possible worlds. The literature of the classroom cannot be seen either as a stable platform from which the authentic 'personal voice' of the author, the teacher or the student may speak, nor as a democratic exercise in the avoidance of ascribing textual criteria. Students need to understand that the making of private connections is no guarantee of inclusion in evolving interpretive communities (Fish, 1980), and that 'personal' voices are achieved only through participation in the cultural and historical processes of making the world by making meaning. What is needed, certainly, is a translation of Bakhtin's (1981) notion of polyglossia into the classroom. This will involve the admission of a range of voices, with all the hybrid uncertainty that this opening out of the discourses of the classroom involves. What I have in mind is White's (1984) description of the operation of polyglossia in *Ulysses* and *Finnegan's Wake*, where 'blocks and fragments of language interanimate one another, recontextualizing familiar class, gender and racial styles so that each is reinflected, made strange or even made questionable by the mobility of context'.

In those classrooms, then, where frequent opportunities are provided for self-conscious (reflexive) analysis of *both* cognitive and cultural reading strategies, the status of some enigmatic strategies can be retheorized. Reading logs or response journals, for example, have been used as an opportunity for students to engage in a range of cumulative annotations, imagings, speculations, anticipations, interrogations, revisitings, and simple relishings of the process of reading

(Jackson, 1982; Hackman, 1987; Corcoran and Evans, 1987; Thomson, 1987). At the same time, the journal has run the risk of becoming a loosely disguised form of confessional writing or even as an exercise in faking something called personal voice for the teacher (Gilbert, 1989). Alongside some of the entirely relevant purposes just listed, the journal needs to provide a space for the student to experiment at becoming a multiple reading voice, a sort of composite reader who questions the *objective*, *subjective* and *intersubjective* elements of an emergent social text. Viewed from a dialogical perspective, Morgan (1987) argues, the journal could become a useful genre for putting 'a more active, collective and contradictory subject on the agenda', and for 'freeing student writers from the account sheet of an essentialized romantic self'.

Similarly, the relationship between *readerly*, *re-readerly* and *re-writerly* activities sets resistant reading in the context of something more than an 'artistic' control over a range of stylistic conventions. To rewrite scenes, incidents, chapters, endings from various points of view is to recognize how minor characters, in particular, come to be marginalized and how their meanings (or significances) are suppressed while other perspectives are correspondingly valorized or privileged. Similarly, there is something more than artificial paraphrase involved in modernizing passages from older texts for the purpose of uncovering the assumptions and ideology embedded in the original and rewritten language. The inevitable outcome of a symptomatic reading is the way in which history foregrounds the absences in texts. To re-read Joyce's *Eveline* (1967), for example, is to trade a relatively uncomplicated pre-feminist idea that it is difficult to leave a world of drudgery for a post-feminist questioning of how a female develops autonomy in a man's world.

We are left, then, with the suggestion that to read and write in a literate culture is to be able to join in (or to be excluded from) a series of situated, *circumtextual* and *intertextual* conversations. As Wolf (1988) argues, to read 'resonantly' is to be able to hear the 'conversations in a work', to recognize particularly how subsequent re-readings of particular texts result from the inevitable historical positioning of new readers in new and different discourses, and how students therefore need a sense of their own reading histories. Wolf recalls a teacher who was introducing her students to a play called *Ma Rainey's Black Bottom* (1985) where the writer, August Wilson, had included a prefatory essay which begins:

> It is early March in Chicago, 1927. There is a bit of a chill in the air. Winter has broken but the wind coming off the lake does not carry the promise of spring. The people of the city are bundled and brisk in their defence against such misfortunes as the weather, and the business of the city proceeds largely undisturbed.
>   Chicago in 1927 is a rough city, a bruising city, a city of millionaires and derelicts, gangsters and roughhouse dandies, whores and Irish grandmothers who move through the streets fingering long black rosaries. Somewhere a man is wrestling with a taste of a woman in his cheek. Somewhere a dog is barking. Somewhere the moon has fallen through a window and broken into thirty pieces of silver.

What interests me most is how the teacher challenges the students to talk about 'all the other stories that these lines trigger', and *not just* the 'personal ones like having been cold or looking out a window at night' but the 'stories you have heard or read'. And so the stories flood in – 'Of Chicago and gangsters. The "Untouchables", the fight between good like Eliot Ness and evil like Al Capone. Quick getaways and bootleggers'; of 'something about the opposites: millionaires and derelicts, whores and grandmothers'; of the musical, metrical patterns heard in church, 'Bundled and brisk . . . *Somewhere a* man, *Somewhere a* dog, *Somewhere the* moon*'; 'all kinds of stories of people landing in big cities, immigrants coming in'; or the 'autobiography of Billie Holliday. The way she gets beaten up by the city – that's the part about how bruising the city is'; or back further still to 'a kid's book, a picture book, the moon seemed like a metal plate'.

But there are no stories of Judas and the thirty pieces of silver! 'We'll read it', the teacher says, guaranteeing her own proprietary rights to a re-reading, and the students' rights to a potentially resistant reading, 'before we get through the play'.

Bibliography

Adams, D. (1979). *The Hitch Hiker's Guide to the Galaxy*. London: Pan.
Adams, R. (1972). *Watership Down*. London: Collings.
Adler, M. (1982). *The Padaeia Proposal*. New York: Macmillan.
Ahlberg, J. and Ahlberg, A. (1978). *Each Peach Pear Plum*. Harmondsworth: Kestrel.
Ahlberg, J. and Ahlberg, A. (1982). *The Baby's Catalogue*. Harmondsworth: Kestrel.
Ahlberg, J. and Ahlberg, A. (1986). *The Jolly Postman or Other People's Letters*. London: Heinemann.
Aiken, J. (1968). *The Whispering Mountain*. London: Jonathan Cape.
Aldridge, J. (1986). *The True Story of Spit MacPhee*. Harmondsworth: Kestrel.
Althusser, L. (1971). 'Ideology and ideological state apparatuses'. In Althusser, L., *Lenin and Philosophy and other Essays*. London: NLB.
Althusser, L. (1984). *Essays on Ideology*. London: Verso.
Anderson, R. L. and Pearson, P. D. (1984). 'A schema-theoretic view of reading comprehension'. In Pearson, P. D. (ed.), *Handbook of Reading Research*. Harlow: Longman.
Anderson, R. L. and Pearson, P. D. (1987). 'Instructional research on literacy and reading: Parameters, perspectives, and predictions'. In Tierney, R. J., Anders, P. L. and Mitchell, J. N. (eds), *Understanding Readers' Understanding: Theory and Practice*. Hillsdale, NJ: Lawrence Erlbaum Associates Inc.
Applebee, A. (1978). *The Child's Concept of Story*. Chicago, Ill.: University of Chicago Press.
Applebee, A. (1982). 'Literature in English'. In Mitzel, H. E. (ed.), *Encyclopedia of Educational Research*, 5th edn. New York: Free Press.
Applebee, A. (1985). 'Studies in the spectator role: An approach to response to literature'. In Cooper, C. R. (ed.), *Researching Response to Literature and the Teaching of Literature: Points of Departure*. Norwood, NJ: Ablex.
Applebee, A. (1989). *The Teaching of Literature in Programs with Reputations for Excellence in English*. Albany, NY: Center for the Learning and Teaching of Literature.
Association for Supervision and Curriculum Development, with the American Library Association (1983). *A Five Year Study of Censorship in US Schools*. Washington, DC: ASCD.
Avery, G. (1971). *A Likely Lad*. London: Collins.
Bakhtin, M. (1981). *The Dialogic Imagination* (translated by C. Emerson and M. Holquist). Austin, Tex.: University of Texas Press.
Ballantyne, R. M. (1858). *The Coral Island*. London: Nelson.

Barone, D. (1989). Young children's written responses to literature: Exploring the relationship between written response and orthographic knowledge. Unpublished doctoral dissertation, University of Nevada-Reno.

Barone, T. E. (1988). 'Curriculum platforms and literature'. In Beyer, L. E. and Apple, M. W. (eds), *The Curriculum: Problems, Politics, and Possibilities*, pp. 140–65. Albany, NY: State University of New York.

Barr, M. (in press). 'The California Literature Initiative'. In Farrell, E. J. and Squire, J. R. (eds), *Fifty Years of Literature as Exploration*. Urbana, Ill.: National Council of Teachers of English.

Barrs, M., Ellis, S., Hesler, H. and Thomas, A. (1988). *The ILEA Primary Language Record*. London: ILEA Centre for Language in Primary Education.

Barstow, S. (1960). *A Kind of Loving*. London: Michael Joseph.

Barstow, S. (1969). 'The fury'. In Barstow, S. (ed.), *The Human Element*. Harlow: Longman Imprint Series.

Barthes, R. (1970). *S/Z*. Paris: Seuil. (Translated by R. Miller. New York: Hill and Wang, 1974.)

Barthes, R. (1982). 'Inaugural Lecture, College de France'. In Sontag, S. (ed.), *A Barthes Reader*. New York: Hill and Wang.

Bawden, N. (1975). *The Peppermint Pig*. London: Gollancz.

Beach, R. (1985). 'Differences in autobiographical narratives of English teachers, college freshmen, and seventh graders'. *College Composition and Communications*, **38**, 56–69.

Beach, R. and Brown, K. (1987). 'Discourse convention and literacy inference'. In Tierney, R., Anders, P. and Mitchell, J. (eds), *Understanding Readers' Understanding: Theory and Practice*, pp. 147–73. Hillsdale, NJ: Lawrence Erlbaum Associates Inc.

Beach, R. and Brunetti, G. (1976). 'Differences between high school and university students in their conceptions of literary characters'. *Research in the Teaching of English*, **10**, 259–68.

Beach, R. and Hynds, S. (1990). 'Research on the learning and teaching of literature: Select bibliography'. In Farrell, E. J. and Squire, J. R. (eds), *Transactions in Literature*. Urbana, Ill.: National Council of Teachers of English.

Beach, R. and Wendler, L. (1987). 'Developmental differences in response to a story'. *Research in the Teaching of English*, **21**, 286–97.

Beckson, K. and Ganz, A. (1961). *A Reader's Guide to Literary Terms*. London: Thames and Hudson.

Belsey, C. (1980). *Critical Practice*. London: Methuen.

Bennett, W. (1988). *James Madison Elementary School*. Washington, DC: OERI.

Benton, M. and Fox, G. (1985). *Teaching Literature: Nine to Fourteen*. Oxford: Oxford University Press.

Benton, M., Teasey, J., Bell, R. and Hurst, K. (1988). *Young Readers Responding to Poems*. London: Routledge.

Berger, P. and Luckman, T. (1967). *The Social Construction of Reality*. Harmondsworth: Penguin.

Bettelheim, B. (1978). *The Uses of Enchantment*. Harmondsworth: Penguin.

Bleich, D. (1978). *Subjective Criticism*. Baltimore, Md.: Johns Hopkins University Press.

Bleich, D. (1986). *Readings and Feelings: An Introduction to Subjective Criticism*. Urbana, Ill.: National Council of Teachers of English.

Bogdan, D. (1985). 'The justification question: Why literature?' *English Education*, December, 238–48.

Bogdan, D. (1986). Literary experience as total form: Stasis and dialectic or in and out of love with literature. Paper presented at the NCTE Conference, San Antonio, Texas, USA, November.

Bogdan, D. (1989). 'Joyce, Dorothy, and Willie: Literary literacy as engaged reflection'. In Page, R. (ed.), *Proceedings of the Forty-fifth Annual Conference of the Philosophy of Education Society*, San Antonio, Texas, April 1989. Normal, Illinois.

Bogdan, D. and Yeomans, S. (1986). 'School censorship and learning values through literature'. *Journal of Moral Education*, 15(3), 197–211.

Booth, W. (1961). *The Rhetoric of Fiction*. Chicago, Ill.: University of Chicago Press.

Booth, W. (1988). *The Company We Keep: An Ethics of Fiction*. Berkeley, Calif.: University of California Press.

Brecht, B. (1965). *The Jewish Wife and other Plays*. New York: Grove Press.

Brecht, B. (1976). *Bertolt Brecht: Poems* (Willett, J. and Mannheim, R., eds). London: Eyre Methuen.

Bridge, C. (1987). 'Strategies for promoting reader–text interactions'. In Tierney, R., Anders, P. and Mitchell, J. (eds), *Understanding Readers' Understanding: Theory and Practice*, pp. 283–306. Hillsdale, NJ: Lawrence Erlbaum Associates Inc.

Britton, J. (1963). 'Literature'. In Britton, J. (ed.), *The Arts and Current Tendencies in Education*. London: Evans/London Institute of Education.

Britton, J. (1969). *Language and Learning*. Harmondsworth: Penguin.

Britton, J. (1977). 'Response to literature'. In Meek, M., Warlow, A. and Barton, G. (eds), *The Cool Web*. London: Bodley Head.

Britton, J. (1982). *Prospect and Retrospect: Selected Essays* (Pradl, G., ed.). Upper Montclair, NH: Boynton/Cook.

Britton, J. (1989). 'The spectator as theorist: A reply'. *English Education*, 21(1), 53–60.

Britton, J., Martin, N., McLeod, A. and Rosen, H. (1975). *The Development of Writing Abilities*. London: Macmillan.

Brown, A. L. (1975). 'Recognition, reconstruction and recall of narrative sequences by preoperational children'. *Child Development*, 48, 156–66.

Bruner, J. (1986). *Actual Minds, Possible Worlds*. Cambridge, Mass.: Harvard University Press.

Bunbury, R. (1985). 'Levels of response to literature'. *Australian Journal of Reading*, 8, 220–28.

Burningham, J. (1977). *Come Away from the Water, Shirley*. London: Cape.

Bussis, A. M., Chittenden, E., Amarel, M. and Klausner, E. (1985). *Inquiry into Meaning: An Investigation of Learning to Read*. Hillsdale, NJ: Lawrence Erlbaum Associates Inc.

Calfee, R. (1987). 'Reading comprehension'. In Wittrock, M. (ed.), *Handbook of Research in Teaching*. New York: Macmillan.

California State Department of Education (1987). *Handbook for Effective Teaching of Literature*. Sacramento, Calif.: State Department.

Carlsen, G. R. and Sherrill, C. A. (1988). *Voices of Readers: How We Come to Love Books*. Urbana, Ill.: National Council of Teachers of English.

Carpenter, H. (1985). *Secret Gardens*. London: Unwin.

Carter, P. (1980). *The Sentinels*. Oxford: Oxford University Press.

Cawley, W. (1974). *Gran at Colegate*. Oxford: Oxford University Press.

Chatman, S. (1978). *Story and Discourse: Narrative Structure in Story and Film*. Ithaca, NY: Cornell University Press.

Chew, C., DeFabio, R. and Hansbury, P. (eds) (1986). *Reader Response in the Classroom*. Liverpool, NY: New York State English Council.

Christopher, J. (1970). *The Guardians*. London: Hamish Hamilton.

Clifford, J. (ed.) (1988). *Reader: Essays in Reader-oriented Theory, Criticism, and Practice*, **20** (entire issue on Louise M. Rosenblatt).

Cohan, S. and Shires, L. (1988). *Telling Stories*. London: Routledge.

Coles, R. (1989). *The Call of Stories*. Boston, Mass.: Houghton Mifflin.

Cooper, C. R. (ed.) (1985). *Researching Response to Literature and the Teaching of Literature: Points of Departure*. Norwood, NJ: Ablex.

Corcoran, W. and Evans, E. (eds) (1987). *Readers, Texts, Teachers*. Upper Montclair, NJ: Boynton/Cook.

Cormier, R. (1975a). *I Am the Cheese*. New York: Bantam Books.

Cormier, R. (1975b). *The Chocolate War*. London: Gollancz.

Cormier, R. (1979). *After the First Death*. London: Gollancz.

Cox, B. (chair) (1989). *English 5–16: Report of the National Curriculum English Working Group (The Cox Report)*. London: DES.

Crago, M. and Crago, H. (1983). *Prelude to Literacy*. Carbondale, Ill.: Southern Illinois University Press.

Croall, J. (1983). *Neill of Summerhill*. London: Routledge.

Culler, J. (1975). *Structuralist Poetics: Structuralism, Linguistics, and the Study of Literature*. London: Routledge and Kegan Paul.

Culler, J. (1980). 'Prolegomena to a theory of reading'. In Suleiman S. and Crosman, I. (eds), *The Reader in the Text*. Princeton, Guildford: Princeton University Press.

Culler, J. (1981). *The Pursuit of Signs: Semiotics, Literature, Deconstruction*. Ithaca, NY: Cornell University Press.

Culler, J. (1983). *On Deconstruction*. London: Routledge and Kegan Paul.

Cullinan, B., Harwood, K. and Galda, H. (1983). 'The reader and the story: Comprehension and response'. *Journal of Research and Development in Education*, **16**, 29–38.

Davies, A. (1978). *Conrad's War*. London: Blackie.

Davis, L. J. (1987). *Resisting Novels*. London: Methuen.

Davis, M. M. (1989). *Television is Good for Your Kids*. London: Hilary Shipman.

Derrida, J. (1978a). *La Verite en Peinture*. Paris: Flammarion.

Derrida, J. (1978b). *Writing and Difference* (translated by A. Bass). London: Routledge and Kegan Paul.

Desai, A. (1982). *The Village by the Sea*. London: Heinemann.

Dias, P. (1987). *Making Sense of Poetry: Patterns in the Process*. Ottawa: Canadian Council of Teachers of English.

Dias, P. and Hayhoe, M. (1988). *Developing Response to Poetry*. Milton Keynes: Open University Press.

Dickinson, P. (1976). *The Blue Hawk*. London: Gollancz.

Dixon, J. (in press). 'Students exploring literature across the world'. In Farrell, E. J. and Squire, J. R. (eds), *Fifty Years of Literature as Exploration*. Urbana, Ill.: National Council of Teachers of English.

Dixon, J. and Brown, J. (1985). *Responses to Literature – What is Being Assessed?*, Parts I, II and III. London: Schools Council Publications.

Dixon, J. and Stratta, L. (1987). *Narrative and Beyond*. Ottawa: Canadian Council of Teachers of English.

Dollerup, C. *et al.* (1981–8). 'Folktale: A cross-cultural interdisciplinary study of the experience of literature'. *Eight Reports on the Danish–Turkish Folktale Project*, Copenhagen.

Donald, J. (1985). 'Beacons of the future: Schooling, subjection and subjectification'. In

Beechey, V. and Donald, J. (eds), *Subjectivity and Social Relations*. Milton Keynes: Open University Press.

Durkin, D. (1966). *Children Who Read Early*. New York: Teachers College Press.

Eagleton, T. (1988). 'J. C. Austin and Jonah'. *New Blackfriars*, April, 146–68.

Eco, U. (1979). *The Role of the Reader: Explorations in the Semiotics of Texts*. Bloomington, Ind.: Indiana University Press.

Eeds, M. and Wells, D. (1989). 'Grand conversations: An exploration of meaning construction in literature studies groups'. *Research in the Teaching of English*, **23**(1), 4–29.

Egan, K. (1988). *Teaching as Story Telling*. London: Routledge.

Everett, B. (1986). *Poets in Their Time*. London: Faber.

Fanslow, J. (1973). Responses of Puerto-Rican adolescents to four short stories. Unpublished doctoral dissertation, Teachers College, Columbia University.

Farrell, E. J. (in press). 'Response to literature'. In Farrell E. J. and Squire, J. R. (eds), *Fifty Years of Literature as Exploration*. Urbana, Ill.: National Council of Teachers of English.

Farrell, E. J. and Squire, J. R. (eds) (1990). *Transactions in Literature*. Urbana, Ill.: National Council of Teachers of English.

Faulkner, W. (1935). *As I Lay Dying*. London: Chatto and Windus.

Favat, F. A. (1977). *Child and Tale: The Origins of Interest*. Urbana, Ill.: National Council of Teachers of English.

Finlay, L. and Faith, V. (1987). 'Illiteracy and alienation in American colleges: Is Paolo Freire's pedagogy relevant?' In Shor, I. (ed.), *Freire for the Classroom*. Portsmouth, NH: Heinemann.

Fish, S. (1980). *Is There a Text in this Class? The Authority of Interpretive Communities*. Cambridge, Mass.: Harvard University Press.

Fisher, C. J. and Natarella, M. A. (1979). 'Young children's preferences in poetry'. *Research in the Teaching of English*, **16**(4), 339–54.

Flood, J. and Lapp, D. (in press). 'Reading comprehension'. In Flood, J., Jensen, J., Lapp, D. and Squire, J. R. (eds), *Handbook of Research on the Teaching of the English Language Arts*. New York: Macmillan.

Flood, J., Jensen, J., Lapp, D. and Squire, J. R. (eds) (in press). *Handbook of Research on the Teaching of the English Language Arts*. New York: Macmillan.

Foucault, M. (1977). *Language, Counter-memory, Practice: Selected Essays and Interviews*. Ithaca, NY: Cornell University Press.

Fowles, J. (1963). *The Collector*. London: Jonathan Cape.

Frye, N. (1970). *The Stubborn Structure: Essays on Criticism and Society*. London: Methuen.

Galda, L. (1982). 'Assuming the spectator stance: An examination of the responses of three young readers'. *Research in the Teaching of English*, **16**, 1–20.

Galda, L. and Pellegrini, A. (eds) (1986). *Play, Language and Stories*. Norwood, NJ: Ablex Publishing Corp.

Gare, N. (1966). *The Fringe Dwellers*. Melbourne: Sun Books.

Garfield, L. (1966). *Devil in the Fog*. Harmondsworth: Kestrel.

Garner, A. (1967). *The Owl Service*. London: Collins.

Gibbs, A. (1970). 'The test'. In Bennett, B., Cowan, P. and Hay, J. (eds), *Spectrum Two*. Harlow: Longman.

Gilbert, P. (1988). 'Authorship and creativity in the classroom'. In Hart, K. (ed.), *Shifting Frames: English/Literature/Writing*, pp. 24–39. Geelong, Centre for Studies in Literary Education: Deakin University.

Gilbert, P. (1989). *Writing, Schooling and Deconstruction: From Voice to Text in the Classroom.* London: Routledge and Kegan Paul.

Ginzburg, C. (1976). *The Cheese and the Worms.* London: Routledge and Kegan Paul.

Giroux, H. (1983a). 'Theories of reproduction and resistance in the new sociology of education: A critical analysis'. *Harvard Educational Review*, 53(3), 257–93.

Giroux, H. (1983b). *Theory and Resistance in Education: A Pedagogy for the Opposition.* South Hadley, Mass.: Bergin and Garvey.

Golding, W. (1954). *Lord of the Flies.* London: Faber.

Griffith, P. (1987). *Literary Theory and English Teaching.* Milton Keynes: Open University Press.

Hackman, S. (1987). *Responding in Writing: The Use of Exploratory Writing in the Literature Classroom.* Exeter: Short Run Press for NATE.

Handlan, B. (1946). 'The fallacy of free reading'. *English Journal*, 25, 182–7.

Hansson, G. (1973). 'Some types of research on response to literature'. *Research in the Teaching of English*, 7, 260–84.

Harding, D. W. (1937). 'The role of the onlooker'. *Scrutiny*, 6, 247–58.

Harding, D. W. (1962). 'Psychological processes in the reading of fiction'. *British Journal of Aesthetics*, 2, 133–47.

Harding, D. W. (1963). *Experience into Words.* Cambridge: Cambridge University Press.

Hardy, B. (1975). *Tellers and Listeners.* London: Athlone Press.

Harker, J. (1987). 'Literary theory and the reading process: A meeting of perspectives'. *Written Communication*, 4(3), 235–52.

Harris, J. (1988). 'The spectator as theorist: Britton and the functions of writing'. *English Education*, 20(1), 41–50.

Havelock, E. (1986). *The Muse Learns to Write.* New Haven, Conn.: Yale University Press.

Hayhoe, M. and Parker, S. (1984). *Working with Fiction.* London: Edward Arnold.

Hayhoe, M. and Parker, S. (1988). *Words Large as Apples: Teaching Poetry 11–18.* Cambridge: Cambridge University Press.

Heaton, M. (1955). 'Introduction'. *Reading Ladders for Human Relations*, 2nd edn. Washington, DC: American Council on Education.

Hemingway, E. (1951). 'The faithful bull'. In *The Complete Short Stories of Ernest Hemingway.* New York: Charles Scribner.

Hemschemeyer, J. (1984). 'We interrupt this broadcast'. In Janeczko, P. (ed.), *Strings: A Gathering of Family Poems.* New York: Bradbury.

Hickman, J. (1980). 'Children's response to literature: What happens in the classroom'. *Language Arts*, 57, 524–9.

Hickman, J. (1981). 'A new perspective on response to literature: Research in an elementary school setting'. *Research in the Teaching of English*, 15, 343–54.

Hickman, J. (1983). 'Everything considered: Response to literature in an elementary school setting'. *Journal of Research and Development in Education*, 16, 343–55.

Hirsch, E. (1987). *Cultural Literacy: What Every American Needs to Know.* Boston, Mass.: Houghton Mifflin.

Holland, N. (1968). *The Dynamics of Reader Response.* New York: Oxford.

Holland, N. (1975). *Five Readers Reading.* New Haven, Conn.: Yale University Press.

Holland, N. (1985). 'Reading readers reading'. In Cooper, C. R. (ed.), *Researching Response to Literature and the Teaching of Literature: Points of Departure*, pp. 3–21. Norwood, NJ: Ablex.

Hughes, T. (1968). *The Iron Man.* London: Faber and Faber.

Hughes, T. (1970). 'Myth and education'. *Children's Literature in Education*, 1, 55–70.

Hughes, T. (1984). *What is the Truth?* London: Faber.

Hunt, P. (1988). 'What do we lose when we lose allusion? Experience and understanding stories'. *Signal*, 57, 212–22.

Hunt, R. and Vipond, D. (1987). 'Aesthetic reading: Some strategies for research'. *English Quarterly*, 20(3), 178–83.

Hutchins, P. (1968). *Rosie's Walk*. London: Bodley Head.

Hynds, S. (1986). 'Interpersonal cognitive complexity and the literary response process'. *Research in the Teaching of English*, 19(4), 254–68.

Hynds, S. (1989). 'Bringing life to literature and literature to life: Social constructs and contexts of four adolescent readers'. *Research in the Teaching of English*, 23(1), 30–61.

Iser, W. (1974). *The Implied Reader: Patterns of Communication in Prose Fiction from Bunyan to Beckett*. Baltimore, Md.: Johns Hopkins University Press.

Iser, W. (1978). *The Act of Reading: A Theory of Aesthetic Response*. Baltimore, Md.: Johns Hopkins University Press.

Jackson, D. (1982). *Continuity in Secondary English*. London: Methuen.

Jackson, D. (1983). *Encounters with Books: Teaching Fiction 11–16*. London: Methuen.

Jackson, S. (1970). 'After you my dear Alphonse'. In Bennett, B., Cowan, P. and Hay, J. (eds), *Spectrum Two*. Harlow: Longman.

Janssen, T. and Rijlaarsdam, G. (1989). What do pupils learn from literature teaching? Paper presented at the International Convention on Literature and Response, University of East Anglia, Norwich, UK, April.

Jauss, H. (1982a). *Aesthetic Experience and Literary Hermeneutics* (translated by M. Shaw). Minneapolis, Minn.: University of Minnesota Press.

Jauss, H. (1982b). *Toward an Aesthetics of Reception*. Minneapolis, Minn.: University of Minnesota Press.

Johnson, M. (1988). 'Hell is the place we don't know we're in: The control dictions of cultural literacy, story reading, and poetry'. *College English*, 50(3), 309–17.

Joyce, J. (1967). *Eveline*. Harmondsworth: Penguin.

Juel, C. (1988). 'Learning to read and write: A longitudinal study of 54 children from first through fourth grades'. *Journal of Educational Psychology*, 80(4), 437–47.

King-Smith, R. (1983). *The Sheep-Pig*. London: Gollancz.

Kress, G. (1986). 'Reading, writing and power'. *ALAA Occasional Paper*, 9, 98–117.

Lacan, J. (1977). *Ecrits: A Selection* (translated by A. Sheridan). London: Tavistock.

Leaf, M. and Lawson, R. (1937). *The Story of Ferdinand*. London: Hamish Hamilton.

Leaper, J. D. (1984). 'Responses of adolescents to poetry'. *English in Australia*, 68, 16–23.

Lee, H. (1960). *To Kill a Mockingbird*. Philadelphia, Pa.: J. B. Lippincott.

Leeson, R. (1985). *Silver's Revenge*. London: Collins.

Lehr, S. (1988). 'The child's developing sense of theme as a response to literature'. *Reading Research Quarterly*, 23, 337–57.

Llosa, M. V. (1984). *Aunt Julia and the Scriptwriter*. London: Picador.

Loban, W. (1954). *Literature and Social Sensitivity*. Urbana, Ill.: National Council of Teachers of English.

Lorimer, R. and Long, M. (1979). 'Sex-role stereotyping in elementary readers'. *Interchange*, 10(2), 35–45.

Lunzer, E. and Gardner, K. (1979). *The Effective Use of Reading*. London: Heinemann Educational.

McCaughrean, G. (1988). *A Pack of Lies*. Oxford: Oxford University Press.

McClure, A. (1986). Children's response to poetry in a supportive literary context. Unpublished doctoral dissertation, Ohio State University.

McCormick, K., Waller, G. and Flower, L. (1987). *Reading Texts: Reading, Responding, Writing*. Lexington, Mass.: D. C. Heath.

McIntosh, M. M. (1988). Feeling like a fraud. Paper presented at the R. Freeman Butts Lecture at the Conference of the American Educational Studies Association, Toronto, 2–6 November.

MacLachlan, G. (1988). 'The (set) text as genre'. *Typereader*, 1, 13–18.

Maclean, M. (1988). *Narrative as Performance*. London: Routledge.

Magorian, M. (1981). *Goodnight Mister Tom*. Harmondsworth: Kestrel.

Mandler, J. and Johnson, N. (1977). 'Remembrance of things parsed: Story structure and recall'. *Cognitive Psychology*, 9, 111–51.

Mark, J. (1980) *Nothing to be afraid of*. Harmondsworth: Kestrel.

Martin, B. (1981). *A Sociology of Contemporary Cultural Change*, Oxford: Blackwell.

Martinez, M. and Roser, N. (in press). 'Children's response to literature'. In Flood, J., Jensen, J., Lapp, D. and Squire, J. R. (eds), *Handbook of Research on the Teaching of the English Language Arts*. New York: Macmillan.

Meares, P. (1988). '"Personal growth" as a frame for teaching literature'. In Hart, K. (ed.), *Shifting Frames: English/Literature/Writing*. Geelong, Centre for Studies in Literary Education: Deakin University Press.

Meckel, H. (1946). An exploratory study of the responses of adolescent pupils to situations in a novel. Unpublished doctoral dissertation, University of Chicago.

Meckel, H. (1953). 'Research on teaching composition and literature'. In Gage, N. L. (ed.), *Handbook for Research on Teaching*, pp. 966–1006. Chicago, Ill.: Rand McNally.

Meek, M. (1987). 'Symbolic outlining: The academic study of children's literature'. *Signal*, 53, 97–115.

Meek, M. (1988). *How Texts Teach What Readers Learn*. Stroud: Thimble Press.

Meek, M., Warlow, A. and Barton, G. (1977). *The Cool Web: The Pattern of Children's Reading*. London: Bodley Head.

Meek, M., with Armstrong, S., Austerfield, V., Graham, J. and Plackett, E. (1983). *Achieving Literacy: Longitudinal Case Studies of Adolescents Learning to Read*. London: Routledge and Kegan Paul.

Mellor, B., O'Neill, M. and Paterson, A. (1987). *Reading Stories*. Perth: Chalkface Press.

Miller, J. (1986). *Women Writing about Men*. London: Virago.

Milner, J. O. and Milner, L. F. M. (eds) (1989). *Passages to Literature*. Urbana, Ill.: National Council of Teachers of English.

Moi, T. (ed.) (1986). *The Kristeva Reader*. Oxford: Blackwell.

Montefiore, J. (1987). *Feminism and Poetry: Language, Experience, Identity in Women's Writing*. London: Pandora.

Morgan, B. (1987). 'Three dreams of languages: Or, no longer immured in the bastille of the world'. *College English*, 49(4), 449–58.

Mosenthal, P. (1987a). 'The goals of reading research and practice: Making sense of the many means of reading'. *Reading Teacher*, 40, 694–8.

Mosenthal, P. (1987b). 'The reader's affective response to narrative text'. In Tierney, R. J., Anders, P. L. and Mitchell, J. N. (eds), *Understanding Readers' Understanding: Theory and Practice*, pp. 95–106. Hillsdale, NJ: Lawrence Erlbaum Associates Inc.

National Council of Teachers of English (1985). *Proceedings of the Business Meeting, Annual Convention*, Detroit, Michigan, November 1984. Urbana, Ill.: NCTE.

Needle, J. (1982). *The Wild Wood*. London: Methuen Children's Books.

Nelms, B. (ed.) (1988). *Literature in the Classroom: Readers, Texts, and Contexts*. Urbana, Ill.: National Council of Teachers of English.

Noel, E. (1984). *Changing Faces.* Sydney: IBBY.

Norvell, G. W. (1950). *The Reading Interests of Young People.* Boston, Mass.: D. C. Heath.

Norvell, G. W. (1958). *What Boys and Girls Like to Read.* New York: Silver Burdett.

O'Neill, M. H. (1983). 'Identification of educational and psychological characteristics of verbally gifted children'. *Education Research and Perspectives,* 10(1), 59–67.

O'Neill, M. H. (1984a). Conceptual frameworks for English curriculum. Unpublished dissertation, University of Western Australia.

O'Neill, M. H. (1984b). 'Functions of response to literature'. *English in Australia,* 68, 24–34.

O'Neill, M. H. (1987). 'English curriculum: A kind of anarchy'. *English Education,* 19(1).

O'Neill, M. H. and Reid, J. (1985). *Educational and Psychological Characteristics of Students Gifted in English.* Canberra: Commonwealth Schools Commission and University of Western Australia.

Ong, W. (1982). *Orality and Literacy: The Technologizing of the Word.* London: Methuen.

Paley, V. G. (1981). *Wally's Stories.* Cambridge, Mass.: Harvard University Press.

Pearson, P. D. (1986). *A Decade of Change in Reading Comprehension.* Lexington, Mass.: Ginn and Co.

Pearson, P. D. and Tierney, R. (1984). 'On becoming a thoughtful reader; learning to read like a writer'. In Purves, A. and Niles, O. (eds), *Becoming Readers in a Complex Society: 83rd Yearbook of the National Society of the Study of Education.* Chicago, Ill.: University of Chicago Press.

People for the American Way (1984, 1986, 1989). *Attacks on the Freedom To Learn.* Washington, DC: PAW.

Peseroff, J. (1988), 'Adolescent'. *Harvard Magazine,* July–August, 50.

Petrosky, A. R. (1975), Individual and group responses of fourteen and fifteen-year-olds to short stories, novels, poems and thematic apperception tests. Unpublished doctoral dissertation, State University of New York, Buffalo. *Dissertation Abstracts International,* 36, 8527.

Petrosky, A. R. (1985). 'Response: A way of knowing'. In Cooper, C. R. (ed.), *Researching Response to Literature and the Teaching of Literature: Points of Departure,* pp. 70–86. Norwood, NJ: Ablex.

Peyton, K. M. (1969). *Flambards.* Oxford: Oxford University Press.

Pilling, A. (1985). *Henry's Leg.* Harmondsworth: Kestrel.

Prince, G. (1973). *A Grammar for Stories.* The Hague: Mouton.

Pritchard, K. S. (1972). *Coonardoo.* Penrith: Modern Australian Library, Discovery Press.

Probst, R. (1988). *Response and Analysis: Teaching Literature in Junior and Senior High School.* Portsmouth, NH: Boynton/Cook Heinemann.

Propp, V. (1968). *The Morphology of the Folktale.* Austin, Tex.: Austin University Press.

Protherough, R. (1983). *Developing Response to Fiction.* Milton Keynes: Open University Press.

Protherough, R. (1986). *Teaching Literature for Examinations.* Milton Keynes: Open University Press.

Protherough, R. (1987). 'The stories that readers tell'. In Corcoran, W. and Evans, E. (eds), *Readers, Texts, Teachers.* Milton Keynes: Open University Press.

Purves, A. (1971). 'Evaluation of learning in literature'. In Bloom, B. S., Hastings, J. T. and Madaus, G. F. (eds), *Handbook on the Formative and Summative Evaluation of Student Learning.* New York: McGraw-Hill.

Purves, A. (ed.) (1972). *How Porcupines Make Love.* Lexington, Mass.: Xerox.

Purves, A. (1975), 'Research in the teaching of literature'. *Elementary English,* 52, 463–6.

Purves, A. (1981). *Achievement in Reading and Literature: The United States in International Perspective*. Urbana, Ill.: National Council of Teachers of English.

Purves, A. (in press). 'Growth in literature and the effect of the American gardener'. In Farrell, E. J. and Squire, J. R. (eds), *Fifty Years of Literature as Exploration*. Urbana, Ill.: National Council of Teachers of English.

Purves, A. and Beach, R. (1972). *Literature and the Reader*. Urbana, Ill.: National Council of Teachers of English.

Purves, A. with Rippere V. (1963). *Elements of Writing About a Literary Work*. Urbana, Ill.: National Council of Teachers of English.

Purves, A., Foshay, L. and Hansson, G. (1973). *Literature Education in Ten Countries: An Empirical Study*. New York: John Wiley.

Ravitch, D. and Finn, C. (1987). *What Do Our Seventeen Year Olds Know?* New York: Harper and Row.

Reid, I. (ed.) (1987). *The Place of Genre in Learning: Current Debates*. Geelong: Deakin University Press.

Reid, I. (1988). *Enlarging Literature: An Inclusive Role for Australian Writing*. Canberra: Commonwealth Schools Commission.

Reid, I. *et al.* (1988). *Writing with a Difference*. Melbourne: Thomas Nelson.

Rhys, J. (1966). *The Wide Sargasso Sea*. London: Andre Deutsch.

Richards, I. A. (1929). *Practical Criticism*. London: Routledge and Kegan Paul.

Richards, I. A. (1943). *How to Read a Page*. London: Routledge and Kegan Paul.

Riffaterre, M. (1978). *Semiotics of Poetry*. Bloomington, Ind.: Indiana University Press.

Rimmon-Kenan, S. (1983). *Narrative Fiction: A Contemporary Poetics*. London: Methuen.

Robinson, J. (1987a). 'Literacy in society: Readers and writers in the worlds of discourse'. In Bloome, D. (ed.), *Literacy and Schooling*. Norwood, NJ: Ablex.

Robinson, J. (1987b). *Radical Literary Education: A Classroom Experiment with Wordsworth's 'Ode'*. Madison, Wis.: University of Wisconsin Press.

Rose, P. (1985). *Parallel Lives: Five Victorian Marriages*. Harmondsworth: Penguin.

Rosenblatt, L. (1938). *Literature as Exploration*. New York: Modern Language Association.

Rosenblatt, L. (1978). *The Reader, the Text, the Poem: The Transactional Theory of the Literary Work*. Carbondale, Ill.: Southern Illinois University Press.

Russell, D. (1970). *The Dynamics of Reading*. Boston, Mass.: Ginn and Co.

Russell, D. and Shrodes, C. (1950). 'Contributions in bibliotherapy to the language arts program'. *School Review*, **58**, 335–42, 411–20.

Saunders, I. (1988). 'The solitary reader'. *Southern Review*, **21**(1), 99–103.

Schlee, A. (1979). *The Vandal*. London: Macmillan.

Schlee, A. (1981). *Rhine Journey*. New York: Holt, Rinehart and Winston.

Scholes, R. (1982). *Semiotics and Interpretation*. New Haven, Conn.: Yale University Press.

Scholes, R. (1985). *Textual Power: Literary Theory and the Teaching of English*. New Haven, Connecticut: Yale University Press.

Sebestyen, O. (1979). *Words by Heart*. New York: Bantam Books.

Shuman, A. (1986). *Story Telling Rights*, Cambridge: Cambridge University Press.

Sillitoe, A. (1959). *The Loneliness of the Long Distance Runner*. London: Allen.

Simmons, J. (1986). 'The young adult novel: Looking down the road'. *The ALAN Review*, Winter, 26.

Simonson, R. and Walker, S. (1988). *The Greywolf Annual Fire: Multi-cultural Literacy*. St Paul, Minn.: Graywolf Press.

Sims Bishop, R. (in press). 'Fifty years of exploring children's books'. In Farrell, E.J. and Squire, J. R. (eds), *Fifty Years of Literature as Exploration*. Urbana, Ill.: National Council of Teachers of English.

Slatoff, W. (1970). *With Respect to Readers: Dimensions of Literary Response*. New York: Cornell University Press.

Spencer, M. (1987). 'Emergent literacies – a site for analysis', *Language Arts*, 63(5), 442–53.

Squire, J. R. (1963). *The Responses of Adolescents to Four Short Stories*. Urbana, Ill.: National Council of Teachers of English.

Squire, J. R. (ed.) (1968). *Response to Literature*. Urbana, Ill.: National Council of Teachers of English.

Squire, J. R. (1969). 'English literature'. In Ebel R. (ed.), *Encyclopedia of Educational Research*, 4th edn. New York: Macmillan.

Squire, J. (1985). 'The crisis in literary education'. *The English Journal*, 73(6), 18–21.

Squire, J. and Applebee, R. (1969). *The Teaching of English in England*. Urbana, Ill.: National Council of Teachers of English.

Stead, C. (1970). *The Man Who Loved Children*. Harmondsworth: Penguin.

Stein, N. and Policastro, M. (1984). 'The concept of a story: A comparison between children's and teachers' viewpoints'. In Mandl, H., Stein, N. L. and Trabasso, T. (eds), *Learning and Comprehension of Text*. Hillsdale, NJ: Lawrence Erlbaum Associates Inc.

Stowe, H. B. (1852). *Uncle Tom's Cabin*. Boston, Mass.: John P. Jewett.

Sulzby, E. (1985). 'Children's emergent reading of favourite storybooks: A developmental study'. *Reading Research Quarterly*, 20, 458–81.

Sulzby, E. and Teale, W. (1987). *Young Children's Storybook Reading: Longitudinal Study of Parent–Child Interaction and Children's Independent Functioning*. Final Report to the Spencer Foundation. Ann Arbor, Mich.: University of Michigan Press.

Taba, H. (1955). *With Perspective on Human Relations*. Washington, D.C.: American Council on Education.

Taxel, J. (1988). 'Children's literature: A research proposal from the perspective of the sociology of school knowledge'. In De Castell, S., Luke, A. and Luke, C. (eds), *Language, Authority and Criticism: Readings on the School Textbook*. Lewes: Falmer Press.

Taylor, M. (1977). *Roll of Thunder, Hear My Cry*. New York: Avon Press.

Terry, A. (1974). *Children's Poetry Preferences*. Urbana, Ill.: National Council of Teachers of English.

Thomas, R. (1987). *The Runaways*. London: Hutchinson.

Thomson, J. (1987). *Understanding Teenagers Reading: Reading Processes and the Teaching of Literature*. New York: Nichols/Melbourne: Methuen Australia.

Tierney, R. J., Anders, P. L. and Mitchell, J. N. (eds) (1987). *Understanding Readers' Understanding: Theory and Practice*. Hillsdale, NJ: Lawrence Erlbaum Associates Inc.

Todorov, T. (1975). *The Fantastic*. New York: Cornell University Press.

Van Dijk, T. (1977). *Text and Context: Explorations in the Semantics and Pragmatics of Discourse*. Harlow: Longman.

Van Peer, W. (1988). *The Taming of the Text*. London: Routledge.

Venezky, R. *et al.* (1987). *The Subtle Danger*. Princeton, NJ: Educational Testing Service.

Walker, A. (1982). *The Colour Purple*. New York: Harcourt Brace Jovanovich.

Walker, J. L. (in press). 'Reading preferences'. In Flood, J., Jensen, J., Lapp, D. and Squire, J. R. (eds), *Handbook of Research on the Teaching of the English Language Arts*. New York: Macmillan.

Walsh, J. P. (1972). *Goldengrove*. London: Macmillan.

Walsh, J. P. (1976). *Unleaving*. London: Macmillan.

Walsh, J. P. (1983). *A Parcel of Patterns*. Harmondsworth: Kestrel.

Warren, A. and Welleck, R. (1949). *Theory of Literature*. London: Jonathan Cape.

West, A. (1987). 'The limits of discourse'. *The English Magazine*, 18, 18–22.

White, A. (1984). 'Bakhtin, sociolinguistics and deconstruction'. In Gloversmith, F. (ed.), *The Theory of Reading*. Sussex: Harvester Press.

Willard, B. (1973). *The Iron Lily*. Harmondsworth: Kestrel.

Willinsky, J. (1987). 'The seldom-spoken roots of the curriculum and the new literacy'. *Curriculum Inquiry*, 17(3), 267–91.

Wilson, A. (1985). *Ma Rainey's Black Bottom*. New York: Farrar.

Wilson, J. R. (1966). *Responses of College Freshmen to Three Novels*. Urbana, Ill.: National Council of Teachers of English.

Wimsatt, W. (1970). *The Verbal Icon: Studies in the Meaning of Poetry*. London: Methuen.

Winton, T. (n.d.). 'Neighbours' (as published on Western Australia TEE paper).

Wolf, D. (1988). *Reading Reconsidered: Literature and Literacy in High School*. New York: College Entrance Examination Board.

Woodman, M. (1985). *The Pregnant Virgin*. Toronto: Inner City Books.

Wynne Jones, D. (1977). *Charmed Life*. London: Macmillan.

Zimet, S. (1979). *Print and Prejudice*. London: Hodder and Stoughton.

Zipes, J. (1983). *The Trials and Tribulations of Little Red Riding Hood: Versions of the Tale in Socio-Cultural Context*. South Hadley, Mass.: Bergin and Garvey.

Index

Aborigines, 88
academic reader, 47
accomodation, in reading, 137
active reader, 143
'actual reader', 136
Adams, Douglas, *The Hitch Hiker's Guide to the Galaxy*, 76
Adams, Richard, *Watership Down*, 108
ADE (Association of Departments of English of the Modern Language Association), 62–4
Adler, Mortimer, 19
advertising revenue, and children's books, 112–13
afferent reading, 18, 21, 23–4
age differences, and definition of stories, 29, 32, 33
Ahlberg, J. and Ahlberg, A., 76
  The Baby's Catalogue, 10
  Each Peach Pear Plum, 10
  The Jolly Postman, 10–12, 138
Alabama, 116, 117, 118–19, 122
Alabama State Textbook Commission, 117
ALAN review, 122
Althusser, L., 134, 137
ambivalence, value of in response, 70
American Bar Associations, 121
American Civil Liberties Union (ACLU), 115, 119, 120, 121–2
American Educational Studies Association, 62
American Library Association, 117
Anderson, Hans Christian, *Stories*, 118
Anderson, R. L. and Pearson, P. D., 14, 137
Angelou, Maya, *I Know Why the Caged Bird Sings*, 117
Anglo-American Seminar at Dartmouth College, 15
Applebee, A., 14, 15, 20, 21–2, 143
  The Child's Concept of Story, 25–6
Aristophanes, *Lysistrata*, 119, 120
Arkansas, 116
Arnold, M., 133

Asterix the Gaul, 5
Australia, 88–9
  new literature, 75
Australia, Western, literature teaching, 84
author, intentions of, 135

Bakhtin, M., 132, 144
balanced reader, 47
Baldwin, James, *Invisible Man*, 19
Ball, Lucille, 37
Ballantyne, R. M., *The Coral Island*, 81
Barone, D., 14, 20
Barone, T., 23
Barr, M., 13, 15, 23–4
Barstow, Stan, *A Kind of Loving* 88–9
  'The Fury', 90–2
Barthes, Roland, 49–50, 80, 133, 135, 136, 143
Baum, Frank, *The Wizard of Oz*, 118
Bawden, Nina, 112
Beach, R., 18
Beach, R. and Brown, K., 18
Beach, R. and Brunetti, G., 14
Beach, R. and Hynds, S., 15, 16, 20, 21
Beach, R. and Wendler, L., 14, 20, 21
Beckson, K. and Ganz, A., *A Reader's Guide to Literary Terms*, 25
behaviourist psychology, and reading, 1
Beloff, Lord, 113
Belsey, C., 66, 67, 137, 144
Bennett, W., 13
Bentley, 14
Benton, M. *et al*, 16
Benton, M. and Fox, G., 6, 140
Beowulf, 126
Berger, P. and Luckman, T., 88
Bettelheim, B., 133
Bible, influence of, 97, 146
Biggles, 4
Black, Judge Susan, 120
Black Like Me, 17
Bleich, D., 15, 43, 133, 140

Blyton, Enid, 81, 125
  The Famous Five, 113
Boccacio, 4
Bogdan, Deanne, 78, 83
  'Joyce, Dorothy and Willie: Literary literacy
    as engaged reflection', 63, 65–70
Bogdan, Deanne and Yeomans, S., 77, 78
Book Marketing Council, 110
  Top Teenage Reading list, 109
Booker Prize, 112
Books for Keeps (journal), 111
Bookseller, The, 110
Booth, Wayne, 14, 136
boredom in reading, 9–10
Boston Globe/Horn Book award, 112
Bradbury, Ray, 'The Whole Town's Sleeping',
    141
Brecht, Bertolt
  The Caucasian Chalk Circle, 79
  Children's Crusade, 79
  The Exception and the Rule, 79, 80
Brennan, Justice William, 117
Brice Heath, Shirley, 8
Bridge, C., 18
Bridgers, Sue Ellen, 44
Briggs, Raymond, *The Snowman*, 8, 12
Britton, James, 6, 14, 15, 20, 63, 69, 85
  The Development of Writing Abilities, 60
Brontë, Charlotte, *Jane Eyre*, 80
Brontë, Emily, *Wuthering Heights*, 119
Brooks, C., 43
Brown, A. L., 26
Bruner, J., 9, 10
Bunbury, R., 23
Burningham, John, *Come Away from the Water,
    Shirley*, 138
Burns, Robbie, *Tam o'Shanter*, 4
Bussis, A. M. *et al*, 8

Calfee, R., 18
California Assembly, 122
California Board of Education, 121
California Literature Initiative, 13
Carey, Peter, 80
Caribbean literature, 75
Carle, Eric, *The Very Hungry Caterpillar*, 6
Carlsen, G. R., and Sherrill, C. A., 15, 21,
    23
Carnegie Award, 109, 111
Carpenter, H., 74
Carroll, Lewis, *Alice in Wonderland*, 17, 126
categorization, and definition of stories, 30–1
censorship, 73, 78, 115–23
  abridging of texts 118, 121
  book-banning 115–21
  focus on ideology, 121–2
  and fundamentalism, 73, 116, 118–19, 121
  and role of secular humanism, 122
Center for the Learning and Teaching of
    Literature, 21

Centre for Studies in Literary Education,
    Deakin University, 49, 52–9
Chambers, Aidan, 25
character, as plot-function, 81
  students' assumptions about, 86
Chatman, S., 136
Chaucer, Geoffrey, 'The Miller's Tale', 119,
    120
Chew, C., *et al*, 15
children, censorship of books for, 115–23
  developmental sequence in response to
    fiction, 32
  learning to read, 138
  losing interest in reading, 124
  and sense of story 25–6
  society's attitude to books for, 107, 111–14
  see also home stories; reading programmes
Children's Book Groups, Federation of, 109
Childress, Alice, *A Hero Ain't Nothin But a
    Sandwich*, 115
Christian Educators, Association of, 116
Cinderella, 118
circumtextual framing, 50, 54–5, 59–60, 61
Citizens United for Responsible Education,
    116
class, and perspective of reader, 70, 88,
    132–3, 144
classroom, decentred 62
  and framing, 54–5
  as interpretative community, 43
  neutrality of, 85–6, 144
  see also reader; teacher
Clifford, J., 14
codes, 80, 135–7, 141
  contrasted with framing, 49–50
  cultural code 136
  hermeneutic code, 136
  'ideological overcoding', 139
  proairetic code, 136
  semic code, 136
  symbolic code, 136
Cohan, S. and Shires, L., *Telling Stories*, 25
Cole, Michael, 8
Coles, Robert, 14, 15, 17, 19
Columbia City School, Lake City, Florida,
    119, 120, 121–2
community, portrayal of in Great Tradition, 75
  portrayal of in realist literature, 74
competence, literary, 33
Concerned Women of America, 116, 118
content, and definition of stories, 31–2
conviction, and definition of stories, 30, 31
Cooper, C., 15
Corcoran, W. and Evans, E., 15, 22, 140, 145
Cormier, Robert, 80
  After the First Death, 79
  The Chocolate War, 82
  I Am the Cheese, 119, 120
Cox Report (1989), 2, 8
Crago, M. and Crago, H., 26

Crane, Stephen, *The Red Badge of Courage*, 119
'creation science', teaching of, 116
Croall, J., 127
Culler, J., 5, 49, 132, 136, 138
Cullinan, B., 14, 20–1, 23
cultural assumptions, 86, 88–90
cultural code, 136
cultural heritage position, 133
cultural studies, 3
cultural values, making reading compatible
    with, 86

Dahl, Roald, 112
D'Alemberte, Talbot, 121
Danish Folktale Project, 17
Dartmouth Report on Response to Literature,
    17
Davies, Andrew, *Conrad's War*, 108, 109, 112
    Marmalade Atkins series, 112
Davis, Lennard, 74
Davis, M. M., 8
de Man, Paul, 49
    Allegories of Reading, 6
Deakin University, Centre for Studies in
    Literary Education, 49, 52–9
deconstructive criticism, 70
Defoe, Daniel, *Robinson Crusoe*, 81, 126
Departments of English, Association of
    (ADE), of the Modern Language
    Association, 62–4
Derrida, Jacques, 50, 135
Dewey, John, 14, 20
Dias, P., 23
Dias, P. and Hayhoe, M., 16, 23, 142
Dickens, Charles, 76
divided reader, 47
Dixon, J., 19, 20, 21
Dixon, J. and Brown, J., 2, 21
Dixon, J. and Stratta, L., 18, 23
Dollerup, C. *et al*, 17
Donald, J., 132, 139
Durkin, Dolores, 20

Eagle Forum, 116, 121
Eagleton, Terry, 6–7, 12
Early Margaret, 23
Eco, U., 133, 135, 137, 138
Educational Research Analysis Corporation,
    116
Eeds, M. and Wells, D., 37
efferent reading, 18, 21, 23–4, 42, 47
Egan, K., *Teaching as Story Telling*, 25
Eliot, T. S., 4
engagement, definition of, 63
    as 'engaged reflection', 62, 65, 69–70
    and literary conditioning, 68–9
    as a poetic value, 67–8
English Studies, 62, 70
epic theatre, 79–80
estrangement, 79–80

European literature, 75
evaluation, and definition of stories, 30, 31
Everett, Barbara, 7–8
evolutionary theory, 116
extratextual framing, 50–1, 59–60, 61

fairy tales, children's,
    categorization of, 26, 27, 32
    establishment of markers, 33
    and intertextuality, 139
Fanslow, J., 14
fantasy, role in home stories, 125, 127
Farrell, E. J. 17, 18, 19
Farrell, E. J. and Squire, J. R., 14
Faulkner, William, *As I Lay Dying*, 87–8
Favat, F. A., 20
Federation of Children's Book Groups, 109
feminist criticism, 3, 4–5, 88–9, 140–1
    content analysis, 143
    and response journals, 63
    and Romanticism, 63–70
fictionality, and definition of stories, 30, 31
Fine, Anne, 112
Finlay, Linda Shaw and Faith, Valerie, 46–7
Fish, Stanley, 42, 43, 44, 63, 136, 140, 144
Fisher, C. J. and Natarella, M. A., 17
Flood, J. and Lapp, D., 23
Foucault, M., 135
Fowles, John, 'The Collector', 87
framing, 49
    circumtextual, 50, 54–5, 59–60, 61
    extratextual, 50–1, 59–60, 61
    intertextual, 51, 60, 61
    intratextual, 51, 60, 61
    and reframing, 57–61
Frank, Anne, *The Diary of Anne Frank*, 117,
    118
free association, 34–6, 46–7
'free' reader, 139
'free' response, 139
Frye, N., 64
fundamentalism, and censorship, 73, 116,
    118–19, 121

Galda, L., 15, 21
Galda, L. and Pellegrini, A., *Play, Language
    and Stories*, 25
Gardam, Jane, 112
Gare, N., *The Fringe Dwellers*, 88
Garfield, Leon, 74
GCSE 2, 12, 73
gender, and perspective of reader, 56, 59–60,
    70, 88, 132–3, 141–2
gender differences, and definition of stories,
    29
genres, 81, 138–9
Gibbs, A., 'The Test', 88
Gilbert, Pam, 59, 145
Ginzburg, Carlo, 8
Giroux, H., 132, 137–8, 142

Golding, William, *Lord of the Flies*, 81, 81–2, 126
Grahame, Kenneth, *The Wind in the Willows*, 80
Grass, Gunter, 80
Great Tradition, The, 75–6, 84
Grey, Zane, 4
Griffith, P., 15
Guardian adult fiction award, 110
Guardian Award for children's books, 107–12
Guardian, The, 109, 111

Hackman, S., 145
Hand, Judge W. Brevard, 116, 118–19, 120
Handlan, B., 18
Hansson, G., 14, 23
Harding, D.W., 14, 15
Hardy, Barbara, 25
Hargreaves, Roger, 125
Harker, J., 138
Harris, J., 69
Hatch Amendment to education bill (US), 116
Hatch, Senator Orrin, 116
Havelock, Eric, 124
Hawkins County, Tennessee, 118, 122
Hayhoe, M. and Parker, S., 140
Hazelwood, Missouri, 117, 120, 121, 122
Heaton, Margaret, 16
Hemingway, Ernest, *The Faithful Bull*, 60, 61
Henschemeyer, Judith, 'We Interrupt this Broadcast', 36–40
hermeneutic code, 136
Hickman, J., 14, 15, 20, 20–1
Hirsch, E. D., 19, 142
'historical reader', 136
Holland, N., 2, 14, 15, 43, 133
home stories, 124–31
    immediacy of, 126–7
    limits of, 128–9, 131
    personal nature of, 125, 127–8
    personal vocabulary of, 125
    and plagiarism, 125, 126
    rambling nature of, 125, 126
    scatological element, 125–6, 128
    use of by teachers, 129–31
Homer, *The Odyssey*, 81
How Texts Teach What Readers Learn, 10
Hughes, Ted,
    The Iron Man, 9–10, 138
    'Myth and education', 9
    'View of a Pig', 84
The Humanities: Cultural Roots and Continuities, 119
humour, in 'home stories', 125–6, 128
Hunt, Peter, 1
Hunt, R. and Vipond, D., 64
Hutchins, P., *Rosie's Walk*, 138
Hutchinson (publishers), 112
Huxley, Aldous, 4

Hynds, S., 14, 48
Hynds, S. and Chase, 16

Ibsen, Henrik, *A Doll's House*, 117
ideal reader, 136
'implied reader', 136
individualism, 49
    portrayal of in realist literature, 74
'informed reader', 136
Inquiry into Meaning, 8
International Convention on Reading and Response, 27, 120
interpellation, concept of, 137
interpretation, 144
    dialogue, 144
    equivocal, 144
    univocal, 144
interpretative communities, 42–3
intersubjective elements, 145
intertextual framing, 51, 60
intertextuality, 5, 10–12, 51, 60, 80, 138, 145
intratextual framing, 51, 60, 61
Iser, W., 41, 63, 133, 136, 140, 144
    Act of Reading, 15
Island Trees School Board, 115, 117

Jackson, D., 140, 145
Jackson, S., 'After You My Dear Alphonse', 88
Jacksonville, Florida, 120
James Madison Elementary School, 13
Janssen, T. and Rijlaarsdam, G., 14
Jauss, Hans Robert, 63, 136
Johnson, M., 142
Johnson, Samuel, 64
Jonah, Book of, 6–7
Joyce, J., *Eveline*, 145
Joyce, James
    Finnegan's Wake, 144
    Ulysses, 144
Juel, C., 23

Keats, John, *Ode to a Nightingale*, 7–8
Kerr, Judith, *The Tiger who Came to Tea*, 6
King, Stephen, 44, 45
King-Smith, Dick, *The Sheep-Pig*, 108, 109
Kingsley, Charles, *The Water Babies*, 17
Knights, L. C., 14
Kress, G., 139
Kristeva, Julia, 51

Lacan, J., 134
Lake City, Florida, 119, 120, 121–2
language studies, 3
Lasky, Kathryn, *Beyond the Divide*, 44
Last Gentleman, The, 17
Lawrence, D. H., *Sons and Lovers*, 17
Lawson, Robert, 60
Leaf, Munro, *The Story of Ferdinand*, 60, 61
Leaper, J. D., 84
Leavis, F. R., 1, 75, 133

Leavittown School, Long Island, 115, 117
Lee, Harper, *To Kill a Mockingbird*, 17, 75, 88
Leeson, R., *Silver's Revenge*, 80
Lehr, S., 20
Liberty Forum, 116
library services, 113
literary excellence, concept of, 19, 107, 109, 113
literary history, and literature teaching, 99–101
literary language, use of, 96, 99
literature, reawakened interest in schools, 13
literature teaching, attitudes of prospective teachers, 34–6, 43–4
    classification scheme for objectives, 96–9
    conflicts within, 44–5
    focus of, 16
    and 'hard cases', 82–3
    learner reports, 96–106
    literary history approach, 99–101
    moral arguments for, 76–8, 83
    in the Netherlands, 94–106
    outcomes of, 104–6
    provision of variety of texts, 18
    'story analysis' syllabus, 101
    and structural analysis, 101–2
    and textual experience, 102–3
    to foster enjoyment of reading, 100, 102–3
    in Western Australia, 84
Little Red Riding Hood, 87, 139
Lively, Penelope, 112
Llosa, Mario Vargas, *Aunt Julia and the Scriptwriter*, 79
Loban, W., 14, 15, 16–17
London, Jack, *Call of the Wild*, 119
Lorimer, R. and Long, M., 142
Louisiana, 116
ludic reader, 47
Lunzer, E. and Gardner, K., 142
Lytle, Susan, 20

McCaughrean, Geraldine, *A Pack of Lies*, 108, 110
McClure, A., 14
McCormick, K., 142
McIntosh, Margaret Means, 'Feeling like a fraud', 62
MacLachlan, Gale, 54
Maclean, Marie, *Narrative as Performance*, 59
Macmillan (publishers), 112
magic realism, 75
Magorian, Michelle, *Goodnight Mister Tom*, 108, 109
Mandler, J. and Johnson, N., 137
markers, application of, 33
    circumtextual, 54–5
Mark, Jan, 'William's version', 138
Marquez, Gabriel Garcia, 80
Martin, B., 73
Martinez, M. and Roser, N., 20, 22
Marvell, Andrew, *Bermudas*, 81

Marxist criticism, 70
Meares, P., 143
Meckel, H., 14, 16
Meek, M., 14, 15, 16, 23, 138
    The Cool Web, 8–9
Mellor, B. *et al*, 141
Melville, Hermann, 121
Miller, Jane, *Women Writing about Men*, 4
Milner, J. O. and Milner, L. F. M., 15
Milton, John
    Areopagitica, 4
    Paradise Lost, 2, 4
Minneapolis, Minnesota, 118
Mobile, Alabama, 116, 118–19, 122
modernism, not represented in children's literature, 76
Moi, T., 51
Montefiore, Jan, *Feminism and Poetry: Language, Experience and Identity in Women's Writing*, 64
Morgan, B., 145
Morris, Desmond, *The Naked Ape*, 115
Mosenthal, P., 17
Moviegoer, The, 17
Mowat, Farley, *Never Cry Wolf*, 119
Mowat Junior High School, Panama City, Florida, 119
multicultural classroom, 144–5
mythology, 97

Nabb, Magdalen, *Josie Smith*, 110
narrative, embedded, 51
    students' assumptions about, 86
narrative grammar, 80
National Council of Teachers of English (NCTE), 118, 119
    1988 Conference, 63
National Curriculum, 73, 142
National Legal Foundation, 116, 118
NCTE (National Council of Teachers of English), 63, 118, 119
Needle, J., *The Wild Wood*, 80
Neill, A. S., 127
Nelms, B., 15, 40, 143, 144
Netherlands, teaching of literature, 94–106
New Criticism, 1, 2–3, 44, 63, 81, 84, 133
    conflict with reader-response theory, 44–5
    enduring influence of, 21–2
New Literacy, 62–5, 63, 69
    and poetry, 64–70
Newbery award for children's books, 111
Noel, E., 25
Norvell, G. W., 17

O'Brien, Flann, 80
O'Connor, Sandra Day, 116
O'Neill, Marnie, 84
O'Neill, Marnie and Reid, J., 84
Ong, W., 4, 8, 124
opposition, role of in reading, 132, 137

oral tradition, 124–31
and children's response, 20, 21
Orwell, George, *Animal Farm*, 119
Oxford English Dictionary, 25
Oxford University Press, 112

Paley, Vivian, 26
Panama City, Florida, 119
parents, influence in schools, 73, 116–22
passive reader, 143–4
passive synthesis, 40–1, 143
Paterson, Katherine, 44
Paul, Dr. Lissa, 129
Pearson, P. D., 15, 16, 23
Pearson, P. D. and Tierney, R., 22
People for the American Way, 117–18, 120, 121
Attacks on the Freedom to Learn, 120
personal growth model of teaching, 84, 90, 92–3, 140, 143
Peseroff, Joyce, 'Adolescent', 65–72
Petrosky, A. R., 14
Pfeffer, Susan, *About David*, 119
picture books, 10–12, 61, 76, 79, 109, 138
plagiarism, children's use of, 7
in 'home stories', 125, 126
plot, study of, 81
Poe, Edgar Allan, 121
poetry, 100
difficulties of, 39
and New Literacy, 64–70
polyglossia, 144
popular culture, 3, 8
Powell, Justice Lewis, 120
prayer, place of in schools, 116
pressure groups, and book-banning, 116–22
Primary Language Record, 6
Prince, G., *A Grammar for Stories*, 26, 28
Pritchard, K. S., *Coonardoo*, 88
proairetic code, 136
Probst, R., 15, 16, 18, 140
Propp, V., 137
Protherough, R., 16, 33, 140, 143
Developing Response to Fiction, 3
pseudo-literature, 19
Purves, A., 14, 20, 21, 96–7, 138
Purves, A., and Beach, R., 14–15
Purves, A. and Rippere, V., 14

race, and perspective of reader, 70, 88, 89–90, 132–3
and response, 143–4
Ransome, Arthur, 81
Ravitch, D. and Finn, C., 19
reader, academic, 47
active reader, 132
'actual reader', 136
balanced, 47
composite reader, 145
cultural framing of, 143
defined by text, 136

definition of, 132–3
divided, 47
efferent, 47
'free', 138
'historical reader', 136
'ideal reader', 136
'implied reader', 136
importance of primary response of, 85
'informed reader', 136
ludic, 47
'Model reader', 135, 136
passive, 144
resistant reader, 132
and successful reading of text, 135–40
strong reader, 132
'superreader', 136
in text, 135–6, 137
reader-response theory, 1, 80–1, 132–3
application to pedagogy, 43
applied to society, 107
conflict with New Criticism, 44–5
and engagement, 63
historical development of, 14–15
psychoanalytic versions, 133
psychological perspective, 135–6
transactional versions, 133
see also codes
reading
active, 143
analysis of dynamics of, 140
assumptions, 39–40, 85–6
attitudes to, 100–6
and behaviourist psychology, 1
and boredom, 9–10
classification scheme for content and behaviours, 96–9
close, 7–8
and cultural values, 86
developmental differences, 20–1, 23–4
experience of, 77
and framing, 49
and individualism, 49
as learned behaviour, 87–8
and minority values, 124
oscillation between engagement and detachment, 78
passive, 144
personal nature of, 132
and reflexivity, 142
and responding model, 40–2
and role of accommodation, 137
and role of opposition, 132, 137
and role of resistance, 132–3, 137
zones of, 132, 133, 142–3
reading histories, 3, 5, 46
reading inventories, 46
reading lists, 19, 99, 100
reading preference studies, 17
reading programmes, 18, 19, 22
'response-oriented', 19

reading protocols, 46
reading schemes, 138
Reagan, Ronald, 116, 120
realism, 73–6
  and 'Golden Age' of literature, 74
  'magic', 75
  and 'The Great Tradition', 75–6
Reid, I., 52, 54, 59, 139
religion, and perspective of reader, 132–3
resistance, 141–6
  reading, 143–4
  and rewriting, 143–6
  role in reading, 88–9, 90–3, 132–3, 135, 137
response, definitions of, 1
  influences on, 16–17
  international differences in, 21
  and Purves' classification scheme, 96–9
  and questions, 2
  social context, 3
  students' assumptions about, 86
  studies of, 14–15, 84
  value of ambivalence, 70
response journals, 62, 63, 65–70, 121, 145
response theory, see reader-response theory
'response-oriented' reading programmes, 19
responsibility, 3, 12
retelling, 8-12
rewriting, through resistant reading, 142–6
Rhys, Jean, The Wide Sargasso Sea, 80
Richards, I. A., 19
  How to Read a Page, 3
  Practical Criticism, 2–3, 14, 54
Riffaterre, M., 136
Rimmon-Kenan, S., 136
Robinson, J., 135
  Radical Literary Education, 65
Romanticism, feminist critique of, 63–70
Rose, P., 78
Rosen, Harold, 7
Rosenblatt, Louise, 1, 18, 23, 24, 42, 44, 63, 69, 85, 88, 133, 139
  Literature as Exploration, 14, 16
  The Reader, the Text, the Poem, 13, 14, 15, 16
Rossetti, Christina, 4
Rushdie, Salman, The Satanic Verses, 113
Russell, D., 14, 16
Russell, D. and Shrodes, C., 14, 22

Saroyan, 'The Great Leapfrog Contest', 142
Saunders, I., 49
Schafly, Phyllis, 121
schema theory, 15
Schlee, Ann, Rhine Journey, 112
Scholes, Robert, 10, 16, 40–1, 138, 144
  Textual Power, 78
science fiction, 75
Scott-Foresman (publishers), 118
Sebestyen, O., Words by Heart, 144
semic code, 136

semiotic account, 133, 144
Sendak, Maurice, Where the Wild Things Are, 61
Shakespeare, William, 119
  Hamlet, 17, 118
  King Lear, 2, 17
  Macbeth, 132
  Romeo and Juliet, 17, 118, 121
  The Tempest, 81
Shuman, A., Story Telling Rights, 25, 48
Sillitoe, Alan, The Loneliness of the Long-Distance Runner, 17, 88–9
Simmons, J., 'The young adult novel: Looking down the road', 122
Simonson, R. and Walker, S., 19
Sims Bishop, Rudine, 18, 19
Slatoff, W., 133
social issues, not central in realist literature, 74
socialization, through stories, 25
Sophocles, Oedipus Rex, 119
Spencer, M., 9
Squire, J. R., 14, 15, 16, 17, 18, 20, 23
  Response of Adolescents to Four Short Stories, 46
stage theory, 23
State Textbook Adoption Commission (Texas), 121
Stead, Christina, The Man who Loved Children, 129
Stein, N. and Policastro, M., 26
Steinbeck, John, 121
stereotypes, 19
Stevenson, Robert Louis, Treasure Island, 17, 80
stories, children's recognition of, 26–33
story, as literary term, 25
Stowe, Harriet Beecher, Uncle Tom's Cabin, 77
structural analysis, and literature teaching, 101–2
structuralism, 80–1
  and role of teacher, 133–5
structure, and definition of stories, 31–2
  students' assumptions about, 86
Sulzby, E. and Teale, W., 20, 21
Summerhill School, 127
'superreader', 136
Supervision and Curriculum Development, Association of, 117
Swift, Jonathon, Gulliver's Travels, 126
symbolic code, 136
Synge, John Middleton, 'Riders to the Sea', 17
systematic ambiguity', 3

Taba, H., 14
Taxel, J., 144
Taylor, M., Roll of Thunder, Hear My Cry, 144
teacher, constructed by text, 135
  greater choice in selection of texts, 73
  perceptions of outcomes of work, 103–6
  popular antagonism towards, 73
  role of, 133–5, 143–6

teacher, constructed by text – *cont.*
role of in decentred classroom, 62
role in response-centred classroom, 43
as transmitter of literary culture, 133
use of home stories, 129–31
television, 37, 76
and literacy, 3
as resource for reframing, 52–3, 57–9
use of stereotypes, 19
Tennyson, Alfred, Lord, *The Lotos Eaters*, 81
Terry, Ann, 17
Texas State Board of Education, 121
text, closed, 138–9
'closed/open', 133–5
conversation with, 41
criticism of, 41–2
engagement with, 77–8
evocation of, 40–1
as ideology, 135–6, 137, 139
interpretation of, 41
open, 138
'readerly/writerly', 133–5
'real' (for learning to read), 121, 122, 138
resistant reading of, 92–3
as stimulus, 1
as structured language, 135–6, 137–9
'textoids', 64, 67
textoids', 64, 67
textual power, 10
textuality, increasing awareness of, 78–83
as purpose of literary study, 40
Thomas, 23
Thomas, Ruth, *The Runaways*, 108
Thomson, J., 141, 143, 145
Tierney, R. J. *et al*, 16
Todorov, T., 138
Tolkien, J. R. R., *The Hobbit*, 126
Townsend, John Rowe, 107, 108
translations, 75, 80
Treasure Islands' (BBC Radio 4), 111
Twain, Mark, 45

United States, reader-response, 13–24
US Congress, 115–16
US Constitution, First Amendment, 115, 116, 117, 118–19, 120, 121, 122
US Supreme Court, 115, 118, 120, 121

Van Dijk, T., 136
Van Peper, W., 15
Venezky, R., 18

verbal icon concept, and role of teacher, 133
Vienna, Virginia, 118
Vinson, Judge Roger, 120
vocabulary, personal nature of in 'home stories', 125, 128–9
Vonnegut, Kurt, 75
Slaughterhouse Five, 115

Walker, Alice, *The Colour Purple*, 75
Walker, J. L., 15, 17
Walpole, Hugh, *Fortitude*, 16
Walsh, Jill Paton, 80
Goldengrove, 79
A Parcel of Patterns, 79
Unleaving, 79
Walwicz, Anna, 'so small' 52–5
Warren, A., 43
Warren, A. and Welleck, R., *Theory of Literature*, 25
Webb, Bill, 107
West, A., 143
White, A., 144
White, E. B., *Charlotte's Web*, 18–19
White, Justice Byron, 120
whole language programmes, 20
Williams, William Carlos, 48
Willinsky, John, 64–5
Wilson, August, *Ma Rainey's Black Bottom*, 145
Wilson, J. R., 14
Wimsatt, W., 133
Winnicott, D. W., 9
Winton, Tim, 'Neighbours', 89–90
Wolf, D., 145
Women's Studies, 62–70
Woodman, M., 70
Woolf, Virginia, 4
Wordsworth, Dorothy, journals, 65–70, 72
Wordsworth, William, 63
'I wandered lonely as a cloud', 65–9
Intimations Ode, 65
Preface to the Lyrical Ballads, 64, 65, 67, 69
writer, in text, 135–6, 137
writing, and reframing, 57–61
Writing with a difference, 57

young adult' novels, 109, 122, 123

Zimet, S., 142
Zipes, J., 139